BUT I TRUSTED YOU

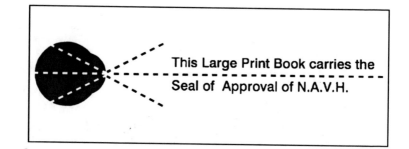

This Large Print Book carries the
Seal of Approval of N.A.V.H.

BUT I TRUSTED YOU AND OTHER TRUE CASES

ANN RULE'S CRIME FILES: VOL. 14

ANN RULE

LARGE PRINT PRESS
A part of Gale, Cengage Learning

GALE
CENGAGE Learning

Detroit • New York • San Francisco • New Haven, Conn • Waterville, Maine • London

LIBRARY OF CONGRESS CATALOGING-IN-PUBLICATION DATA

Rule, Ann.
   But I trusted you / by Ann Rule. — Large print ed.
     p. cm. — (Ann Rule's crime files ; vol. 14)
   Originally published: New York : Pocket Books, 2009
   ISBN-13: 978-1-4104-2140-1 (alk. paper)
   ISBN-10: 1-4104-2140-6 (alk. paper)
   ISBN-13: 978-1-59413-382-4 (pbk. : alk. paper)
   ISBN-10: 1-59413-382-4 (pbk. : alk. paper)
   1. Murder — United States — Case studies. 2. Murderers —
United States —Case studies. I. Title.
HV6529.R82 2009
364.152'30973—dc22

                    2009037618

Published in 2009 in arrangement with Pocket Books, a division of Simon & Schuster, Inc.

Printed in the United States of America
  2 3 4 5 6   13 12 11 10 09

ED357

To the late Sheriff Chris Hansen of Montcalm County, Michigan, my grandfather. Our grandfather inspired me and all my cousins with his ability to talk to almost anyone, his understanding of human nature, his skill as an investigator, and his compassion.

Many decades ago, Robert Ripley chose Chris Hansen for his feature "Believe It or Not" because he never had to fire his gun during his long career as a lawman. The Hansen descendants are spread all over America now, and most of us chose to be police officers, lawyers, social workers, prosecutors, parole and probation officers, teachers, or writers.

We all owe a lot to our grandfather, a Danish immigrant who settled in Michigan!

ACKNOWLEDGMENTS

There are so many cases in *But I Trusted You,* and so many real people in each of them, that this will be a long list. I could not possibly have learned this many details without a great deal of help from detectives, prosecutors, witnesses, jurors, and victims' families.

Thank you to Brad Pince and Jim Scharf of the Snohomish County Sheriff's Office, Eloise Schumacher and Peyton Whitely of the *Seattle Times,* Susan, Lieutenant Frank Chase, Ted Forrester, Rolf Grunden, Bruce Morrison, Jerry Harris, Mike Gillis, Harlan Bollinger, Len Randall, Mark Fern, and the late Sam Hicks of the King County Sheriff's Office. Billy Baughman, Dick Reed, Ted Fonis, Wayne Dorman, "Bud" Jelberg, Bob Holter, and John Boatman from the Seattle Police Department, and to Sergeant L. E. Robinson of the Enumclaw Police Department and Park Ranger Harry De Lashmutt.

Chief of detectives Bill Patterson of the Chelan County Sheriff's Office helped me a great deal, and so did Lieutenant Walt Kezar of the Oregon State Police, the Oregon State Board of Parole, and special thanks to Rob Romig of the *Eugene Register-Guard*.

Thanks to Chuck Wright, Gerry Hay (my first reader, always), Ken Heide, Donna Anders, Kate Jewell, Shirley Hickman, Marni Campbell, Mike Hare, and all the Jolly Matrons from Willamette University and the University of Washington (faded but still lovely): Joan Kelly, Susie Morrison, Betty May Settecase, Shirley Coffin, Alice Govig, Sue Dreyer, Tricia Potts, Val Szukavathy, Gail Bronson, and Shirley Jacobs.

To Dawn and Gary Dunn, Matt Parker, Justin Robison, and to the ARFs (Ann Rule Fans — long may they wave!). And my gratitude to those readers who haven't yet become certified ARFs knows no bounds. I couldn't have even one book without you.

My thanks to my longtime literary agents — Joan and Joe Foley, my theatrical agent — Ron Bernstein of ICM, my editor — Mitchell Ivers, and to Jessica Webb, who helped me every step of the way! My attorney, Felice Javits, checks everything I write to be sure it is absolutely factual.

I haven't forgotten the production crew at

Pocket Books, who remind me graciously about looming deadlines: Carly Sommerstein, Sally Franklin, Lisa Litwack, and Ayelet Gruenspecht.

Thank you also to Theresa Leonard, Sandy Biscaro, and Reisa Schmidt.

CONTENTS

FOREWORD

There are infinite variations on the motive, means, and excuses for the darkest crime of all: murder. Some are unpremeditated and leave the killer full of remorse, while other homicides sink to the cruelest depths imaginable and the murderers feel absolutely no twinge of conscience. Most of us would be capable of taking another person's life, but only to save ourselves or someone vulnerable. Mothers — both human and animal — kill without a thought to protect their young. And that isn't truly murder. Soldiers shoot to kill on the battlefield, and police officers sometimes have no choice but to use deadly force. Any cop will tell you that the officer who is responsible for a death in the line of duty "suffers as much or more than the criminal."

"Conscience doth make cowards of us all," William Shakespeare wrote in *Hamlet*. But he was wrong. There are human beings who have no conscience. They don't feel remorse, or regret, or guilt about the horrible crimes they have committed. They may shed crocodile tears, and they cry when they are caught, but they weep only for themselves.

The cases in this book — ranging in time from a few years ago to more than three decades into the past — are about homicides that were both devious and complicated. The killers planned their crimes, and drew victims in to a point where they placed their confidence in someone who was both sly and deadly. In hindsight, their machinations seem blatant and easy to recognize.

But in the beginning, their "masks," and their ability to say just the right thing at the right time, were often impenetrable.

The longest case, and the title case I explore in *But I Trusted You,* is about a couple whose meeting was romantic, whose marriage seemed fated, and whose final separation was unbelievable. They had it all — at least to anyone looking at them from the outside of their relationship, and even to many who knew them well. Of the two, the husband seemed the more bizarre. He often watered their lawn or picked up the morning paper in minimal clothing, but their neighbors had long since become used to it. His jubilant personality won them over.

The couple lived in a kind of fishbowl. From the living room of their charming house on a picturesque lake, visitors could peer through the glass floor and view the king-sized waterbed below.

He was a school counselor, and she operated a small resale shop — modest and respectable professions, and yet theirs is one of the strangest and most multifaceted stories I have ever come across.

"Death in Paradise" may not have been a betrayal of trust at all; perhaps what happened in the tropical waters off Papeete was only a sad series of accidents. I have to admit that we may never know the complete truth, but the ill-fated journey of the *Spellbound* will never be erased from my own memory — not until the hidden aspects of a case that sounds more like fiction than fact are revealed. It will undoubtedly haunt you, too, just as it haunts those who survived.

In "Sharper than a Serpent's Tooth," I explore another case of a disappearance that suggested a violent and deadly end. No one knew for sure if Lorraine Millroy left her comfortable home of her own volition or if she had no choice. She had many of the usual problems that divorced, middle-aged women face. Still, she wasn't depressed, or, rather, she didn't seem to be. Family problems cropped up occasionally, but money wasn't an issue. On a bitter cold night, detectives searching her home for some hint of where she might be came across items of evidence that gave them a sense of foreboding. As anxious as they were to locate Lorraine, whether she was alive or dead, they hoped they hadn't focused on the right suspect. It was someone whom Lorraine loved, counted on, held high hopes for, and, yes, trusted.

"Monohan's Last Date" reflects the mores of a brief period in American history. The 1960s were all about the love generation, but as the decade eased into the 1970s, love gave way to an intense curiosity about sex. *Cosmopolitan* editor Helen Gurley Brown shocked America with her book *Sex and the Single Girl* in 1962. Her basically innocuous book opened up the floodgates. Masters and Johnson's research and subsequent publications shocked the public deliciously, and *The Joy of Sex* came along ten years later, along with the movie *Bob and Carol and Ted and Alice.*

"Swinging" and "wife swapping" intrigued couples whose marriages had become mundane, but in most cases the results were disastrous, and it wasn't long before they ended up in divorce court.

In "Monohan's Last Date," a highly successful business man, who had been recently divorced, became involved with a group of swingers through a magazine called *The Seekers.* Their leader was friendly and fast-talking, and his CB handle was "Dudley Do-Right." Frank Monohan liked him and his lifestyle, and he saw no danger behind "Dudley's" broad smile.

But, of course, there was. Frank Monohan placed his confidence in the wrong man.

This case began in the thick brush at the summit of a lonely mountain pass, stumped detectives in four jurisdictions — including the FBI — and led them on a four-year chase across the United States. But, in the end, they untangled the mystery of a peculiar liaison that led inexorably to murder.

In "Run as Fast as You Can," a killer's motivation can be traced directly to a horrific bloody attack he witnessed as a small child. Whether any amount of counseling might have mitigated the psychological damage he suffered is a moot point. His parents were brilliant and wealthy, and they lived in an upscale neighborhood near a scenic park. His many trips to the waterfront park seemed a totally wholesome pastime. In reality, he was there to watch and to stalk, hiding in the trees and shrubs while he chose his targets.

"The Deadly Voyeur" demonstrates that we are often most in danger when we feel safe. Everyone should set an alarm bell in their subconscious minds. If they are suddenly threatened or accosted, they will then have an automatic plan to use in those precious seconds they have to escape from a potentially deadly situation. If they don't make the right choice, they are trapped. The young couple who met a prowling monster were not prepared for such an event. Even in their worst nightmares, they couldn't have imagined there were minds like his.

"Dark Forest: Deep Danger" is about a case I first investigated in the 1970s. In some sense, it remains almost as mystifying today as it was then. Even so, as I reinvestigated this inscrutable tragedy, I may have come upon an answer to what happened to a family of four who went into an Oregon forest to have a picnic and an outdoor adventure.

And vanished.

As time went by, they were found, but the discovery only brought about more questions. Perhaps a reader will have the answers that will finally put a horrendous mystery to rest forever. Possibly readers will agree with my theory.

■ ■ ■ ■

BUT I TRUSTED YOU

■ ■ ■ ■

CHAPTER ONE

The slender strawberry blonde and the school counselor whose home was three thousand miles away in Washington State met in such a seemingly romantic way that they seemed destined to be with one another: he was in New Orleans for a ten-day educational conference, and she was a concierge at a fine hotel in the Mardi Gras city. It would have been better, perhaps, if his judgment hadn't been somewhat obscured by the romance of it all. In retrospect, she undoubtedly knew exactly what she was doing.

It was 1988 when their story began. Teresa Gaethe was twenty-seven then, and she had deep roots in Louisiana and Florida. Trying to trace those roots, however, is almost impossible. Gaethe was her first husband's surname; her maiden name was probably Jones, but she didn't tell Charles "Chuck" Leonard that. She said her maiden name was Goldstein before she married a stock broker named Gary Gaethe, and she subtly alluded to her family's wealth, only the first of the many exaggerations and downright lies she would tell Chuck. Teresa's family — two sisters and a brother, and her parents — met Gary Gaethe only twice, once before she married him and once again when they attended their daughter's wedding. Teresa said she and Gary had lived aboard a wonderful sailboat during their brief marriage.

It was a somewhat bizarre celebration. Lois Patois,* Teresa's older sister who had always tried to look after her siblings, recalled, "My whole family went to Teresa's wedding, and there was a gentleman that had come down from like a balcony area, and he had a gun — a big gun."

From then on, Teresa's family wondered if their sister's bridegroom was involved in some things that "weren't normal." Teresa said nothing to disabuse them of that impression; she enjoyed having mysteries in her life. She stayed married to Gary Gaethe less than two years, actually living with him for only a few months.

As they sipped cocktails far into the night,

*The names of some individuals have been changed. Such names are indicated by an asterisk (*) the first time each appears in the narrative.

Teresa gave Chuck the impression that she worked not out of necessity but because she enjoyed interacting with the guests who patronized the hotel where she was employed.

When Chuck told her that he had a master's degree from a highly rated Jesuit college — Seattle University — and that he was working to be qualified as a school principal, she volunteered that she had a college degree. She probably didn't, but following her tangled background to its sources is akin to untangling a ball of yarn after a kitten is through playing with it.

Teresa was five feet, six inches tall, but she was small-boned and sometimes appeared to be far more delicate than she really was. In truth, she had a backbone of steel and usually got what she wanted. Her green eyes gave her a seductive quality. She knew how to attract and please men, and she spent a great deal of time on her clothes, hair, and makeup. Sometimes, she looked like Sharon Stone, and then again she could be as guileless and innocent as Doris Day.

She had a cute little pug nose and thick blond hair, and a good, if somewhat boyish, figure. She kept her nails long and lacquered bright red. But she wasn't technically beautiful; she also had a "spade chin," too elongated for her face to be perfect, and she didn't like her nose.

Haltingly, Teresa told Chuck that she felt lucky to be alive; she said she had survived open-heart surgery when she was a child, but she assured him that she was in good health now. She showed him the scars left from her cardiac operations, and he worried about her. He thought she might be protesting too much when she said she had no lingering effects from such drastic surgery at a young age.

Chuck Leonard was a very complicated man. He was a natural-born caretaker, but he was also something of a hedonist. Chuck Leonard was, as his sister, Theresa (with a name close to Teresa) said, "a rescuer." He was five years older than his only sibling and he'd always been a caring big brother and he liked that role. The women in his life tended to be younger than him — and somewhat dependent and needy.

Probably Teresa Gaethe appealed to him both because she was very attractive and because she seemed lost and in need of a strong shoulder to lean on. It may have been the story she told him about her bad heart.

More likely, it was because Teresa was skilled at figuring out what different men wanted. And she quickly deduced that Chuck wanted someone who needed him, women

24

he could mentor into a more fulfilling life. And, in certain ways, Teresa fit into that category.

Like Gary Gaethe, Chuck Leonard was twenty years older than Teresa, but he didn't act or look his age. He had a trim, muscular build, and handsome even features with clear light eyes beneath hooded lids. Chuck had a thick head of hair that his barber cut in the latest style. Sometimes he had a crew cut, and occasionally, he let it grow below his ears and down to his shoulders. When Teresa met him, he had a thick, brushlike mustache.

During the many evenings they spent together, he told her about his waterfront home in Washington State, his great job with the school district, his airplane, and his vintage sports cars. That was all true, but Chuck's cars and plane were older models. And he'd built his house and property into what they were by dint of his own hard physical labor.

Teresa assumed he was wealthy. One Washington detective surmised that each of them thought the other had no money problems. "In the end, they both got fooled — but Chuck got fooled more."

Actually, Chuck didn't care if Teresa had money, and he didn't deliberately mislead her. He was making a fairly good salary, and he was able to afford those things he wanted. He owned property beyond the house he remodeled, and he lived comfortably.

Oddly, Teresa told Chuck she was two years older than she really was — a switch on the usual adjustments women make to their true ages. Perhaps she wanted him to think that their ages weren't that far apart.

When Teresa and Chuck fell in love his friends thought it was because of a mutual physical attraction and not because either was a fortune hunter. Or so it seemed. In retrospect, one could wonder if Teresa would have allowed herself to become deeply involved with Chuck so rapidly if she knew he didn't really have the assets of a truly wealthy man. But she did miss him a lot when the educational conference ended and he flew back to Washington.

He missed her more. Chuck wrote to Teresa three times a day, mailed sentimental cards, and sent her flowers from his own garden, carefully packed in green tissue paper with water-filled glassine tubes so that they arrived in good condition.

Teresa's heart wasn't totally devoted to Chuck Leonard. In 1987, before she met Chuck, she had carried on an intense affair with another man for six months. His name was Nick Callas,* and she'd met him when she went to Hawaii to work. Callas was a realtor and Teresa went to his office inquiring about housing. They were both single and they could not deny the immediate chemistry between them.

But after six months Nick still hadn't made any move toward a permanent relationship, so Teresa returned to New Orleans. They exchanged cards and phone calls from time to time. After she met Chuck, Teresa wrote to Nick and told him that she would be living in Washington State.

Not long after, Callas married someone else. And he lived even farther away from New Orleans than Chuck did — in Hawaii. Nick was the same age as Chuck, but beyond that they didn't resemble each other. Callas was well on his way to becoming rich, while money mattered little to Chuck. Like most men of Greek heritage, Callas was dark and swarthy, and boldly handsome, with a head of thick wavy black hair.

Teresa tended to gravitate toward older men; the three she was closest to were all almost two decades older than she was. Perhaps she was searching for a father figure. As the doors of her secret life slowly opened over the years, one could understand why.

Gary, Nick, and Chuck all fit that role; they were all kind to her and concerned about her — at least initially.

Teresa knew Nick was wealthy because he'd shown her many of the properties he owned. She sometimes wondered what her life would have been like if Nick had chosen her instead of his wife, Grace.*

Eventually, in about 1989, Nick seemed to disappear from Teresa's life. After her loneliness and frustration in trying to balance not one but two long-distance relationships, it wasn't difficult for Chuck to persuade Teresa to visit him at his Snohomish County home on Lake Goodwin near Stanwood, Washington. She had been married once, and Chuck had one or two ex-wives, but he'd been divorced for years.

"Chuck thought he had found his soul mate," his sister Theresa said. "Teresa came out for Thanksgiving in November 1988."

Chuck had seemed to be a confirmed bachelor for decades. His first wife, Reisa, had been a sixteen-year-old high school student and he'd been twenty-one when he proposed.

"It wasn't romantic at all," Reisa recalled. "We'd been dating and I knew Chuck wanted to avoid being drafted and sent to Vietnam. He didn't want to go to Canada, either. He picked me up at school one day and told me we were going to get married, and if I didn't say yes, he would find another girl."

Reisa wasn't happy at home and she did care about Chuck, so she agreed. Chuck wasn't nearly ready to settle down, but their marriage did delay his being drafted for a few more years. However, they had no children and eventually Chuck's draft number came up. He was sent to Fort Lewis — south of Tacoma, Washington, for training.

Reisa Leonard was very fond of Chuck's family. She and his sister Theresa bonded, and she liked his natural mother, Ann, who was fun to be around. Chuck's father, Fred, resembled Humphrey Bogart with his cigarette hanging from his mouth. "He was a good-looking man," Reisa said, "and he was interesting."

And so was his son, who always had some new plan and was filled with energy.

"When Chuck was at Fort Lewis, he got a brilliant idea," Reisa recalled. "Those poor kids from the Midwest missed their mothers' cooking, so Chuck went into the pie business. Ann made wonderful pies, and she taught me how to make them, too. We would make a bunch of them and take them to Chuck at Fort Lewis. He sold out of his locker for a good profit."

But it was against army rules, and his sergeant found out and made Chuck eat all the pies left in his locker.

Chuck was sent to Germany. In one of his few sentimental gestures toward Reisa, he gave her an engagement ring and wedding ring he'd won playing cards in his barracks. She was touched, even though the set had only small diamond chips.

After almost four years, Reisa and Chuck's marriage died of its own weight, and they divorced. Although she stayed close to Theresa, Reisa went thirty-five years without seeing her young ex-husband. She took a job with the Kitsap County Sheriff's Office, married twice more, and had a son.

Whether Chuck Leonard married again before he met Teresa Gaethe is questionable. He did have a daughter during one of his short affairs, but they were not close. When she grew up, she looked for him and they had begun a tentative relationship that looked promising.

Teresa totally captivated Chuck, and for the first time in decades he actually thought about forming a permanent bond with a woman.

When Teresa saw Chuck's house, she was impressed. Painted a soft gray, it rose three stories and was set right on the lake. A small emerald velvet plateau of grass paralleled the shoreline; it looked as if it had been trimmed with manicure scissors. Chuck was a perfectionist when it came to things like his house, his property, and his cars. He obviously had a green thumb; there were flowers blooming all over his property, along with pine, cedar, and fir trees. He was justly proud of his home. He explained to Teresa that he had built it from a cabin, digging out the hill at the lake level to facilitate two extra floors. It was beautifully maintained and welcoming, even though it wasn't quite the big lodge that Teresa had pictured in her mind. And she had no intention of becoming a gardener; it would ruin her nails.

Still, she told Chuck that she was very impressed with his house and landscaping and praised him for his work on the place.

Chuck had excellent taste in furniture, and he'd hung his grandmother's oil paintings. His former girlfriends had picked out rugs, lamps, and other items that didn't always match. The result was eclectic, but it complemented the inside of the lake house, just as the landscaping did the exterior.

Teresa didn't know anything about cars, so she didn't realize Chuck's prize Porsche was powered by a Volkswagen engine. He had had sports cars since he was a young man and took pride in his expertise at rebuilding engines and other car parts. Some of Chuck's detailing of his assets had been all flash and little substance, but he obviously loved his home, his cars, and his plane.

And he couldn't do enough to make Teresa happy. Heretofore a ladies' man who often dated several women in the same time period, Chuck Leonard was bedazzled by his Southern love. He believed her when she told him she was Jewish and her family name was Goldstein, and warned his parents and other relatives not to serve pork or ham for Thanksgiving. He gave Teresa Hannukah cards, and did everything he could to acknowledge her religion. What her purpose was in claiming to be Jewish remains a mystery; sometimes it seemed that she just enjoyed being untruthful — it gave her some kind of control.

"She was aloof," Chuck's sister recalled, "even though everyone tried to please her, and we carefully followed whatever Jewish customs Chuck said were important to her."

Teresa seemed to care for Chuck, and he adored her — and that was what mattered to his family.

Chuck's sister Theresa noted almost immediately that Chuck's new bride was nice enough to her when he was around, but dismissive when they were alone. As long as Theresa agreed with her new sister-in-law, things went fairly well. And yet she sensed an odd seething anger just below Teresa's surface.

"She could cut you out of her life and be incredibly cold," Chuck's sister said. "She kept me at arm's length. I hated that we had the same name."

Theresa wondered why Teresa didn't try a little harder to fit in with the family. Chuck's relatives had been prepared to welcome his new love, but she was more often a prickly pear with them instead of an affectionate relative. She was warm — even seductive — with Chuck and his father. The older man was quite taken with her.

At first.

CHAPTER TWO

Teresa never returned to New Orleans to live, and she visited only once more. Her sister, Lois, who grew up to marry a sergeant with the Louisiana State Police and to teach children with special needs, talked about the terror she and her two sisters had suffered in their home. No one ever helped them because they didn't tell. They were raised never to confront their father — Ervin R. Jones — who was a steamship captain for the Lykes Brothers Steamship Company when they were small and was rarely home. Later, his daughters longed for those days.

The three younger children were girls, and they had a brother, Frank,★ who was eight years older than Lois. Teresa was six years younger than Lois, and Macie★ was the youngest.

There was information that suggested Ervin Jones had fathered a child outside of his marriage — a boy. He had written tu-

34

ition checks to a private boys' school for a long time.

It would be many years before the Jones girls' memories were voiced. There were secrets upon secrets in their home — which looked, from the outside, like a typical middle-class family lived there. This is so often true: shame and fear keep sexual abuse victims silent.

Teresa's mother's maiden name wasn't where Teresa got the Jewish name she preferred. Her mother's maiden name wasn't Gloria Goldstein; it was Gloria Sheehan in some documents, a good solid Irish name. On her birth certificate, Gloria's last name is listed as Miecikowski.

Teresa told Washington acquaintances that she and her mother went to Texas every year on vacation — just the two of them. That wasn't true.

Gloria Jones passed away of cirrhosis of the liver in October 1990, and Teresa flew back to New Orleans for the funeral. Her sisters picked her up and they sat together in the funeral parlor.

They didn't have long to talk. Lois and Macie weren't really sure where Teresa had been over the years. The sisters were together only sporadically and much of her life was a mystery to them. Lois was very surprised when Teresa told her she had a son, and his name was Taylor. Lois couldn't recall later if she had seen Taylor's photograph, but she didn't think she had.

Two years later, their father died in December 1992. He also had cirrhosis of the liver. Teresa didn't go to his funeral. All three sisters mourned their mother, but not their father. They blamed him for their mother's death, and for their own years of abuse at his hands. Teresa said she didn't even know where he was living when he passed away, "somewhere in the Midwest."

By the time her parents died, Teresa was so removed from her family emotionally and geographically that local police in Washington State had to track her down and notify her of their passing.

Teresa Jones aka Gaethe aka Goldstein and Chuck Leonard were living together on Lake Goodwin. They cohabited for more than a year before Chuck agreed to marry her. He had some reservations, but he loved her and thought they could work out whatever problems they had once they were married.

Chuck's friends were often baffled by some of Teresa's stories which seemed to have no basis in fact. She told them she was a "world-class water-skier," but even though she and Chuck lived on a lake, no one ever saw her water-ski — or snow-ski in the Cascade Mountains.

"She also told us that she was due to come into a huge inheritance," a female neighbor said. "But as far as I know, it never happened."

Chuck and Teresa had set a date for their wedding: June 1990. The wedding itself would be a simple "city hall"–type of ceremony with friends as witnesses. But that would be followed a few days later by a large reception for family and friends at the lake house.

"It was almost as if they had a secret ceremony," Chuck's sister remembers.

Teresa didn't invite any of her family members to either her civil wedding or to the reception. Her mother was ill, and she didn't want her father there. As it turned out, the Joneses of Louisiana weren't nearly as wealthy as Teresa had implied. She came from a working-class clan, and she'd had to work. Chuck could not have cared less. He was happy to take care of her.

After their wedding, Chuck's smile was even wider than usual as he posed in his wedding tuxedo, a sprig of lily-of-the-valley in his lapel and his new gold wedding band gleaming on his finger.

Their wedding reception at Chuck's Lake Goodwin home began with a lot of laughter and toasts as Chuck's friends arrived to congratulate them. Oddly, the new bride had hired a bouncer to be present at the reception. He was a tall, muscular man she worked with at the Bon Marché department store.

There was one very embarrassing incident at the reception. One of Chuck's neighbors, an old friend named Jan, brought an uninvited date. She was one of Chuck's many former girlfriends. Everybody else who showed up was welcome. It wasn't as if Teresa's security guard was checking off names at the front door, and it had been a long time since Jan's date had dated Chuck. They hadn't even gone out for long. Even so, Teresa was livid, wild with jealousy. She asked her bouncer to throw Jan and the woman out. Incredulous and humiliated, they left, along with several of the other guests, who moved the party down the street to Jan's house.

Chuck was mortified by the whole episode.

The next day, Jan came by to talk with Chuck. "You've made a big mistake," he told Chuck.

Rather than being angry, Chuck answered sadly, "I know."

And suddenly, Chuck disappeared for two or three days to decide what to do about his fledgling marriage and Teresa's bizarre behavior.

"He was gregarious and had lots of friends," his sister recalled. "But he was a private person, and incredibly introspective."

It would have been impossible for Chuck not to discover some of Teresa's lies. She had brought her car with her when she moved from New Orleans to Washington State, and then it disappeared. She told everyone that it had been stolen.

"That wasn't the case," one neighbor said. "It was repossessed."

Chuck had never thought to check out Teresa's background; he'd always taken her at her word, even when her past seemed tilted and full of missing pieces. So far, none of the half-truths had hurt their relationship severely enough to drive them apart. He pondered his choices and realized he still loved her.

Chuck came back from his solitary trip. After much thought, he had decided to stay with Teresa, but he had glimpsed a side of her he hadn't really recognized before. She resented not only his former girlfriends but also his male friends. He realized that if she had her way, he would cut them all completely out of his life. He wasn't about to do that.

According to his sister and many of his close friends, Chuck Leonard was "bigger than life." He got along with everyone.

"That was what drew people to him," Theresa said. "He always had a laugh, a broad smile, and a complex inner life."

"But Teresa was nasty to everyone," the same neighbor said. "And sarcastic. She ignored Chuck's friends. The men didn't like her, and she made their wives cry. She would say things like 'Oh, are we having a nice day?' but it didn't sound like she cared — it was sarcastic and derisive."

Teresa was much harder to read than Chuck. It was difficult to know just what she was feeling. Sometimes it was impossible for her sister-in-law to make eye contact with her. Teresa's expression was a mask — a façade, blocking anyone from getting close to her.

Now that she and Chuck were married, it seemed that Teresa set out to deliberately alienate his friends' wives and fiancées even more. The men naturally opted out of the Leonards' social circle when the women in their lives weren't welcome or came away hurt or insulted by the way Teresa had treated them.

Chuck and his sister Theresa had grown up in the navy base town of Bremerton, Washington, and he was "extremely loyal" to his friends. Even though the paths of their lives had diverged, once someone was Chuck Leonard's friend, he remained so. Some of them went back to his childhood and he cherished them. One of his closest friends had been a best pal back in Bremerton when they were fourteen.

But as Teresa insulted more and more people, Chuck's world became smaller. He didn't always know what she had done or said to hurt people, but she was adept at making others feel unwelcome.

Her pattern was much like that of men who "own" the women in their lives. Teresa succeeded in isolating Chuck from a large number of the people who mattered to him. Still, once committed, he was determined to make their marriage work. He made excuses for her behavior — if only to himself. She had had a difficult life, full of illness and sadness before he had "rescued" her, and he kept believing she would change if only she felt safe enough with him.

Chuck continued counseling teenagers — first at Cascade High School, and then at North Middle School.

Left behind in his desk at the former

school was a love letter from some woman in his life. Teresa didn't know about that, and it probably wasn't important to him. If it had been, he would have taken it with him.

But Teresa was suspicious of Chuck's contact with any female over sixteen. She told people that Chuck had been seen behaving inappropriately with one of his female students. This wasn't true.

In some ways, Teresa appeared to be a good sport. When she had realized that she would have to work to help pay their bills, she'd found a full-time position as a Liz Claiborne specialist at the Bon Marché (now Macy's) in a nearby shopping mall. She was an excellent saleswoman, bonding with a loyal clientele, and she did well with her salary and commissions. She was always impeccably dressed with perfect hair and makeup.

Teresa Jones-Goldstein-Gaethe-Leonard was a woman of many names, many faces, and many moods. She may well have had more surnames than even Chuck knew about. One of Chuck's friends said a long time later that she had seen a suitcase belonging to Teresa that was full of papers and cards for different identities.

She was a seductress of both men and women — if not physically, then psychologically. Teresa had an innate ability to recognize what people wanted from her, and could use that to get back what she sought from them.

A number of women who knew Teresa described her as "sweet." She was popular with most of her female coworkers and friends, especially those who were younger and far less experienced than she was. She became a role model for them. They thought her life sounded so exciting and listened avidly as she related fascinating anecdotes. They believed her without questioning.

Basically, Teresa was a "man's woman," and didn't care all that much for women, unless they were in a position to better her life.

With her female friends, her mien was either that of a naive, vulnerable woman — a role in which she was also believable — or she was a living, walking soap opera for female friends whose own lives weren't nearly as interesting as hers.

One of Teresa's customers at the Bon Marché became a very close friend. Joyce Lilly* dropped by regularly to buy Liz Claiborne products, and they often had lunch together. Eventually, Joyce, too, got a job at the Bon Marché, and their friendship became even closer.

Teresa hinted to a few intimate friends that she had suffered at the hands of men. She was attracted to men, but deep down she didn't trust them. It gave her a common ground of experience with a lot of women she met, and those who had bad experiences with men were drawn to her.

Still, she couldn't see a way to have the kind of life she wanted without letting down her guard with certain men. For the moment, Teresa felt Chuck was the man who could help her the most. Like almost all the other men in her life, he was considerably older that she was. She appealed to older men, and may have sought them out — looking for a father figure to cherish her. . . or to punish.

Chuck Leonard was undecided about having children; he was past forty and he had never particularly wanted children of his own. When he was much younger, he had fathered his daughter, who was placed for adoption. He wasn't mature enough to be a parent then. Chuck cared a lot about the teenagers he counseled and showed affection and concern for them. It was a moot point anyway, because Teresa had confided to him she could not have children.

That wasn't the truth, however; Teresa had never been told she was barren. And she had confided to someone she worked with that she hoped to have a child or children.

"Children open doors for you," she said. The other woman had no idea what Teresa meant.

Teresa's relationship with her sister-in-law remained abrasive and dismissive. Neither trusted the other very much, and Chuck's sister worried about her brother's happiness. Maybe the two women — Teresa and Theresa — were just too different. Like Chuck, his sister was highly educated, a no-nonsense woman who was independent and capable.

She also tried to make excuses for Teresa. It might be possible that Chuck's new wife was trying too hard to establish her position with him and as part of the family. Perhaps she was shy and awkward in social relationships, although that seemed unlikely. Theresa backed off, always hoping that one day they might become friends.

"Teresa liked to give people advice," Theresa Leonard, who has a master's degree in psychology, said. "So I made a point of asking her opinion on decorating and clothes, and things like that, hoping it might give us something in common. But it didn't."

It came to a point where Chuck's sister no longer saw him and his wife very often.

Theresa's efforts to bond somehow with

Chuck's wife became even more important when Teresa and Chuck announced nineteen months after their wedding that they were expecting a baby.

Theresa became "Aunt Theresa." At least it helped to spell out which one of them was Chuck's sister and which one was his wife.

And so it turned out that Teresa was not infertile after all. (What had become of her son Taylor — if, indeed, he had ever existed — no one knew. Probably Chuck never even heard of this son Teresa told her sister about.)

Chuck was taken completely off guard by her pregnancy. She had flat-out lied to him about her ability to bear a child, and she'd made many visits to a fertility expert without telling Chuck.

At this point, he was quite willing to accept a baby into his life, realizing this might be his last chance to actually raise a child. He wasn't sure how Teresa felt about being pregnant.

Even though she had visited doctors so that she could bear a child, now that she was pregnant, Teresa acted as if she was ambivalent about the prospect.

Chuck told Teresa, "It's up to you if you want to keep it or not. I'll go along with whatever you decide."

She considered having an abortion, but finally decided to have the baby.

Teresa's labor was induced on December 30, 1991. Teresa was annoyed at what she considered Chuck's insensitivity when he dashed out to get fast food and brought it back to the labor room to eat when she was in pain. She later said her labor progress stalled and her obstetrician decided her pelvic canal was too narrow to deliver her baby, necessitating a caesarean section. Again, she lied; she delivered normally.

She gave birth to a daughter, whom they named Morgan. Her father and mother both adored her. Chuck, especially, was thrilled with his beautiful baby girl and spent hours gazing at her.

"He was over the top in love with her," his sister said. "He'd never realized it would be that way."

As Morgan grew bigger, he took her to the lake in warm weather and watched as she paddled around; he took her to fairs, where she rode on the merry-go-round, and to his school to show her off to his fellow teachers. It was clear that Chuck Leonard loved every minute of being a father, much to his own surprise.

Teresa had experienced labor once (possibly

twice), and she didn't want to go through it again. During a routine checkup after Morgan's birth, her gynecologist found that she had a small fibroid tumor. Many women develop fibroids in their thirties and forties, but they are almost never cancerous and invariably shrink after menopause. Teresa didn't have heavy bleeding with her periods or any of the other indications that the fibroids were large enough to necessitate removing her uterus. Even so, she demanded a hysterectomy, and she was resolute about her decision.

Once more, Chuck acceded to her decision and she got her way, but she asked about having her eggs saved and frozen, just in case she wanted to use them in the future. Teresa had a partial hysterectomy in July 1993. At her request, her surgeon left one ovary and one fallopian tube. She would still have plenty of female hormones, and would produce viable eggs — which could be implanted into another woman's uterus by an in vitro process. She could never carry a child herself, but through modern technology, she would be able to be the biological mother of a child.

To the casual observer, the Leonards appeared to be a happy couple. Teresa didn't want to work full-time away from home now that she had Morgan, so with Chuck's blessing, she rented some space in a shedlike building in the nearby small town of Marysville, Washington, and opened a store called The Consignment Shop.

She painted it pink and decorated the windows and the building itself with cartoon drawings of fashionably dressed women. Teresa told a lot of people she owned a "boutique," but that was stretching the meaning considerably.

Many hamlets in Snohomish County had become meccas for shoppers seeking out antiques, vintage jewelry, and gently used high-end clothing lines. The stores flourished when shoppers from Seattle, Bellingham, and even British Columbia discovered them and told their friends.

Teresa brought in a number of her wealthy customers from the Bon Marché; she'd kept her customer list. She was clever at deciding what would sell in her tiny store, and she kept careful records of items people had left for her to sell on contingency. Some of her Bon Marché customers placed expensive clothing and other treasures with her. When something sold, she kept a small percentage of the price and gave the rest to the seller. She enjoyed her small business, and while she wasn't making a munificent living, she did well enough to buy things for Morgan and clothes for herself, and eventually to hire employees.

Teresa's shop worked well for her because she had a real knack for putting together outfits for would-be customers. Teresa could take a plain dress, add a scarf or some jewelry and a coordinating purse — all second-hand — and make it look like a thousand-dollar outfit. She'd always done that with her own clothes, and now she used her talent in her consignment store. She was extremely professional, even waxing the clothes racks so that garments slid easily, and she kept meticulous books so that she could pay her bills and her consignors promptly.

Most important to Teresa, she could take Morgan to work with her; her two clerks or friends who dropped by were there to share the babysitting duties. She seemed to be a good mother, almost idolizing Morgan. Her friends believed that Teresa's whole life revolved around Morgan.

And so did Chuck's. Morgan always seemed delighted when her father came to pick her up. "She was maybe a little bit spoiled, though," one woman said. "If she was playing with her toys, she wouldn't go with either one of them."

There was no question that both Chuck

and Teresa loved their small daughter, but as the years passed, the bloom was fading fast from their love for each other. Of course all marriages settle in as the years pass, and the emotional highs and lows tend to smooth out, but with the Leonards, it was more than familiarity or boredom. Chuck had always been the man in charge, someone with an expansive personality, who did pretty much what he wanted to. But now, his friends and family noted that Teresa controlled him, chose which of his friends she liked, pouted when she didn't get her way, or, worse, flared into anger. Chuck tried hard to please her and keep a semblance of a happy home — mostly for Morgan's sake.

Chuck was willing to do anything to be able to stay with Morgan.

Teresa began to think a lot about Nick Callas, wondering if she should have let her Hawaiian love go. To test the waters, she sent him a Christmas card. Nick contacted her and they renewed their friendship. From then on, Teresa and Nick stayed connected, but he remained with his wife. Although Grace had helped Nick get a foothold in business, it was his skill and charisma that had built his company to the top levels it now reached. By 1995, he owned prize property all over the islands.

There was no question that Nick Callas was rich enough to give Teresa all the luxuries in life that she longed for, along with credit cards and a healthy stock portfolio. They began an intense correspondence and talked about meeting once again. He promised to send her a first-class ticket if she decided to come to Hawaii to visit him. She was sorely tempted.

Callas's wife, Grace, often went to southern California with their adopted son, who was two months older than Morgan. Grace was a nervous woman who complained of chronic health problems and stayed with her sister while she sought the best possible medical treatments.

Nick had dated many willing females when he was single, but it didn't take long for Teresa to rise to the top of his list as a lover. He'd never forgotten her, but he had chosen Grace, and her family's money had helped him in his mortgage and real estate business.

Like Chuck, Nick was easily distracted by pretty women.

Not surprisingly, Teresa's marriage to Chuck Leonard had foundered, growing worse each year. He hadn't been the answer to her search for happiness after all.

Was it even possible for Teresa to find happiness? She wanted so much, and it didn't appear to matter to her what happened to people who got in her way. Now, the wants and needs of Chuck Leonard or even her own daughter came after her thirst for wealth and love. She felt her husband had never given her what she had needed and expected from him.

Chuck was Chuck, and it amazed some of his friends that he had married at all: they knew him as a guy who dated many women. He was an individual, a little bizarre at times. He was a free spirit. When he got home from work, he started tossing his clothes on furniture and on the floor as he walked through his house. He probably would have been happier in a tropical climate. His neighbors had long since grown used to seeing him out in his yard, gardening or watering his precious grass patch next to the lake, often nearly nude in a bikini bathing suit and flip-flops. It had never really bothered anyone.

He was a good-natured guy and a good neighbor. Chuck was far handsomer than he had any right to be for a man of his age, and women often came on to him. In the first years of his marriage, he began a physical relationship with a female coworker whom he'd known for seven or eight years. Her name was Michelle Conley,* and she was an attractive teaching intern, a few years older than Teresa. Michelle responded to him in a way his wife hadn't for a long time.

They first became intimate when Teresa was pregnant with Morgan. The Leonards had something of an open marriage. Whether they both knew it and discussed it with one another is questionable.

At least outwardly, neither Chuck nor Teresa appeared to be unhappy with their relationship. Chuck had a real rapport with teenage students, and his counseling helped many of them who were suffering through some of the more difficult times of life. He had saved some of them from suicide.

Along with Morgan, those kids gave him a reason to be happy. After he had his second daughter, no one could say Chuck hadn't tried to keep their family together, even if it was probably because he loved Morgan so much. He made no promises to Michelle, but, as Teresa grew colder to him, he felt closer to Michelle, and she definitely wanted to marry him if she could. The more Teresa pulled away from him, the more Chuck sought out Michelle. However, like most men, he wasn't interested in getting divorced and remarried.

There was Morgan and she came first.

In July 1992, Chuck and Michelle were involved in an embarrassing incident, more likely to happen to teenagers than middle-aged educators. A Marysville police officer approached Chuck's car where it was parked on a quiet street at six in the evening. His police report said he found Michelle, whose clothing was in disarray, sitting on Chuck's lap, and noted that Chuck was completely naked. They were both removed from the vehicle, handcuffed, and placed in the back of the police unit. Michelle was cited for disorderly conduct, and Chuck for indecent exposure.

At their trial, they were acquitted of the charges. But naturally, Teresa learned of the incident and it didn't help their already teetering marriage. They stayed together for a few more years, but it became more of an adversarial relationship, held together only by their shared love for Morgan.

And then, quite suddenly, the Leonard marriage was over. Teresa had seen brighter prospects on the horizon: she was in touch regularly with Nick Callas. Nick was rich now, and it didn't matter to Teresa that he was married.

In early 1995, Teresa took three-and-a-half-year-old Morgan and moved out of Chuck's house at Lake Goodwin into an apartment on Everett Mall Way, an hour's drive away.

Teresa had written to Nick Callas, telling him that she was coming to Hawaii with a friend and she would like to see him. He responded with plane tickets and the promise of a place for them to stay.

It hadn't taken long for Teresa to feel quite secure in her affair with Nick Callas, and she fully expected they would marry in the foreseeable future. She invited Joyce Lilly to join her on a vacation to Maui in February 1995, the first of four trips to Hawaii where Joyce accompanied her. Over the next two years, Teresa would visit Callas once a month or more.

The two women would stay in one of Nick's more luxurious condominiums, and when they arrived, there were exotic fresh flowers waiting for them in the Napili Shores condo. Nick came by a few hours later, and Joyce watched as he and Teresa hugged and kissed, and then Teresa sat on his lap while the three visited.

The next morning, Joyce was awakened at 5:30 a.m. by someone sitting on her bed. It was Nick, who apologized profusely. He had meant to wake Teresa up. He moved to the other bed, wakened her gently, and then the two of them walked out to the veranda.

Joyce realized that Teresa wasn't exaggerating about her affair with Nick Callas; they certainly seemed to be entranced with one another. By July 1995, Teresa confided that Nick sent her the monthly first-class tickets to Maui, and checks for $1,000 to $1,250 as regularly. During the weeks that Chuck had custody of Morgan, she would sometimes spend several days in Hawaii with Nick.

When Teresa was in Washington, despite Nick's involvement in his many business interests, they usually called each other up to ten times a day. Nick called Teresa more than she called him, but they were constantly in contact. Nick would recall later that they talked mostly about his son Jack* and Morgan.

"Sometimes we talked about movies," Nick remembered. "We had brief calls that ended when someone came into her little shop, or people walked into my office, but sometimes we talked for a couple of hours."

In July 1995, Teresa filed for divorce.

Teresa's divorce action against Chuck seemed to be more a threat than a reality. In any event, neither Teresa nor Chuck pursued it avidly. Chuck consulted an attorney, who advised him to keep the divorce unsettled. That would establish a pattern of joint custody and help him gain custody of Morgan.

After much wrangling, they worked out a grudging custody arrangement, agreeing that Morgan would stay with each of them during alternate weeks. As long as Chuck knew that his little girl was living close by, he would do whatever was necessary to be with her, even stall a divorce that he wanted as much as Teresa — or more.

Morgan gave Teresa leverage with Chuck, and she felt confident that he would do what she wanted: all she had to do was threaten to take Morgan far away from him. And that is what she planned to do — but not yet.

Morgan had become a pawn, someone Teresa could use to advance her own goals. She seemed unable to understand that taking Chuck away from Morgan, robbing her of her father, would be a cruel thing to do — and a great loss in her daughter's life. Teresa's Hawaiian lover could never care for the child the way Morgan's real father did. Nick had never even seen Morgan, although Teresa had met his little boy a few times.

Teresa Gaethe-Leonard had a plan in mind, but the logistics involved were going to be tricky. Until she was absolutely sure that she had a safe and luxuriant landing place, she was not going to divorce Chuck. Her lover, Nick Callas, was still very married. Although she didn't admit it to her friends,

Nick and she had never even discussed his getting divorced.

Teresa was even a business boost for Nick. She worked as an outside salesperson for Orca Travel and she often connected clients and her lover when they were looking for high-end housing in Hawaii. The referrals she occasionally sent him were a good cover, too. Although Nick had special phone lines set up for them to talk, if Grace ever wondered about the calls, he would say that Teresa was a business contact.

Nick continued to buy Teresa round-trip tickets to Hawaii, she had an American Express card with his name on it, and he provided lodging in one of his plush condos whenever she could fly to the islands. But he was content with the way things were, and he believed she was, too. Among her many talents, she was a persuasive actress.

Teresa was the perfect mistress. She never discussed anything depressing with Nick. "Teresa shares only positive things with me," he said once, "not negative things."

In the two years of their passionate affair, he learned virtually nothing about her early years in Louisiana with her family. If Nick asked her anything about them, she became quiet — but offered no information. There were secrets within secrets in her past that

Nick didn't know, and Teresa meant to keep it that way.

In Nick Callas's memory, they hadn't talked about any unhappy aspects of their affair because there weren't any. Their time together was joyous and relaxing, full of passion. They were able to step out of their own everyday lives and enjoy each other whenever Teresa came to Hawaii. Sometimes, Nick came to the Northwest for a few days and they took trips together to ski lodges and resorts. They never discussed marrying one another, and Nick felt neither of them expected or wanted that to happen. He was unaware of plans for Teresa and Morgan to move to Hawaii, and he certainly had no intention of divorcing his wife.

"I got married once," he said later. "I waited until I was forty-one years old to get married, and that was it for me. I was only going to be married once."

Teresa was a woman who bolstered his confidence, gave him her constant approval, delighted him in bed, and demanded nothing of him. Nick Callas had no hint that Teresa had built a maze of complicated plans for them. He never saw a bad side of her, and she was always smiling and bubbly when they were together. Almost any man who fantasizes about being unfaithful to his wife

60

would probably gravitate toward someone like Teresa.

No nagging. No strings. No problems.

Callas had no biological children, but he loved his adopted son Jack — who was born in October 1991, as if he was the child of his own loins.

Teresa secretly believed that if she gave Nick a child with his own genes, his own Greek heritage, he would be so happy and grateful that he would leave his wife and marry her. Since Teresa had insisted on a hysterectomy after Morgan's birth, that was going to be tricky. Now, she truly could not conceive, but she had already planned for that.

Teresa had visited her gynecologist on May 10, 1995. She wanted to know exactly how in vitro fertilization worked. She knew she still produced eggs, and she told her doctor that "an old friend" who lived in Hawaii had agreed to furnish sperm.

"How often do you see this man?" the female surgeon asked.

"Every two weeks." It was, of course, a lie.

"Have you discussed in vitro with him?"

"Yes — and he's very supportive of it." This, too, was a lie. Nick had no plans to have a baby with Teresa. Teresa believed that Nick and his wife had adopted Jack because of some fertility problem with Grace. But it wasn't Grace who couldn't conceive; it was Nick's problem.

Although he had never confided in Teresa about it, he believed that he was incapable of fathering a child. He and Grace had tried for years to conceive, traveling to southern California to confer with top fertility specialists. They had first tried seven in vitro procedures, mixing Grace's eggs with Nick's sperm in a petri dish, hoping their doctor could implant viable embryos in Grace's uterus.

But no pregnancies resulted. It had been expensive, but the emotional pain was the worst part of that. Again and again, Grace failed to become pregnant.

They hadn't given up, but they tried another way. Although they worked with medical experts, Nick called it the "turkey baster method." Over five years, they tried seven times. In two instances his sperm was injected in two different extremely fertile surrogate mothers, who had each become pregnant in their own marriages on the first try. Both of the female subjects were prepared to carry a resultant embryo to term. They were disappointed when neither potential surrogate mother became pregnant.

Nick Callas, as masculine as he looked, had a very low sperm count. They didn't know why. His doctors eventually diagnosed him as having too many clusters of veins and arteries in his testicles for sperm to survive long. They offered him surgery to remove them, but gave him no promises of success. He opted not to have the operation.

Whether Teresa was aware of this is questionable. Had Nick told her he could not father a child? Nick would insist later that they had never discussed having a child together. There was no reason to share his most intimate physical problems with her.

But Teresa believed what she believed, and she was given to "magical thinking" where everything would turn out as she visualized it. She rapidly erased any truth that interfered with her plans.

Teresa lied once more to her doctor, saying that she had a close female friend who would offer her a "surrogate womb" to carry her own fertilized egg to term.

In Teresa's mind, the baby would be hers and Nick Callas's child, just as much as if conception had taken place the old-fashioned way. And biologically that would be true.

Teresa had studied up on all kinds of infertility, and state-of-the-art insemination procedures. The "friend" who had volunteered to carry her baby was probably another exaggeration. If she moved to Hawaii, Teresa planned to find a surrogate mother and pay her to carry a baby after in vitro fertilization with Nick's sperm. If Teresa's eggs were no longer usable for some reason, she realized she might have to forgo her genetic participation. Whatever it took, she would see that Nick had a child who was partly his own, and then he would marry her and they would raise that child — and Morgan, and, hopefully, Nick's son — together.

Her plan sounded more like an extremely complicated science project than a baby born out of love. And, short of a miracle, it was doomed from the beginning.

Her doctor warned Teresa of legal pitfalls. She cited cases she had read about where the surrogates refused to give up the babies after they were born. "That can be a sticky situation," she said, advising her that she should consult with an attorney before she began such a process.

"And it would help any case that came up against you if you were married to the baby's biological father," she added.

Teresa's gynecologist knew very little about her current marital status. She gave her the names of some fertility specialists, explaining that she didn't have the additional training needed to harvest and implant eggs.

Teresa was jubilant when she left her office, heedless of all the warnings she'd been given. She knew her plans weren't going to be easy to carry off, but she was sure she could do it. Of course, it was all pie in the sky.

There was the problem of Chuck. Teresa expected him to dig in his heels and refuse to let her take Morgan to Hawaii to live. There was no question about it, and she at least accepted that.

Although Chuck had felt a weight lift from his shoulders when Teresa moved out, he missed living full-time with Morgan. Having her with him every other week just wasn't the same as being her dad every day. When Teresa occasionally mentioned that she intended to live in Hawaii, Chuck worried.

He would die before he would let Teresa take his little girl so far away. He may even have used that phrase when she brought up the subject.

Outwardly, Chuck Leonard wasn't a serious man. He had an active social life, and he was still dating Michelle. Michelle was probably the perfect woman for him. She wasn't the jealous type, and she believed that he was faithful to her, but she hadn't asked for that. She lived with Chuck during the weeks that

Morgan wasn't staying there, and she worried about his getting home safe at night. They had a great time together, and she was easygoing and devoted to him.

Chuck didn't miss Teresa, but he was deadly serious about Morgan. He loved her with all the devotion in his body. He was fifty-two and not likely to have more children. Morgan meant the whole world to him, and he looked forward to the weeks when his daughter lived with him.

On the other hand, Teresa often left Morgan with near-strangers as babysitters. She made friends with a man named Bill Pursley* who lived in the same apartment building she did and often asked him to look after Morgan. Chuck's friends, Sandy and Jan — who had once warned Chuck that he'd made a terrible mistake marrying Teresa — regularly looked after Morgan when Teresa was away or busy.

And she often was. Teresa loved Morgan, but she needed time for herself, too.

How was Teresa going to coordinate a medically precarious pregnancy with her lover, a nonacrimonious divorce from her husband, and her lover's divorce from his wife, and be sure all the pieces dovetailed? It was essential that nobody became angry enough to block her plans. She walked on eggshells, testing all the men in her life and balancing them like a juggler with more and more plates in the air.

Teresa believed, albeit erroneously, that Chuck's girlfriend was a recent high school graduate and that he was acting unethically. That would give Teresa another weapon to use against him. Actually, Michelle was a few years older than Teresa.

Teresa still had her consignment store. Chuck never shorted her on child support and he paid for so many other things that Morgan needed. Nick Callas was always willing to buy her tickets to Hawaii for a liaison with him. She was convinced he loved her or, at the very least, found her too sensuous and desirable to walk away from.

If Teresa wrote down her goals, they would have read like this:

1. Gain full legal custody of Morgan.
2. Finalize divorce from Chuck.
3. Move to Hawaii.
4. Have a child with Nick, one way or the other.
5. Convince him to leave his wife.
6. Marry Nick and live happily ever after.

Goals four and five could happen in any order as far as Teresa was concerned. Nick

Callas was probably the biggest challenge she'd ever faced. He was quite content with his life, even though he was also devoted to Teresa. Sexually, she probably was the most enchanting woman he knew. But Nick was fifty, and he had come to realize that sex wasn't the most important thing in the world. He got along well enough with his wife. And if he weighed a love affair against how much it would cost him to get a divorce, his bank account would come first. He had spent years building up a fortune and a marriage, and if he divorced his wife, at least half of that would be gone. More than that, he would probably lose custody of Jack. Ironically, like Chuck, Nick didn't want to do anything that would take his son out of his life. He and Grace had raised the little boy from birth, carrying him straight from the hospital to their home, and he was a wonderful little boy.

Nick fully expected to maintain both his marriage and his affair with Teresa. And as much as Nick loved Teresa, he knew she wasn't the average woman. Not at all. "Teresa's probably ninety percent an angel, and ten percent crazy," he once said.

He may have overestimated the angel

percentage.

Thwarted, Teresa had to regroup, although she still believed that when she actually presented Nick with his own baby, he would change his mind.

And so she stalled, living in her apartment with Morgan, operating her little shop, and waiting to follow through on her divorce from Chuck. All things being equal, and if Chuck didn't fight too hard for custody of Morgan, a divorce in Washington State took only three months.

But Teresa dragged her feet on her divorce too long. In January 1996, the Snohomish County Superior Court informed both Teresa and Chuck that the court was dismissing their divorce case because there had been no action on it for a year.

The Leonards' relationship was in limbo. Neither of them wanted to reunite, but Chuck didn't seem to be upset that they had to refile if they wanted to be legally and finally separated forever. He would wait Teresa out if he had to.

They were deeply in debt, although Teresa always maintained that Chuck was well off and should have paid her more in child support. As it was, he was paying her all he could afford.

It was a paradox, but, with the insurance he carried and his other assets, Chuck Leonard was worth more dead than alive. In the financial statements he presented in their initial divorce action, they were more than $46,000 in debt. Teresa cleared only $300 a month from her shop. That baffled Chuck; she had told him she had a business degree, and he thought she should have made more than that. He offered her $334 a month for Morgan, while she said he could easily pay her $825. In essence, with all the extras he paid for his daughter, he was paying her more than $800.

Teresa didn't reveal that Nick Callas was sending her more than $1,000 a month. He told people that she worked as a travel agent, and she sometimes sent people to him to rent condos; at least he would later say that that was why he wrote checks on the accounts of his various condo rental properties to her. His wife knew nothing about this.

In a will drawn up in 1991, a will still in force, Chuck had stipulated that Teresa would get everything he had, both separate property (which he owned before they married) and community property (that had accumulated during their marriage). And that added up to a considerable amount. By 1996, Chuck's estate was substantial. He had

$95,000 in insurance, $95,000 in retirement benefits from the Everett School District, the $240,000 house on Lake Goodwin, his final payroll from North Middle School of over $11,000, and various properties he had inherited near Bremerton and Camano Island worth over $120,000. On top of that, Teresa and Morgan would receive Social Security payments. Even when his final debts were paid, Teresa stood to receive well over $300,000 as his sole heir, plus Social Security payments every month until Morgan was eighteen.

A year passed. Chuck was happy with Michelle Conley. She had her own place, but she was at Chuck's lake house more than she was home, an arrangement that she and Chuck attempted to keep secret. His best friends knew about Michelle, but most other people didn't.

And Teresa was happy in her relationship with Nick Callas, although she was planning feverishly to accelerate that into much more.

In January 1997, Chuck filed papers to keep his divorce in progress, knowing that that would probably confuse her. She wouldn't be able to take Morgan far away until it was all settled. He was ready to finalize the divorce, but he had no intention of letting her take Morgan to Hawaii.

Oddly, or perhaps not, Teresa was furious when she realized that she no longer had the chilling control over Chuck that she'd maintained since the night she met him. No other woman in his life had ever been able to bend him to her will.

"The cat was going to lose her mouse," Aunt Theresa said flatly. "She was very jealous of Chuck's connection to Morgan."

It had taken Chuck a long time to move forward on his divorce. He'd asked for advice from friends before he made his final decision. Should he let Teresa back in — but only if she agreed to counseling — for Morgan's sake?

None of them thought it was a good idea.

Teresa finally realized that Chuck was prepared to fight her fiercely if she attempted to take Morgan to Hawaii to live, even if she agreed to let Morgan spend the summers and vacations with him.

They were at an impasse.

Teresa and Morgan were close, and Morgan thought her mother was perfect. Moreover, she believed everything Teresa told her. Most five-year-olds accept their mother's word without doubt. Teresa told Morgan that her daddy didn't really own the house on Lake Goodwin. It really belonged to her grandmother — Teresa's mother, who had passed away, leaving it to Teresa. She said Gloria Jones had been an antiques dealer.

Teresa planted ideas about Chuck in Morgan's mind, telling her if she was ever afraid when she was with her daddy, she could call her mommy or "Aunt Joyce."

Teresa told Joyce Lilly she was worried that Chuck was sexually abusing their daughter, and Joyce was convinced it was true. The two women gave Morgan teddy bears with secret pockets where they had hidden their phone numbers. Most of the time when Chuck called Teresa at her shop to facilitate Morgan's transfer, Teresa would burst into tears at the end of the conversation, making her salesgirls think that Chuck Leonard must be a bullying monster.

Joyce was almost as gullible as Morgan, worrying about Teresa and her small daughter. The two young women who worked at The Consignment Shop were sympathetic, too. They noted that Morgan, who had once been jumping with excitement while she waited for her father, seemed to hold back. She cried and begged to stay with her mother, saying she didn't want to play with all the toys her daddy had for her.

No one knew exactly what Teresa was telling her.

Probably no one ever will.

Chuck wondered what Teresa was up to. Looking at her, she didn't appear to be dangerous. Still, Chuck — who had come to recognize her lies — sometimes wondered what she was capable of.

In November 1996, Chuck had wakened when Michelle nudged him. She whispered that she had heard a squeak on the stairs leading down to his bedroom. "I think someone's in the house."

He jumped out of bed and they heard the sound of someone running upstairs. Chuck leapt up the stairway to the living room. Soon, he came back, saying he hadn't caught up with whoever it was.

Michelle dressed hurriedly and drove after a car she spotted driving toward the main road that led to the freeway. Its headlights were out. It appeared to have come from a darkened area full of trees that abutted the state park at the end of Chuck's street. As the car passed under a streetlight, she saw the license plate. But the vehicle was soon in the shadows again, and she couldn't see the driver clearly. She was positive about the license plate, however. Then the car pulled away and picked up speed before she could catch up with it. She gave up and called

Chuck, giving him the license plate number.

It was the license number of Teresa's Nissan.

Chuck thought it might have happened again in January 1997. This time, his eyes snapped open with the sense that they were not alone. Half-asleep, he looked past Michelle who lay beside him in bed and thought he saw a dark figure in his ground-floor bedroom. He blinked and the figure was gone.

There was no particular sound of an intruder; it was more a feeling. But Michelle slept quietly, and the fear he'd felt slowly went away. He figured he must have had a bad dream — the fugue state of the nightmare that was already giving way to reality. They had both been jumpy, but not enough for Chuck to lock his doors before heading for bed. He never locked the cat doors because his five cats needed to get in the house if it rained, or if predators like raccoons, coyotes, or an occasional cougar stalked them. He wanted Bear, Chaucer, Zena-the-Warrior-Princess, Tab, and Jezabel to be safe and to come and go as they pleased during the night. A very small person could wriggle through the swinging cat entrances.

"Chuck loved his cats," his sister recalled.

Usually, Chuck liked the clear window in the floor over his waterbed, and the comments it elicited from visitors. It had once been a circular stairway, but he changed that when he remodeled the house, making it more like a ship's ladder than stairs, with a removable see-through hatch cover.

On this chilly night, he shivered at the thought that someone could have been up there in the dark, watching Michelle and him sleep. Maybe someone had been — maybe it was only a nightmare that had evolved from the incident in November. If someone had really been there, the trespasser had left the house on Lake Goodwin without causing any harm or stealing any of Chuck Leonard's possessions. Michelle believed it was Teresa.

Chuck told one of his good teacher friends about his "nightmare," and they tried to rationalize it in the light of day. Finally, they assumed it had been an imaginary thing — a night terror. Chuck had been under a lot of stress recently, and that could account for his feeling that someone was hiding in his house, watching him.

If only it had been.

CHAPTER THREE

Deputy Wynn Holdal of the Snohomish County Sheriff's Office was at the Lake Goodwin Fire Station at a quarter to one in the afternoon of February 20, 1997, when he heard the emergency medical technicians get a call of "Man down" at an address on Forty-second Drive. He prepared to follow the fire fighters to the address when more bells sounded and the station radio blared.

"Man down is DOA — dead on arrival."

This time, Holdal was dispatched to the scene by the sheriff's radio. He arrived by 1:00 p.m. and met with Fire Chief Darryl Neuhoff and Assistant Chief Robert Spencer. They had already strung yellow tape around the carport area of the three-story house; the rest of the yard was fenced off.

It was very cold out, the morning's frost barely burned off by a vapid sun.

Holdal could see the dead man, lying half-naked partially on his back and slightly on

77

his right side on the top step inside the front gate. Oddly, his right arm lay so close to a chain saw that it seemed to cradle it.

A man about forty stood nearby. He was fighting with his emotions, but did his best to tell Holdal what he knew. He gave his name as Douglas Butler and identified the corpse as his friend, Chuck Leonard.

"We both work at North Middle School," he said. "Chuck is — was — a counselor there and I teach shop and wrestling."

Butler said that Chuck hadn't come to work at the school earlier in the day or called in to arrange for a substitute. That wasn't at all like him, and both he and the principal were concerned. Chuck's estranged wife, Teresa Gaethe-Leonard, had called the school looking for him. That was a fairly rare event, too.

"Our principal asked me to check on him," his fellow teacher said.

Doug Butler said he'd gone to Chuck's lakeside house, walked down the sidewalk to the gate, and found it closed. "But I could see through it, and I saw Chuck on the steps. I opened the gate, and I knew he was dead, but I checked for a pulse anyway. There wasn't any."

Butler said that he and Chuck had been good friends for eighteen years, and he'd spent a lot of time at Chuck's house over the years.

No wonder his face was pale and his voice strained. It would have been a horrible shock to find his friend lying on the cold cement in icy weather. Dead.

Deputy Wynn Holdal asked Doug Butler the last time he had seen Chuck Leonard.

"Yesterday — about four p.m."

"He live with anyone?"

"No, not usually. He lives alone — except when his little girl is here — she's just turned five. He has a girlfriend named Michelle who works for the Everett School District. She sometimes stays over. And he's got an ex — or estranged — wife named Teresa. She *never* stays over."

Butler explained that this would have been Chuck's week to have Morgan, but the child had to have some dental work done. Neither Teresa nor Chuck had been able to say no to her about eating candy or going to bed with sugary juice in her bottle when she was much younger, and she'd had dental problems as a result. On this day in February, Teresa had argued that she would do better staying with her mother after seeing the dentist, and Chuck had given in.

"I hope she's not in there," Butler said nervously. He was afraid plans might have changed, and he worried that Morgan could possibly be inside the house, terrified, hiding someplace. Neither he nor Wynn Holdal wanted to think that she had suffered the same fate as her father.

Sergeant Matt Bottin had been dispatched to the scene and arrived at a quarter after one. He walked up to Deputy Holdal, who was standing in front of the carport talking with the aid crew and another man — who he learned was Doug Butler.

Bottin saw the body of Chuck Leonard lying on the top steps. He wore only a gray, bloodstained T-shirt.

He asked Butler about that, and Leonard's long-time friend said that Chuck was in the habit of sleeping either completely naked or wearing just a T-shirt.

"He just doesn't like underwear, and he sometimes answers the door nude when I've gone over to visit him in the morning. That's just him."

Sergeant Bottin crossed the yellow tape and walked close to Chuck Leonard's body. The gate was ajar about two inches. He could see trauma in Leonard's chest area, just above his heart.

"Was the gate like this when you got here?" Bottin asked Doug Butler, who shook his head.

"I pushed it just that far open so I could see if I could help Chuck," he said. "But it was obvious that he was dead, so I backed off without disturbing anything, went to my car and phoned 911 on my cell phone."

Bottin commented that it was odd that the dead counselor had his arm around the chain saw. Butler said that was his saw — that he had loaned it to Chuck a few days before. "It probably was sitting there when he collapsed.

"I'm still concerned about Morgan," he said. "I know she's not in there, but what if she is . . ."

To calm his fears, Bottin and Holdal slipped on rubber gloves and walked past the dead man. They entered the home through the front door, which stood open about six inches. The front door was on the east side of the lake house.

"Deputy Holdal and I would do only a cursory search, and then turn the crime scene over to the homicide detectives, who had been notified.

"There was a trail of blood from the deceased to the threshold of the door, and blood drops and smudges on the door itself. The blood trail continued into the house," Bottin recalled. "Down the hallway, across the living room to the stairs, which led down to Chuck's bedroom."

Doug Butler had told them that Morgan Leonard's room was upstairs, the first door on the left. "It was closed," Bottin said "and I opened it from the back side of the door knob."

Morgan's room was a lovely little-girl's room, full of dolls and toys, and it was completely undisturbed. Thank God, she wasn't anywhere in the house.

Wynn Holdal searched the remainder of the upstairs, while Bottin walked through the kitchen. He noted some open wine bottles and two or three empty wine glasses, which were sitting on the kitchen counter.

The kitchen didn't have a bloody trail. The two Snohomish County officers resumed following the dried blood that led down the stairs to a bedroom, passing by a throw rug that was rumpled as if someone had slipped on it.

Bottin spotted three bullet casings at the bottom of the stairs; they appeared to be for a .45 automatic. There were dried blood smudges on the wall beside the steps.

But they realized they'd found the site of the shooting in the bedroom itself. A large water bed sat in the middle of the room, and the comforter on it was blood-soaked. A bullet hole was evident in the fabric. The pillows at the head of the bed were also stained red. Clearly, the victim had been attacked in his bed, possibly while he was sleeping. The water bed had been pierced; the floor beside it was covered with puddles of water.

At the end of the bed, there was a sofa table with books and magazines on it, and there were blood splatters on top of these, too. A child's Pocahontas wigwam, a large white teddy bear, and children's books were also in the master bedroom.

They glanced behind a bifold door and found a closet inside. Another door led to a small office room. Neither closet area showed any signs of being disturbed.

They touched nothing directly as they looked through the house, and they were vastly relieved that they hadn't found a five-year-old girl inside.

"We turned around and left," Holdal said. "We still hadn't touched anything."

For all intents and purposes, Chuck Leonard had probably been near death from the moment he was shot, but he had managed to leap from his bed, run up the steep captain's ladder stairs after his killer, and keep going until he had bled out in the cold loneliness of his front yard. Even if paramedics had been in his house when he was shot, he probably would not have survived.

There were nine houses along the single-lane dirt road, but only seven were occupied in winter. The beach area was buzzing and alive in the summertime. And Wenberg State Park was just beyond a wooded area at the end of the street. Picnickers and campers filled the park then.

The house just to the north of Chuck's three-story home was occupied year-round by a doctor, who was a good friend of the victim's. In fact, Dr. Les Staunton* let Chuck park his Porsche in his carport. Their homes were about twelve feet apart wall-to-wall, but their decks were only four feet apart.

Bottin opened the door to the west wall of the carport and saw the walkway leading down to the doctor's home. He started down, but Butler stopped him.

"I've already banged on the door, but no one answered."

There was a good reason for that. Staunton had returned from a trip to Venezuela a day or so earlier, and he'd taken a sleeping pill the night before to try to get rid of his jet lag. He'd wakened early and left for his practice.

When he was located at his clinic, he told the investigators that he'd gone to bed a little after midnight and fallen sound asleep, only to be wakened by something — something he couldn't identify. It might have been the motion-detector light on his porch or a strange noise.

"It sounded like somebody with asthma," he said slowly, "a noise that sounded very foreign to me, but it wasn't an actual voice, [and] it wasn't a scream. It was just a wheezing noise, but it was loud enough for me to hear it from my bedroom — which is the opposite side from where Chuck's house is."

Staunton said he'd gotten up and sat on the edge of his bed for "thirty seconds," noticing that the motion-detector light on his porch was on. He listened, but he heard nothing more — no more screams or wheezes or whatever it had been. No sound of a car engine starting. It could have been anything — from an owl in the night to a cougar or even a raccoon fight.

It was difficult for Staunton to set the time he'd been wakened, but he was sure it would have been about three to five hours after he'd taken the sleeping pill. He assumed it was about 5:00 a.m.

He'd woken up again at 7:00 a.m. to the sound of cats fighting. He figured that was probably what he'd heard earlier.

Shocked to hear that Chuck was dead, Dr. Staunton said he'd seen him only the night before at a restaurant called Buck's in downtown Everett. Chuck was there with some friends, a couple of men and a woman he didn't recognize. His neighbor had come over to invite him to join them, and he did — but when Chuck asked Dr. Staunton if he wanted to go to a nearby gambling casino, he'd declined, saying he was headed home to bed.

No one else along the street who might have helped Chuck Leonard had heard anything during the night or in the chill hours of the morning. Maybe it wouldn't have made any difference, but it was sad, nevertheless.

Rigor mortis, the stiffening of a body's joints that begins shortly after death, was well established. His body temperature was very, very low when it was taken at the medical examiner's office.

It was ironic that a man who had spent his whole life surrounded by friends should die all alone. Had someone been familiar with his habits — where he slept, who his neighbors were, who was away in the winter or had their windows tightly closed?

It would take detectives from the Major Crimes Unit to figure that out. Detectives Brad Pince and Jim Scharf arrived, and Bottin walked them through the residence, retracing his original path exactly.

They worked the crime scene meticulously, gathering, bagging, and labeling the .45 slugs and casings, taking samples for typing from the blood that marked the lake house with splashes and pools. The water bed where Chuck Leonard had been shot was punctured by either a bullet or a fragment, and it leaked water that mixed with his life's fluid.

The stairway down to the master bedroom ran along the left side of the living room. The fatally injured victim must have run across the living room and slipped on a few area rugs, which were now askew. When Pince looked down at one, he saw a wedge of transparent material beneath it. As he tugged it aside, he realized it was some kind of window in the floor — a window looking down toward Chuck's room. It wasn't directly over his water bed, but it was close enough.

The dead man had designed his house carefully so that skylights in the ceiling of the lake house were positioned to capture light, which, in turn, focused on the window in the floor, sending more light to the bedroom below. The Plexiglas cover was open now, but could obviously be closed to keep someone from falling through.

If someone had stealthily come into the house in the dark, and the moonlight was just right, he — or they — might have been able to watch Chuck and any female friend who might be staying over.

It gave the detectives pause, a shivery feeling of privacy invaded.

They received a phone call from Detective John Padilla in the Records division. He had left several messages on Teresa's cell phone during the day, and she finally called him back. She asked about Chuck's death. Padilla wasn't positive how she had learned of it, but Doug Butler and other teachers and administrators at North Middle School had known for hours that Chuck was dead — murdered. Word of his shocking demise had spread rapidly through the area.

Padilla said Teresa had left the phone number and address of her best friend — Joyce Lilly — and said she would wait there for the detectives to contact her.

Pince and Scharf were very anxious to talk with Teresa Gaethe-Leonard, but it was ten thirty that evening before they had cleared the lake house. Detectives Joe Ward, Rob Palmer, and Gregg Rinta had done yeoman's work photographing and sketching the layout of the house and the location of all physical evidence before it was bagged and labeled and put safely into the chain of evidence.

Dr. Dan Selove, associate medical examiner for Snohomish County had come to the scene, too. After Chuck Leonard's body was photographed and then removed for autopsy, deputies remained behind to guard the property to be sure that no one crossed the crime scene tapes.

The Snohomish County investigators knew what had happened, but they didn't know who might have shot the popular school counselor or what their motivation might have been.

Sergeant Al Zurlo of the Snohomish County Major Crimes Unit had been assigned to be the incident commander in the investigation of Chuck Leonard's death. At 4:00 p.m. on February 20, he arrived on the scene and signed the crime scene log. He was gratified to see that procedure had been followed perfectly. The whole area was either blocked by barricades or encircled with yellow crime-scene tape.

Zurlo gave out assignments; the investigation would operate on many fronts at the same time.

DETECTIVE BRAD PINCE: lead team, coordinate tasks

DETECTIVE JOHN PADILLA: lead team, interviews and background information

DETECTIVE JIM SCHARF: witness interviews and scene processing

DETECTIVE MATT TRAFFORD: neighborhood canvass, witness interviews

DETECTIVE HALEY: crime-scene sketching, processing

DETECTIVE STICH: crime-scene sketching, processing

DETECTIVE GREGG RINTA: body site, interior crime-scene processing

DETECTIVE ROB PALMER: body site, interior crime-scene processing

DETECTIVE JOE WARD: search warrant preparation, supervise interior crime-scene processing

DETECTIVE STOOPS: exterior crime-scene security, crime-scene log

North Middle School was afire with rumors, and Chuck's friends were appalled. When Detective Brad Pince phoned his father to tell him that his son was dead — murdered — Fred Leonard's voice was full of tears, although he and Chuck were often at odds.

"Was he shot by some jealous husband or boyfriend?" he asked. "I've always been afraid that might happen."

"I don't know," Pince said. "We're trying

to find out."

No one knew at this point who the shooter was.

The investigators knew that first day that Chuck's love life was problematic. Early in the afternoon, Deputy Wynn Holdal called the North Middle School to talk to Everett police officer Dan Boardley who worked security at the school. Boardley said he'd talked to the school's vice principal.

"He told me he spoke with Chuck last night about nine o'clock. Chuck told him he was with a 'skinny blonde' and they were going to Harrah's Club," not the one in Nevada, but a local gambling casino.

Chuck was probably joking, but he'd sounded kind of "down." Boardley got the impression that the woman sitting with him was a casual acquaintance.

From the very beginning there were many possible suspects and motives in the death of Charles Fred Leonard. He was a convivial man who was almost always in a good mood. But he was also a man who walked by himself and lived by his own rules, incurring envy in many men, jealousy in others. He was witty and funny and great to be around. He wasn't legally divorced from Teresa Gaethe-Leonard when he died, but they had been separated for two years.

He was said to be dating at least three attractive young women at the same time, and he had romanced more women in his lifetime than most men could dream of.

Still, if Chuck Leonard had many female friends, he also had lots of male friends who found him generous, a hard worker, a loyal friend, and a good neighbor.

He was over fifty, but he looked much closer to forty, and he had the perfect house for a bachelor or divorcé. The bottom floor of his home, which could only be entered from the outside, was where he made and stored wine. He was as knowledgeable about wine as a sommelier, and proud of his skill.

The next two floors were stacked on top of that with the living room–great room almost at street level. Whoever came and went couldn't be easily monitored by neighbors.

Chuck loved kids, and he enjoyed his job. He had many friends and enough money to get by. His health was great. His biggest worry was that Teresa might take Morgan far away, but so far he'd been able to see his little girl often, and he figured his background would impress a judge more than Teresa's. He didn't even dislike Teresa; she was more an irritant than a threat.

Everyone who mattered to Chuck liked him.

At least so it had seemed until Thursday, February 20, 1997. But someone had hated him enough to shoot him while he slept.

Teresa planned Chuck's funeral. She told Chuck's sister, Theresa, that she was thinking of using some lines from Goethe in the eulogy she was writing; Theresa thought that was pretentious. She doubted that Teresa had anywhere near the education she claimed she had.

Teresa wanted the service to be perfect, but when she arrived, few mourners approached her. Chuck's friends had never cared much for her, and rather than being the star of the event, Teresa was more a wallflower. Basically, no one acknowledged her, except Chuck's uncle. No one spoke to her. When she went into the family room at the funeral parlor, she appeared upset — and intoxicated; she reeked of alcohol. Teresa had maintained close ties with Chuck's father and stepmother; Caroline Leonard felt sorry for her and patted the chair next to her. The elder Leonards asked Teresa to be in the reception line, but she didn't want to do that, despite her friend Joyce Lilly telling her that she should. Teresa almost fainted, and Joyce took her back to the family room.

Then they went to the cemetery. Bonnie, who had only worked for Teresa for two months at The Consignment Shop, walked up to her and Teresa hugged her for a long time. It seemed as though it was at least ten minutes. Bonnie was surprised and somewhat embarrassed. She really didn't know Teresa well at all. It was as if her boss wanted to show people that she did have friends after all and they cared about her.

A short time later, the funeral director approached Joyce and said, "I think Teresa needs to go."

Teresa sat in Joyce's car, her head down. When they reached the main street, Teresa "just looked up and said, 'Get me the fuck out of here.'"

CHAPTER FOUR

Back on the night of Chuck's murder, detectives Brad Pince and Jim Scharf weren't sure what to expect at Joyce Lilly's house, but they found two rather nervous woman — Joyce more so than Teresa — and a pretty little girl, who was recovering from a visit to the dentist. Her face had puffed up and bruised after her treatment the day before. The two detectives were relieved that this time they didn't have to be the ones who broke the news to a widow. And it soon became obvious that Teresa had had very loose connections to Chuck; they were legally married, but that's about all. Apparently, they'd led separate lives for some time. Although she had called his school asking about where he was, she hadn't returned any calls from the Sheriff's Office.

When Detective John Padilla had notified Michelle Conley about Chuck's murder, he gleaned more information. "They fought

95

like cats and dogs," Michelle said. She explained that the Leonards' separation was anything but friendly, and that Chuck only dealt with her because he cared so much about Morgan.

Teresa introduced the detectives to Joyce Lilly, commenting that they were "best friends."

Only five, Morgan Leonard hadn't been told that her father was dead. If she had known at this point, she couldn't possibly have understood the enormity of her loss or begin to understand that the life she had known up until now had changed cataclysmically. The daddy who had loved her so much was never coming back.

There was nothing particularly overt about either Teresa's or Joyce's actions that made the two Snohomish County detectives suspicious. Joyce excused herself and carried Morgan upstairs so that they could talk to Teresa alone.

"We tentatively considered Teresa a suspect because of their acrimonious divorce, and we had talked to Michelle," Scharf explains. "We always tend to look initially at the people closest to the victim. We didn't know much about the Leonards' history that first night."

Teresa didn't seem grief-stricken, but then

she wasn't a widow in the strictest sense of the word. She told the investigators that she had wanted a divorce for a long time, and that Chuck was the one who wanted to stay married. Her decision to delay a divorce was purely pragmatic. She explained that she wasn't a wealthy woman, and she had had to think about how she and Morgan could get by.

"I've had open-heart surgery," she said, "and I need — needed — Chuck's medical insurance, as I don't know what might happen with my health. I couldn't afford it on my own."

Chuck had been good about his child support payments. He paid her $350 a month regularly. "I work, too, of course," she added. "I've had my consignment shop in Marysville for three years. Before that, I worked for the Bon Marché."

Teresa's clothing resale business, combined with Morgan's child support money and a part-time job with a travel agency, gave them just about enough to pay rent on their small apartment on Everett Mall Way, and to buy groceries and other necessities of life.

Detective John Padilla joined his fellow investigators at Joyce Lilly's house. The three detectives listened intently as Teresa told them what Chuck had been like.

She said that she thought her estranged husband had lots of girlfriends, and that he lived the high life.

"Do you know any of their names?" Pince asked.

She shook her head. "No, I don't."

She suggested that Chuck was careless about safety precautions, and that he didn't always lock his doors at night. "He wanted his cats to be able to come in and out. He liked cats."

When she was asked about the last time she'd been to the lake house, Teresa was emphatic. "I haven't been there for two years — not since the day I left."

Although Morgan spent alternate weeks with Chuck, Teresa said she never went into Chuck's house with her. Instead, they set up meetings somewhere else to facilitate the exchange.

"What kind of father was Chuck?" Pince asked.

"He was a good father," she said softly.

Asked about life insurance, Teresa shook her head. She didn't believe Chuck had any. Nor did she seem to be aware that Morgan would be eligible for Chuck's Social Security survivor benefits now.

"Are you dating anyone?" Pince asked.

"Someone important in your life?

"No, there's no one," she said convincingly.

Teresa painted her deceased and estranged husband as a complete playboy, who had any number of "big-boy toys."

"He has a Cessna airplane at the Arlington Airport, and he keeps his Corvette there, too," she said. "He has a brown-and-cream-colored boat. Chuck spent his money on wine and cars."

She also said that he was addicted to pornographic movies. She spoke quietly and seemed quite vulnerable. Except for his predilection for attractive women, her take on her estranged husband was far different from what they had heard so far from others who knew him. And yet it was difficult to ascertain what Teresa's true emotions were. That was perhaps understandable; Chuck's murder was too fresh.

When Brad Pince asked Teresa how she had spent the previous day — February 19, a Wednesday — she could account for almost every minute. She had taken Morgan to the dentist to have some cavities filled two days before and she was concerned that her daughter's face was swollen and bruised; she wanted the dentist to check Morgan's condition. Then they had run some errands and purchased some soft food that Morgan could eat.

"By the time we got home, it must have been five thirty or six in the evening. Then Joyce came over, and she stayed and visited until nine or nine thirty. I didn't go out at all last night. I went to bed about eleven, and I got up at nine this morning."

It was midnight on a day that seemed to go on forever when Brad Pince and Jim Scharf left Joyce Lilly's home.

They didn't know what to think. The murder investigation had just begun, and it sounded as though there were many people they needed to talk to. Joyce Lilly had practically quivered with anxiety during their visit to her home, while Teresa seemed to be in control. They didn't view the two women's behavior as indicative of innocence or guilt. They had done enough felony investigations to know that people in shock and suffering loss react in all different ways.

Teresa Gaethe-Leonard was a slender, very attractive blonde. She appeared to have a core of strength in her. That was fortunate, the detectives thought. She was really on her own now; she would have to raise Morgan all alone, as best she could. It was easy to feel sorry for her, but homicide detectives always look at the nether side of human behavior;

they have learned to observe with jaundiced eyes. Teresa was almost too calm in the face of searing tragedy.

Maybe the enormity of it hadn't hit her yet.

And then again, Brad Pince and Jim Scharf didn't know yet that Teresa was far from alone. She had lied to them when she said she had no boyfriend. She hadn't mentioned Nick Callas, her rich lover in Lahaina, Hawaii.

Only one thing struck them as strange. Near the end of their conversation with her, it occurred to Brad Pince that Teresa hadn't once asked how Chuck had died.

Odd.

"Do you know what happened to Chuck?" Pince asked her.

"I was told that he died," she said faintly. "But I don't know how or any of the details. From the questions that you've asked me, I can guess at some of those details."

The next forty-eight hours passed in a blur for both the Snohomish County investigators and Chuck Leonard's friends and family. His fatal shooting made the top of television news broadcasts and headlines in Seattle and Everett newspapers. Although it happens more often than most people would like to think, schoolteachers and counselors do become involved in scandals and violent-death investigations, just as some doctors, ministers, politicians, and people in every other demographic do.

But the public is still shocked and, yes, intrigued. There is something about the dichotomy between a victim's public image and a shocking crime that fascinates those not directly affected.

But those who knew Chuck Leonard grieved, including many teenagers he had helped through the problems of adolescence.

Morgan had yet to realize her daddy was gone forever.

Snohomish County detectives and deputies canvassed the neighborhood on the lake where Chuck had lived, although they found little information that helped. One neighbor woman said she had stayed up long after her husband went to bed. She had heard what she thought was a scream. If she had, it had nothing to do with Chuck Leonard. He hadn't been home near midnight when she'd heard that strange sound.

The only likely "ear witness" was Dr. Staunton, Chuck's chiropractor friend who lived next door. There seemed to be no eye-witnesses at all.

Brad Pince talked to Theresa Leonard, who had deep suspicions about who had killed her brother. She didn't want to know what her gut was telling her. She told Pince that she thought Teresa was crazy and left it at that.

"I knew," she said years later. "I just knew Teresa had done it. I did tell our parents that, but it was hard for them to accept."

"You really think she could have done it?" Pince asked.

"I don't know. . . . She's weird — that's all I can tell you for sure."

Initially, Teresa made attempts to bond more closely with Chuck's family. She wanted them to get together and go to the cemetery with Morgan four days after the murder. His father had just had shoulder surgery and wasn't up to going. A week later, Teresa and her father-in-law and Chuck's stepmother had lunch together. When Theresa showed up, too, the new widow was taken off guard; Chuck's sister hadn't been invited.

For the first time Caroline Leonard, Theresa's stepmother, understood her suspicions about Teresa. She watched, shocked, at the way Teresa glared at "Aunt Theresa."

Later, she said, "Boy! She really hates you!"

Theresa tried to see Morgan and asked if

she could take her for a visit for a while.

"No!" Teresa said. "She can't."

A few days later, there was a memorial for Chuck organized by his school, and hundreds of people came, including many former students who eulogized him for making their lives better and for being there when they needed a friend and counselor.

This could have been something that Morgan would remember her whole life, that would make her proud of her father. But Teresa refused to let her attend, telling her that children weren't allowed. That wasn't true: other people's children and teenagers attended the memorial service. When it became too crowded inside, they stood outside, listening as Chuck was praised for his devotion to children.

Many had tears running down their cheeks.

Joyce Lilly worried incessantly about what would become of Morgan, whom she loved dearly. But Joyce had worries of her own. She considered Teresa Leonard her best friend and believed sincerely that their devotion went both ways. Joyce was divorced, Teresa had been separated for two years, and as two women alone, they shared many things in common.

The investigators learned that Teresa was not only popular with men; there were some women who liked her, too. Those who worked for her at her consignment shop adored her.

Then again, there were females who detested her and said so. But not her close friends or her staff.

"She's just the sweetest little thing," one salesclerk told reporters — asking that her name not be revealed. "She's just a nice girl."

Joyce felt the same way, although she had seen glimpses of another side of Teresa that sometimes disturbed her. Teresa was far more confident than she was, and the life she lived sometimes gave Joyce pause.

Now, Joyce had a problem that she didn't think she could discuss with anyone. Usually, she talked things over with Teresa — but that was clearly impossible: Teresa was the problem. Teresa had used Joyce as a sounding board, a patient and supportive friend. She always seemed to be embroiled in one messy incident or another. But Joyce didn't want to get involved in them any longer, although she feared she might already be, and that scared her.

Up until the night of February 19, listening to Teresa's problems had been akin to watching a suspense movie. Joyce had listened, fascinated, and then become a part of Teresa's secret life when they traveled several times to Hawaii so her best friend could have a rendezvous with Nick Callas.

Teresa's life wasn't intriguing now. It was fraught with danger and the possibility that she would have to pay the piper for always taking what she wanted.

CHAPTER FIVE

Teresa might have had good reasons for wanting to escape Louisiana and her early years. According to her older sister Lois, she, Teresa, and their younger sister lived a "life of fear."

"Our family looked just like the typical family," the special-education teacher confided. "Everything looked good on the outside."

No one can see what goes on behind closed doors, and the Joneses — mother and three daughters — were afraid of their husband and father, a steamship captain. Their older brother had seemingly escaped unscathed, leaving home as soon as he could get away. The sisters were grateful when their father was gone, but he always came home, and he apparently wielded power over all of them.

Lois said her father had abused her sexually and that she had tried her best to protect her mother from spousal abuse and her younger sisters from going through what she had. There was a terrible night when she heard her mother crying hysterically. She forced her way into their bedroom and found Ervin Jones choking his wife. She stood up to him and probably saved her mother.

None of the females in their family talked about what was happening, not even to each other. They were in deep denial. "It was really tense in our home. It was very tense. You didn't talk about [such] things. No one knew."

They did their best, according to Lois, to stay out of their brutal father's way, tiptoeing around, hoping he wouldn't notice them.

But secret things went on. Lois and Teresa's baby sister, Macie, often slipped into her room late at night to crawl in bed with Lois.

"She would be crying."

But none of the girls told each other what was happening to them, so the dark secrets continued. Although Lois may have suspected that Teresa was being molested, too, she was never convinced until the summer of 1997, long after Teresa had left Chuck. The three sisters, adults now, had sought out a therapist and Lois said Teresa had finally confessed that their father had sexually abused her.

When she talked about their childhood, Lois cried, her mind going back to a time when they were all helpless to do anything about their situation and their mother was too frightened and weak to protect them.

If her memories were true, that might explain why Teresa hated some men, distrusted others, and continually tried to better her situation by seeking out men she thought had a lot of money. If Lois was embroidering the truth, she might only be the protective big sister who had always done whatever she could to shelter her younger siblings from stress and unhappiness.

But, of course, she couldn't do that. In any murder probe, detectives look first at those closest to the victim or victims. Despite their digging, they had found no one who had a grudge against Chuck Leonard — no one but Teresa, his estranged wife.

Still, the two detectives found it difficult to believe that a small woman would go so far as to sneak into a house she hadn't entered in two years, creep through the dark, and have the nerve to fire into the sleeping man who was at least twice as strong as she was. After all, Chuck could have been awake; she no longer kept track of his habits.

And they had parented a child together, a little girl who loved both of them. If Teresa loved Morgan as much as her sisters and friends said she did, how could she even think of taking her father away from her?

Teresa's plans didn't make a lot of sense; she was basing her future on an almost impossible scenario. Everything — even things that seemed impossible — would have to fall precisely into place for a surrogate to carry Nick's natural child, and for him to leave his wealthy wife and the boy he had adopted, a boy he loved.

Infamous female criminals like Susan Smith, Casey Anthony, and Diane Downs have devised similar schemes, building castles in the sky out of diaphanous threads hooked to weak foundations. They all murdered their own children, sacrificing them to get what they wanted, to find perfect love. And there have been scores more women without conscience who have killed people who trusted them to achieve what they think will make them happy.

Joyce Lilly had heard Teresa's stories about how cruel Chuck was to her. She said that he hadn't been happy at all when she became pregnant. She said he even suggested that she get an abortion because he "didn't need little monsters running around."

Later, detectives who talked with Joyce sometimes wondered if she had been present when Chuck allegedly was mean to Teresa, or if she was going by what Teresa had told her. He was a natural flirt — he always had been, and some of Teresa's friends thought he was coming on to them. Teresa agreed with them that he probably was. That only deepened their suspicion that poor Teresa was living a life of terror and abuse. Whether she told them about her childhood abuse isn't clear, but her staunch supporters gathered around her as sheriff's detectives asked more and more probing questions.

Rick Lilly,* Joyce's ex-husband, called her at 9:30 a.m. on February 20, a few hours after Chuck's body was found but before his death had been reported on the news. Joyce was moving to a smaller place, and Rick had agreed to buy some of her furniture.

Rick had never approved of Joyce's tight friendship with Teresa. He didn't trust Teresa, and thought she was too controlling with Joyce. But he hadn't yet heard that Chuck Leonard was dead, so when Joyce's answering machine picked up the call, he left a brief message asking her to call him back.

She didn't return his call until about four in the afternoon, saying she had slept in because she had been up until three in the morning. "There were some police officers here," she said in a worried voice.

"What are police officers doing at your house?" Rick asked incredulously.

She explained that Teresa's husband had been shot to death, and that the detectives were asking Teresa questions. "I was mostly upstairs with Morgan, playing games and coloring and —"

"Why was Teresa at your house?" he asked next.

"She doesn't have anyone else but me," Joyce said. "I'm the only friend she has, and she's going through a terrible time right now. I'm helping her with whatever I can."

Rick listened, shaking his head. Joyce was such a patsy, always acting without thinking, and now she might have herself in a hell of a mess. Joyce went on talking, and he listened, trying to come up with a way she could detach herself from her good friend, Teresa.

Joyce was trying to do that herself; she wasn't answering or returning calls or pages from either Teresa or Nick Callas.

Rick called her back the next morning. He had thought about Chuck Leonard's murder overnight, and he asked his ex-wife point-blank: "Joyce, do you think that Teresa might be 'dirty'?"

"What do you mean by 'dirty'?"

"You know what I mean. Do you think

that she did it?"

"You don't know Teresa the way I know her," Joyce lied frantically. "She couldn't do anything like this."

"Well, okay, but keep clear of her — this thing doesn't have a good smell to it."

Joyce wanted to tell her ex-husband that Teresa had told her *she* was the one who had shot Chuck, and that she hadn't shown any grief or remorse over it. Now she didn't know what she should do. But she was afraid. She was more afraid after hearing his questions.

Rick Lilly dropped by to see her a few days later. He was taunting her, making up a story — but he was very close to the truth. "They've arrested your pal," he said. "She's in the jailhouse now."

"No, they haven't," Joyce said. "They didn't arrest her. Don't say that."

"Don't you listen to the radio?" he asked, taunting her still more as Joyce kept protesting. Rick wasn't looking at her, but when he turned around, he saw that she had burst into tears, and he apologized.

"I'm just kidding you, Joyce," Rick said. "I was only joking. Teresa didn't get arrested."

Joyce was close to hysteria, sobbing as she gasped, "She killed him, she killed him, oh, why would she tell me? Why? You don't know the story like I do."

And now as she poured out her worries to Rick, he was the one who had a hard time believing her. She told Rick that Teresa had described shooting Chuck three times in the chest. She made him promise not to tell anyone — it would ruin Morgan's life. Joyce couldn't bear for her to be hurt anymore.

Joyce said that she'd moved a white bag that Teresa gave her only hours after Chuck's murder from her car trunk into her garage, hiding it behind some boxes. A few days later as she was cleaning the garage, she reached up to move the bag and it hit a pier support. She heard a dull "clunk."

Trembling, she'd untied the top of the bag and looked in. There was a heavy handgun inside, and some of Teresa's clothes, stiff with dried blood.

"Where's the bag now?" Rick asked, still doubting Joyce.

"I hid it. I don't want to hurt my best friend, but I'm frightened to death. I could go to jail, myself," Joyce cried. "But I had nothing to do with Chuck Leonard's murder. I don't know what to do. Teresa's been calling me every hour, but I don't answer."

Joyce's ex-husband looked at her incredulously as she detailed for him what had her so jittery. Tears leaked from her eyes as she spoke, and her hands shook. She hadn't been able to sleep more than a few hours at night.

Rick shook his head in disbelief: how could she have been so dumb? Every day that had gone by while she hid evidence for her precious Teresa, she had been risking her own reputation, not to mention her freedom. He told Joyce that she could very well go to jail for hiding evidence, and for being an "accessory after the fact."

He wasn't very sympathetic, but he gave her good advice. "You're a fool if you don't call a lawyer right now and tell the police everything you know. I'll go with you."

They had some difficulty finding an attorney who practiced criminal law. Rick's own attorneys said they did not, and they recommended George Cody. But when he called, Rick learned that Cody was already representing Teresa Leonard.

Lilly's civil attorneys next suggested George Bowden. Bowden agreed to meet them. So it was that Friday evening, February 28, eight days after Chuck Leonard's murder, Joyce and Rick walked into George Bowden's Everett office carrying a box of evidence — all the items Teresa had told Joyce to hide.

Joyce poured out her story to Bowden, and he said he would represent her. The sheriff's Major Crimes Unit was closed this late on a Friday night, but Bowden promised her he would go to talk with detectives early Saturday morning. In the meantime, he would lock up the white plastic bag with the .45-caliber handgun, Teresa's clothes and bloodied boots, and other items Teresa had given Joyce in his office.

On Saturday, March 1, 1997, Brad Pince talked to a "very upset" Joyce Lilly. She turned over the bag of evidence. For homicide detectives, it was a bonanza, something they never imagined they would find. More than the physical evidence, they had a witness who could tell them what had happened nine days earlier. While she hadn't actually been present when Chuck was shot, they had the next thing to it in Joyce Lilly.

If she was about to tell them the truth, the deadly puzzle would be solved. That was, of course, a big "if."

Aware now that he and Jim Scharf hadn't heard the whole truth on the evening after Chuck Leonard died, Pince asked Joyce Lilly if she had been honest with them. Tears rolling down her cheeks, she shook her head. She admitted that she'd known then who killed Chuck, but that she had lied for Teresa. As the days passed, Joyce Lilly said she couldn't sleep, and she was close to having a panic attack when she turned to her former husband for advice. Although they were no longer married, she trusted his opinion and she had to talk to someone.

"One night back in November, a couple of months before somebody shot Chuck," Joyce began "Teresa came by to leave Morgan with me to babysit. She was dressed strangely, wearing black sweatpants, a dark fuzzy jacket, and boots."

"It was almost winter, wasn't it?" Scharf asked. "Why was it strange for her to dress like that?"

"It wasn't Teresa's style — not at all," Joyce's words tumbled out. "She said 'How do you like my outfit?'"

Joyce closed her eyes, remembering the incident. "I said, 'It doesn't look like you.'"

"That's the point," Teresa had said succinctly.

Joyce said she'd stared at Teresa, baffled. And then she was shocked when Teresa told her that she would have killed Chuck that night if she'd only had enough time.

That didn't even seem possible, and she had finally decided that Teresa was engaging in some kind of black humor.

"But she seemed serious, even though she didn't mention killing Chuck again. And then the holidays came and nothing happened, and Teresa's custody of Morgan —

sharing with Chuck, you know — went on just like before. One week with Teresa, one week with Chuck —"

Except for the week that included February 17–20, 1997, when Morgan had her dental work done.

On Wednesday, February 19, Teresa told Joyce something unbelievable: "I'm going to whack Chuck tonight."

Joyce had just stared at her friend, open-mouthed. Teresa had that same icy look on her face that she'd had back in November when she'd showed up in her all-black outfit.

While Joyce believed that Chuck had been abusive to Teresa and she felt sorry for her, that was no reason to kill the man. That's what "whack" meant, she thought; she'd heard it on gangster television shows.

But why? Teresa wasn't in danger anymore; she and Chuck didn't live together any longer. They were both involved with other people, and, until last November, Teresa said she hadn't even been in Chuck's house at the lake for a couple of years.

Joyce knew better than to try to talk Teresa out of any plans she made. And besides, she couldn't believe that Teresa would really kill Chuck. She often behaved dramatically — that was part of what made her an interesting friend. Being with Teresa was a little like being in the center of a soap opera.

Telling herself it would be okay, Joyce Lilly was able to get to sleep on Wednesday night. But in the wee hours of February 20, her phone trilled and she woke up instantly, her heart thumping. It was Teresa, and she sounded very upset. She begged Joyce to come to her apartment.

As she always did, Joyce said she'd be there as soon as she could. Teresa hung up before she could ask her any questions. It took her an hour to get dressed and arrive at Teresa's. When Joyce got there, Teresa was smoking and drinking scotch. "She was very shaken — almost quivering," Joyce said, "and Teresa's always in control — always."

Teresa immediately handed her a white plastic bag that was tightly tied at the top.

"I want you to put this in the trunk of your car," she said.

"What's in it?"

"Just do it, and I'll tell you when you come back in."

"You did it?" Rick Lilly asked, disgust and alarm in his voice. "What happened then?"

"I did it. Teresa said, 'I shot Chuck. Three times.' And I asked her 'What?'" Joyce said, sobbing.

Teresa said she'd found Chuck alone,

sound asleep in his bed. She had fired two or three times at him and hit him in the chest.

"He got up out of bed and chased me," Teresa recalled, shivering. At one point, Chuck had gotten close enough to her at the top of the stairs to grab her by the ankle, but then his grip loosened.

"At the top of the stairs, he gasped," Teresa said, "and then he made a noise and fell —"

"What did you do?" Joyce asked. "Did he look at you? Did he look in your eyes?"

"I ran," Teresa said. "Yes . . . he looked in my eyes."

Teresa told her good friend that she didn't know if Chuck was dead. She thought he was alive. "He's so strong," she breathed. "He's so strong . . ."

She didn't seem to know just what time it was when she shot Chuck, but she was sure she was back in her apartment by five in the morning.

Joyce Lilly didn't want to believe Teresa. Teresa was always full of drama and exaggeration. Surely this was another of her fantasies — like the night she dressed in her "camouflage" outfit.

"Where did you get a gun?" Joyce had asked in a doubtful voice.

"I bought it from some guy in a bar," Teresa had said, with a hint of pride in her voice. "It was just like a TV thing."

Joyce Lilly drove home with the white plastic bag in the trunk of her car. Teresa had also given Joyce the key to Chuck's house, even though Joyce didn't want it.

"Well, I can't have it, you need to take it," Teresa said imperiously.

Joyce threw the key away by tossing it in a planter barrel at a Jack in the Box restaurant on her way home.

She was horrified the next morning when the news that Chuck Leonard had been murdered circulated among their friends, and then was on the top of the radio and television news shows around Seattle and Everett.

Still, Joyce didn't look in the bag. She didn't want to know what was in it. It stayed in her car trunk, like a poisonous snake or a time bomb, while she worried about what she should do. She decided, finally, to move it to her garage.

Joyce admitted now to Brad Pince and Jim Scharf that she had known that Teresa was lying to them on the night of February 20 when they came to her house to question Teresa. She told them about Teresa's hair appointment that day, and how she had hidden Teresa's car in her own garage at her request. This was the first time that had ever happened.

She repeated Teresa's statement on the day of Chuck's murder when she said she planned to "whack" him.

Still half-expecting to go to jail, Joyce was reassured when that didn't happen. As she left the sheriff's office, she wasn't confident that it wouldn't occur in the following days and she shuddered every time her phone rang or there was a knock on her door. When days passed and she wasn't arrested, she began to feel somewhat more at ease.

As Joyce continued to clean out her garage, she came across something that she knew she hadn't put there. It was an almost-full box of .45-caliber ammunition.

Again through her lawyer, Joyce Lilly contacted the investigators at the Snohomish County Sheriff's Office. She was a lot calmer than she was the first time she talked to them. And she revealed more hidden things.

"I loaned Teresa a small handgun in October — last fall," she said. "She told me that she needed a gun because she and Morgan lived alone in an apartment and she had no protection. Rick gave it to me a few years ago for the same reason, taught me how to use it, and I fired it once or twice — but I never used it. It made me nervous to have it in my house."

"Do you know what caliber it was?" Pince asked.

"I'm not sure what a caliber is. It was a small silver gun. It seems as though it might have been a .25 or .22, something like that. Teresa took it out in the backyard and fired it into the ground — to see if it worked.

"I haven't seen it since October. It was after she borrowed it that she told me that she had been in Chuck's house one night."

"Do you know when?" Pince asked.

She shook her head. "It would have been a few months ago — before Christmas. Teresa told me she saw Chuck and his girlfriend in bed, so she left."

That would jibe with what Michelle Conley told detectives about the November intruder that she'd followed in her car. But she had lost the intruder in the dark. At the time, she believed it was Teresa's car. However, Chuck had decided not to report the matter to police.

Joyce said she wasn't sure where Teresa was at the moment. She had been avoiding Teresa.

Armed with the new information from Joyce Lilly, Michael Downes, a senior deputy prosecution attorney for Snohomish

County, filed an affidavit of probable cause. He asked for the arrest of Teresa Gaethe-Leonard on first-degree-murder charges. It was granted almost immediately.

On Sunday night, March 2, ten days after Chuck Leonard died, Teresa appeared at the Snohomish County Courthouse in Everett. She did not, however, walk in under her own power to be booked. She was accompanied by her defense attorney, George Cody, who had driven her there, but she was passed out in the backseat of his car, far too intoxicated — or possibly under the influence of drugs — to walk. Cody was very worried about her condition. At length, Cody and Detectives Jim Scharf and John Padilla managed to rouse her and support her as they walked her into the booking area. She was arraigned the next day in district court.

Cody told reporters that she would plead not guilty to the charges against her. He explained that her surrender "doesn't mean she confessed. It means she didn't try to run. She has not made any admission whatsoever to the police in any way of being involved in Chuck Leonard's death."

The judge wasn't so sure that Teresa wouldn't try to run in the days ahead, so he set her bail at $500,000 and directed that it be cash only. This would assure that Teresa would remain behind bars for two more weeks. At that time, Michael Downes would have to refile the case against her in Superior Court.

Teresa was not without support. Her employees asserted that she was still a nice little woman and they didn't believe she was capable of shooting anyone. They sent word that they would keep her shop open for her and help in any way they could. Even her new lawyer found her vulnerable and sweet. He felt sorry for her. Like so many middle-aged men before him, George Cody was already stepping into Teresa Gaethe-Leonard's circle of devoted admirers.

Nick Callas didn't really know what was going on. Teresa had phoned him in Hawaii and told him that Chuck had died suddenly.

"What happened?" Nick asked her at the time.

"They don't know," she'd said. "Some kind of profound trauma —"

Nick said later that his mind had flashed to an automobile accident, and he'd pictured Chuck Leonard hitting a tree or telephone pole while driving one of his sports cars. Teresa hadn't said anything about a gun or murder — nothing but "profound trauma."

Even though he and Teresa had been lovers since 1987, years before Teresa met and married Chuck, Nick Callas knew very little about her life. They had made a pact that they wouldn't talk about unhappy things or her family background. For Nick, Teresa had always been sexy, fun, a woman without problems.

Chuck Leonard had his army of supporters, too. He wasn't a man to talk about his problems either — except to very close friends. He was witty and funny and kind. Everyone had liked Chuck — with the possible exception of Teresa and the friends she had told about his "brutality" toward her.

Somehow, Teresa had managed to keep her juggling act of a life together for years. Of all people, the archaic mystery writer's term "a tissue of lies" fit Teresa. She'd kept her wealthy lover, married Chuck, given birth to Morgan, and managed to convince any number of people that Chuck was abusive toward her. Those who knew him couldn't believe it — any more than Teresa's allies could believe that she would shoot a man to death as he slept.

News stories proliferated each day with more and more shocking details about the Leonards' marriage, and his fatal shooting. The Snohomish County Prosecutor's Of-

126

fice said that they believed Teresa had taken a bead on her estranged husband as he lay sound asleep, and started firing. "He was hit in the arm and twice more in the chest," Michael Downes told District Judge Thomas Kelly. "One of those .45-caliber bullets penetrated his chest — and that was the wound that killed him."

On autopsy, Dr. Selove had found that Chuck had died of exsanguination: he had bleed to death after being shot.

The public had no idea what motive Teresa might have had to kill her husband. The affidavit for probable cause remained sealed.

There were still many secrets about Teresa. She told people that she was thirty-three and that was what her driver's license said, but her divorce papers listed her as thirty-seven.

Her attorney, George Cody, sat beside Teresa in an attorney-client room in the Snohomish County Jail and communicated with the court through a closed-circuit video hookup as he asked for a reduction in her bail. Teresa said nothing.

Cody asked that her bail be lowered to $100,000, since she had willingly talked to detectives at least four times before she surrendered just before midnight on the previous Sunday. "If she was going to flee," he pointed out, "she already would have done so."

Downes argued against a bail reduction. The prisoner had, after all, proven herself a community threat when she shot Chuck Leonard, and had no particular ties to the community: her family was in Louisiana and her wealthy boyfriend was in Hawaii.

Judge Thomas Kelly took both sides into consideration and lowered Teresa's bail to $200,000.

Close to a dozen of Chuck Leonard's relatives and friends observed these arguments about bail. Two of them were attractive women who identified themselves as his former girlfriends. Even though they had long since ended romantic attachments to him, they had remained platonic friends. The group watched and listened and dabbed at the tears that often filled their eyes. What did money matter now that Chuck was gone?

But it did. Enough cash could get Teresa out of jail. The Snohomish County detectives were extremely uneasy about that possibility, fearing that she would "rabbit" on them and disappear.

When she was charged with first-degree murder in Snohomish County Superior Court a week later, her bail was once more raised to $500,000.

Deputy Prosecutor Downes had little difficulty convincing Judge Kathryn Trumbull that Teresa, for all her demure appearance, was a danger to the community, and a flight risk with access to money, and that she might well take six-year-old Morgan and disappear.

Someone was already inquiring about how to wire money to bail her out, someone who didn't seem at all abashed that it would take almost $200,000 to gain her release. The man, who called the sheriff's office from Hawaii, asked to have his name kept private.

It was, of course, Teresa's wealthy lover, Nick Callas. He said he was prepared to wire the money. Callas didn't want to leave Hawaii, and he only grudgingly agreed to meet with Michael Downes, Brad Pince, and John Padilla if they flew to Maui to talk to him.

Michael Downes was not only concerned that Teresa might leave Washington State, but he felt that Joyce Lilly's life might be in danger. If Joyce hadn't gone to the sheriff, Teresa might well have walked away scot-free: no jail, no bail, no trial. And Downes feared that Joyce — who was probably going to be the State's prime witness against her former friend — might seem expendable to Teresa. In the prosecutor's view, Chuck

Leonard had gotten in the way of Teresa's plans to move to Hawaii — and he was dead. Joyce was now a serious impediment to the defendant's freedom and the life she visualized. Although detectives in the sheriff's office were keeping an eye on Joyce, they couldn't be with her all the time.

Now the evidence against Teresa was being slowly unveiled. Although her name was not given to reporters, Joyce Lilly had received immunity from prosecution in exchange for her cooperation with sheriff's investigators.

The white plastic bag that Joyce gave to Brad Pince contained a dark brown polarfleece jacket with some sort of emblem on the shoulder, a pair of sweatpants, light brown leather boots with a large bloodstain on one toe, bullets, and a magazine for a .45-caliber handgun. The gun itself was at the bottom of the bag. It was securely locked in the evidence room at the sheriff's office, each item bagged, sealed, dated, and signed by the investigator who had entered it into the chain of evidence.

George Cody objected to this alleged evidence being admitted into any forthcoming trial, saying, "I can't comment on it because I haven't seen it. I know what they say they've got, but I don't know what they have."

Cody pointed out that Teresa had no

criminal record or history of making threats. And as far as anything the investigation had turned up so far, that was true. He described her as a dedicated mother who would never leave her daughter. Nor would she close down her business. She needed that income to survive.

Everything in the white bag was going to the Washington State crime lab to be tested for fingerprints, hair, DNA, and rug and fabric fibers that might link to Teresa or to someone else.

The sheriff's investigators had searched Teresa's home, her consignment shop, and her car, looking for receipts that might show what she had purchased or where she had been in the days before Chuck's fatal shooting. She obviously hadn't had the .45 back in October 1996, when she borrowed Joyce's handgun, but she had one on the night Chuck died.

Joyce didn't think Teresa had returned her small handgun. Sometime after Chuck's murder and Joyce's accusations about Teresa, Joyce found a backpack in her garage when she was packing to move. At the time she didn't look inside it, assuming it belonged to her twenty-one-year-old son. But in April 1997, she did look. There she found her .25-caliber gun, wrapped in a woman's handkerchief, along with a small box of ammunition. She had no idea how it got there. Apparently Teresa had put it in her garage sometime over the past five months.

The Snohomish County detectives didn't find a receipt for the .45, but they did find a letter from a realtor on Maui, thanking her for her interest in buying property there. Oddly, they found a credit card in the name of Chuck's mother, Ann, who had been dead for almost five years. The card had been issued after her death, and the address was for Teresa's consignment shop — where Ann Leonard had never lived.

George Cody said he didn't find that strange. "It was a cash card that had to be tied to a bank account." He told the judge that Chuck Leonard had often had mail sent to his wife's shop when they were together and that the victim had maintained his bank account jointly with his mother long after she was deceased.

But what was Teresa doing with it?

One person that Pince, Scharf, and Downes wanted to talk to was Nick Callas. Initially, he declined to speak with them, saying through his attorney that there was no advantage to him to become involved. But the Washington State lawmen were not going to back off so easily. Michael Downes threatened to legally summon Callas from Hawaii to Everett at county expense, where he would be expected to give a deposition on what he knew about Teresa, her relationship with her estranged husband — and with him — and the murder of Chuck Leonard. Superior Court Judge Anita Farris agreed with Downes's motion for a subpoena.

Would Callas come? Or would he change his mind about answering questions in Hawaii and decide that that would be a lot easier than a six-hour flight to the Northwest? Actually, Judge Farris had no jurisdiction in Hawaii, but the investigators believed that the rich condo owner might decide that being an "uncooperative witness" was not in his best interest after all. Downes, Pince, and Padilla were still willing to fly to Hawaii to talk with Teresa's purported lover there.

Teresa had not appeared as yet in court in person, her participation having been accomplished through closed-circuit television. Finally Teresa showed up in the courtroom for the first time in a pretrial hearing. There was a murmur in the courtroom as she was led to her chair at the defense table. She was a pretty woman, more slender than ever after weeks of jail cuisine, and so pale and breakable-looking. There were unshed tears in her eyes. The body language and facial expressions on court watchers signaled what they were thinking: *How could this sweet-looking woman kill a man in cold blood?*

Most laymen have preset notions of how a murderer is supposed to look and act. Some of them are true. Mass murderers and serial killers are almost always male, but they don't necessarily look like monsters: many are very attractive. A serial killer is addicted to murder. Mass murderers, of whom we have seen far too many recently, tend to carry rage within them, blaming others for a job loss, a broken marriage, or their inadequacy. They are often insane and suicidal.

But women defendants are usually less predictable. Their motivation revolves around love in its broadest definition (to include jealousy, revenge, sexual attraction) and money. Where poison was once their weapon of choice, in the twenty-first century more female killers use a gun. They kill people who are close to them, relatives, spouses, lovers, and friends who trust them. However, women whose photos were featured in fact-detective pulp magazines from the 1920s to the 1960s tended to be plump and matronly, passing their time in jail knitting or reading their Bibles, or "hussies" who looked like gun molls with dyed hair, too much makeup, and scanty attire.

But Teresa Gaethe-Leonard looked more like a pretty kindergarten teacher or someone serving fruit punch at a church function.

That look had stood her in good stead since puberty. When she cried or trembled from the emotion of it all, she was even more pitiable. And Michael Downes worried that a jury might view her that way.

There was no question at this point that Morgan could live with her mother — Teresa's emotions were too unstable. Under an agreement drawn up by the Washington State Child Protective Services, Teresa was allowed to phone Morgan twice a week for a fifteen-minute monitored call. However, Judge Farris was concerned that Morgan hadn't seen a counselor yet, apparently because Teresa hadn't signed the required paperwork. A guardian was appointed for Morgan who would arrange for her to have sessions with a child psychologist.

On March 12, 1997, Morgan was slated to talk with P. J. Summers, a child interview specialist with the Crimes Against Children Unit of the Snohomish County Sheriff's Office. Since her mother's arrest, she'd been staying with Chuck's father and stepmother, Fred and Caroline, at their home in Concrete, Washington, and her small world was in total upheaval.

Caroline Leonard brought her into the sheriff's office.

Morgan wanted to know where her mother was, and why she couldn't see her.

"She's in a safe place," Pince explained, "but you can't see her right now."

"I need to ask about my daddy," she pressed.

Pince said he would talk to her about that later. Morgan was willing to talk to P. J., whom Pince introduced as a friend of his, but she made him promise to answer some questions for her when she was finished.

Morgan told P. J. Summers that her mother was going to get married in Hawaii and she and her mom were going to move there. "I'm going to be a flower girl at the wedding," she said.

She was clinging to the happy-ever-after ending that her mother had promised her. She said she knew her daddy was dead, but she didn't really understand what had happened.

Pince kept his word and, after Morgan's interview with P. J., he did his best to explain what had happened to her father. He told her that Chuck had been shot. She didn't ask who had done that. They talked a little bit about how anyone could have gotten into his house. Morgan said she knew that he had some guns around the house, but they were kept up high or locked up and she was not allowed to touch them. She didn't think her mother had any guns at all in her house.

Pince was very gentle with her. Morgan was confused about what could have happened. She wanted things back the way they were before.

If only . . .

The Snohomish County investigators talked to dozens of people as they reconstructed the last day of Chuck Leonard's life. He had, indeed, had drinks and dinner with friends at Buck's American Café in Everett on Wednesday night, and he'd been trying to find someone to go to Harrah's Club, a nearby casino, with him. But he had no luck. Les Staunton was tired after arriving home from his South American trip. Michelle wished him good luck, but she was turning in early. She asked him to call her when he left the casino or when he got home.

The "skinny blonde" he'd talked about taking to gamble with him was a former waitress at Buck's. She'd eaten with Chuck and his friends, but hadn't wanted to go to Harrah's so late on a weeknight either.

A cocktail waitress at Harrah's confirmed

that Chuck had been in the gambling casino that night. She said he was usually loud and raucous after a few drinks, and it would be difficult to forget him — although he was also a nice guy who had a great sense of humor. However, on this last night, he'd seemed "down" or "depressed."

Chuck had arrived late — after eleven. He wasn't in her section, so she had no idea how many drinks he had. "By the time I saw him, he was drinking bottled water," she said. "After two a.m., the drinks are cut off."

Chuck Leonard had left Harrah's quietly and probably driven straight home; it wasn't more than a half hour's drive.

They were now eight days away from Teresa's April trial date for the murder of Chuck Leonard.

But like most high-profile trials, Teresa's was delayed. Rather than beginning in April, it was rescheduled for July 1997. And then, quite suddenly, on April 25, after eight weeks in jail, Teresa was released. Her half-million-dollar cash bail had been paid. Her attorney, George Cody, said a group of her friends had raised the money because they were worried that Teresa wouldn't be able to choose who would have custody of Morgan if she had to do it from a jail cell.

But Teresa's friends and relatives weren't anywhere near that rich. In truth, the bail money came almost entirely from one very close friend: Nick Callas. He may not have chosen to divorce his wife and marry Teresa, but he seemed to care deeply for her.

George Cody, too, was very taken with Teresa. He doted on her, and some observers wondered if his feelings for her were more than those of an attorney for his client. Just before Teresa walked free from her jail cell, Detective John Padilla asked Teresa's new lawyer, John Henry Browne, to be present while he photographed Teresa in the clothing she'd worn the night Chuck died.

With a female detective present, too, Padilla began by taking several photographs of the suspect as she looked in her normal clothing.

She was annoyed, and said sarcastically, "Of course you had to do this before my cosmetic surgery."

He wasn't sure if she was kidding or not. Next, he took pictures of Teresa wearing the sweatpants, dark brown fleece jacket, and bloodied boots. He noted that she never looked at him or the clothes; instead she gazed with empty eyes at the door to the room they were in. She didn't seem particularly upset. Rather, she seemed removed, as though she had stepped out of her body, blocking any angst she might feel at seeing the stained items again.

George Cody had found an apartment for Teresa and paid the rent. There was no possibility that she could have Morgan live with her. Chuck's family wouldn't hear of it, and the court felt Teresa wasn't currently stable enough to have her back. But there was more. If Morgan lived with Teresa, what would stop the accused murderess from disguising herself and her daughter and vanishing? Who would prevent Teresa from convincing Morgan of just about anything she wanted her to believe?

Morgan had told her grandparents and her Aunt Theresa that she was going to have a "new daddy" when her mother got married. Fred, Caroline, and Theresa were alarmed.

"And I'm going to have flowers in my hair at the wedding," Morgan burbled. "My mommy said so and she doesn't lie."

Although the case appeared to be growing tighter around Teresa, there were gaps in it, and there were still many people who absolutely refused to think of her as a killer. The men who loved her and the women she'd chosen to be her confidantes still could not equate the bubbly, caring Teresa with their image of a murderess.

Detective John Padilla took advantage of the trial delay to see if he could find out who Teresa really was. He called Lieutenant Steve Buras of the Homicide Division of the Jefferson Parish Sheriff's Office in Louisiana and asked him if he would search his records there for any information on Teresa Gaethe-Leonard. Padilla gave the Louisiana lawmen every possible combination he could come up with about Teresa: her birthdate, Social Security number, her names, parents' names, even her father's date of birth.

Buras called Padilla a few hours later and said he couldn't find any information on Teresa, but he was going to check with the Social Security office in his jurisdiction and see if they might have something on her activities.

Next, Padilla found the phone number for Gary Gaethe, Teresa's ex-husband. He called him in early summer, 1997. Gaethe was most forthcoming with what he knew about her.

According to Gaethe, Teresa had lived most of her life in Pensacola, Florida, and she attended high school there until her parents moved to Metairie, Louisiana. He knew her mother's name was Gloria, and that she had two sisters, but he'd forgotten their names.

"After we divorced," he said cryptically, "I got rid of everything that reminded me of Teresa."

Gaethe's romance with Teresa began much like her involvement with Chuck Leonard. He had been in a department store, buying a present for his mother. They struck up a conversation. He got the impression that she was in her twenties.

"I found out later that she was only a teenager," he said. "We dated for about three years before we got married. She was a fun and exciting person to be with."

Gary Gaethe made good money. He owned a sailboat, a plush condominium, and expensive cars. They took trips together and reveled in an outdoor life.

When they got married, Gary had a BMW and he bought Teresa a Lotus. He moved his sailboat to Pensacola, and they lived together aboard her for a few months. "We had a lot of fun," he recalled.

But it didn't last. Gaethe said there were cracks in their relationship almost from the day they got married. He worked four days a week in New Orleans, while Teresa insisted upon living on their boat. He would have much preferred that they live in his condo in New Orleans and spend their weekends and vacations on his sailboat.

"She became very cold to me," he recalled to Padilla. "She wanted her own apartment. And for the first two months of our marriage, she isolated me from my family."

Thinking back on what might have caused Teresa to be frosty toward him, Gaethe said he believed it started when he suggested they slow down their spending a little. "I told her I didn't want to have the financial pressure of all the bills for things we really didn't need."

That was all it took. His bride set her jaw and turned away from him. She had enjoyed their life as long as there were no restrictions on her spending habits. Shortly thereafter, they separated and lived apart for seven months until their divorce became final.

Gary had loved Teresa and he took the divorce hard. Even so, he wanted to be sure she was okay. He got her an apartment, gave her money to live, and bought her another car and new furniture. He was instrumental in getting her the concierge job at the Sheraton Hotel.

And then she walked out of his life without a backward glance.

"I didn't see her again for about ten years," Gaethe told Padilla. "Not until she called me out of the blue four months ago. It was like nothing had ever happened between us.

She told me she had a beautiful daughter and that she was no longer married. She said she owned a fancy boutique, and that she was coming to New Orleans to see her mother. She asked if she and her little girl could stay with me for a while when they came down."

Gary Gaethe was unaware that Gloria Jones had been dead for almost seven years at that point. Or that Teresa was soon to go on trial for murdering the husband who came after him. Even so, he demurred about having her stay with him. He had long since moved on, and didn't want to open old wounds.

Teresa stayed in Washington. Teresa had been very exciting and fun. "But when it came to reality, she was as cold as ice. She was an accomplished liar — I learned that. You know, I think she even believed her own lies."

"Was Teresa capable of handling a gun?" Padilla asked.

"She sure was. I had a house in the woods, and Teresa and I used to go out there for target practice. We shot all kinds of guns, but primarily a .44 magnum."

Padilla contacted the Registry of Vital Statistics in New Orleans next, and he came up with three names Teresa had used before she became Teresa Leonard: Teresa E. Jones,

Teresa E. Goldstein, and Teresa E. Gaethe. He wondered how many others there were.

Teresa's trial was postponed yet again, to October 1997. She had her new attorney, one of the most effective criminal defense lawyers in the Seattle area. His name was John Henry Browne, the same John Henry Browne who had once advised Ted Bundy on his legal options more than twenty years earlier, and who had defended many of the most high-profile accused killers in the Northwest. Browne was a flamboyant and passionate advocate for his clients, and a successful one, too. He would probably be among the three top choices in the state for someone facing serious criminal charges. How Teresa could afford Browne was a question; perhaps Nick Callas had stepped in once more to rescue her from a long prison sentence.

Nick had always promised he would stand behind her. Indeed, Nick contacted many of Teresa's women friends and asked them to support her emotionally; he was very worried about her.

In late summer, Teresa was in the headlines again. John Henry Browne told reporters that she had barely survived an overdose of prescription drugs. He stressed that she

145

had not attempted suicide — the overdose was accidental. She had been taken to Stevens Memorial Hospital in Edmonds, Washington, on August 28 in a comatose state from a combination of antidepressant and sleeping pills.

"She almost died," Browne had said the day after she was hospitalized, adding that physicians were preparing to do "brain-death studies" to determine if her memory loss was temporary or permanent.

Prosecutor Michael Downes was less sympathetic, asserting that she had deliberately attempted suicide. He asked Judge Ronald Castleberry to raise her bail to $5 million to assure that she would remain in jail until her trial. The judge perused a doctor's report on her condition, and deduced that neither the State nor the Defense was completely accurate. He didn't believe that her condition after overdosing was critical or that she was comatose, but he did think it had all been an accident.

Castleberry denied a raise in Teresa's bail to the almost unheard of amount, but he stipulated that she avoid alcohol and continue all treatment — psychological and medical — and that every doctor who might prescribe medication for her be aware of what she was getting from the others.

Chuck Leonard had been dead for six months, and the path toward trial seemed to be getting slower and slower. Brad Pince and D.A. Michael Downes kept working, gathering more evidence. They continued to find rumors, anecdotes, and accusations about Teresa; she had convinced any number of people — both men and women — that they were essential to her well-being, that she cared a great deal for them and was grateful for all the help they gave her.

Her first attorney, George Cody, was at the forefront of her defenders. Although he was no longer representing her in the murder case, he was overseeing her civil affairs. He had found a new apartment for her and paid all the expenses there through his law firm. He was probably infatuated with Teresa. When she mentioned how much she wanted to have some plastic surgery, he couldn't see why she would need it — but he didn't try to talk her out of it.

Nick Callas was still sending her money, although not as much after he'd put up $500,000 bail money for her. Her loyal employees at The Consignment Shop were keeping it open, knowing she needed that income. Although Joyce Lilly had kept her distance since she turned in evidence and information that led to Teresa's arrest, Teresa had several other female friends who stood by her.

One friend, Carol Fabray,* had given birth to a new son in 1997, and she was touched when Teresa was so interested and concerned for her, despite her own problems. Although they made many appointments to meet so Teresa could give the new baby a present, it wasn't until late fall that Teresa showed up at Carol's home.

CHAPTER SIX

It was close to 9:00 a.m. on November 13, 1997, when Brad Pince walked by Sergeant Al Zurlo's desk in the homicide unit. Zurlo was on the phone and obviously trying to calm down whoever was on the other end of the line. He had written a name on a pad in front of him: Grace Callas.

Pince knew that surname, and he heard Zurlo say, "I'll transfer you to Detective Pince's extension —"

But the woman's voice came through the receiver so loudly that Pince could hear her. He raised his eyebrows questioningly, and Zurlo covered the mouthpiece and whispered quickly, "She says her name is Grace Callas, and she's hysterical. She wants information about her husband's involvement in one of our homicide investigations."

Pince picked up the phone and identified himself. Zurlo was right; the woman was sobbing and screaming into the phone. It was difficult to make sense of what she was saying, but he finally deduced that she was Nick Callas's wife, and, of course, Nick was Teresa Gaethe-Leonard's lover.

"Ma'am, ma'am," Pince said, "I think I know who you are. How can I help you? If you can calm down a little, maybe I can answer any questions you have."

"Two days ago — on November 11 — I found some romantic cards in my husband's business papers," she said, still crying. "They were from someone named Teresa Leonard. When I asked him about where the cards came from, he told me that this . . . this Teresa person is involved in a murder in your jurisdiction. He says he's been dragged into the middle of it."

Not surprisingly Grace Callas wanted to know more about Teresa and what her husband had to do with her.

She had done some detective work of her own before she called the sheriff's office. When Nick left on November 12, she began searching through their computer files. She found two listings for "Teresa." One was for someone associated with Orca Travel in Marysville, Washington. When she called the number given, she reached a consignment shop instead. The woman who answered said she was in the process of buying the store from Teresa Gaethe-Leonard.

Grace Callas had asked her husband who this was. He was angry and said, "You don't know what you're getting into. You have to stop your little detective work. Stop digging and stop asking questions."

But that just spurred her on more. She noted the area code for Marysville and called every law enforcement agency in that region, finally ending up with the Snohomish County Sheriff's Office.

Brad Pince explained carefully that Nick Callas had been interviewed as a "possible witness" in a homicide case involving Teresa Gaethe-Leonard.

"Why?" she asked. "Why on earth? —"

Pince drew a deep breath. "I should explain to you that your husband has been paying Teresa Leonard's legal expenses, and he's posted $500,000 cash to bail her out of jail."

"What?" Grace Callas gasped, much more upset now than when she had originally called the sheriff's office.

"She was barely able to continue the conversation," Pince commented later. "And she kept asking me what she needed to do."

Grace sobbed as she told Pince that her husband was spending all their money, that she herself had no independent resources, and now he was leaving her and their son "high and dry" without any money to pay their bills.

All Pince could do was suggest that she obtain legal help to protect her personal finances.

From her comments, Pince deduced that things were not as rosy in the Callas marriage as Nick had described. Grace said she no longer lived in Hawaii. "I had to move because of my medical condition. The local doctors in Hawaii ran out of ways to treat me, so I had to move to California with my son Jack, and I'm staying with my sister while I undergo treatment. Nick still lives in Hawaii, but he comes to California to visit us."

Grace Callas had not been aware how important Teresa was to him. Until she found the cards, she had never even heard of Teresa. Now she said she was going to contact her family's attorney to see that her assets were protected.

Two hours later, Brad Pince received a call from Grace's lawyer. He said that she was still upset to the point of hysteria, but he would see that she was properly represented, if not by him, then by another attorney.

At four thirty on this same day, Grace Callas called once more and seemed much calmer. Pince explained that he, John Padilla, and Michael Downes had gone to Hawaii to interview her husband earlier in the year, and Pince gave her more details on the death of Chuck Leonard. Grace confided that she had had issues with Nick for years, and had known of several girlfriends he had. "He lies to me, and he can be intimidating. I'm afraid of him."

Knowing now her penchant for high emotion, Pince suspected that Grace Callas could be exaggerating, especially when she said Nick called her several times a day. He appeared to be a man who was constantly on the phone; between his many daily calls to Teresa, and his business calls, and constant calls to his wife, too, it was a wonder the man got anything done, let alone manage to successfully juggle a wife and a mistress and a business.

Pince and Downes were anxious to see the cards Teresa had sent to Nick Callas. They would, perhaps, substantiate that the two did have a very romantic, intimate relationship, far more intense than either of them had admitted. They would need to obtain the actual cards to use as court exhibits; copies wouldn't be as easy for a handwriting expert to examine.

Three days later, on November 16, 1997,

Pince talked once more to Grace Callas. She had retained an attorney — Eleanor Stegmeier — and would turn the cards from Teresa to Nick over to her. As Pince had suggested, she had taken notes during her phone conversations with Nick. He had warned her, she said, to stop snooping into his business.

"Did he tell you anything about Chuck Leonard's murder?" Pince asked.

"He told me that Teresa killed her husband for the insurance money — that she's now saying Chuck abused their daughter, but that that's not true. He said that he had no involvement with Teresa, but that everyone who knew her was being investigated. She wanted the insurance money and she wanted to move to Hawaii."

"Which was it?" Pince asked. "Did your husband say her motive was Chuck Leonard's insurance payoff — or that she shot him because he was molesting their daughter?"

She wasn't sure; she thought that Nick had told her different things at different times.

"I've been told," Pince began, "that the reason Nick can't leave you is because all the money he has is money you brought into the marriage?"

"When I married him in December 1989, I

had about $300,000 — but all of my money has been spent. It's gone now. I have no idea what Nick's assets are worth — he hides that from me," she sighed. "He always tells me he's broke. He wouldn't pay ten dollars for his son to sit on Santa's lap."

Pince didn't have to ask questions; Grace seemed to have an endless list of grievances against her husband of eight years. She said that when Nick left Hawaii on trips, he always suspended her credit cards so she couldn't spend any money while he was gone.

It was like watching an *Oprah* or *Dr. Phil* show on nasty divorces. But the Callases weren't getting a divorce, and Grace insisted they were still married and not really separated — except temporarily, and only for medical reasons.

On December 1, Pince and Michael Downes, the assistant prosecutor, flew to Orange County, California, and met with Grace and her attorney. Although she was willing to let the Washington investigators look at the actual romantic cards Teresa had sent to Nick, and to ask Grace Callas some questions, Eleanor Stegmeier refused to turn over the cards to them.

But they needed the original cards because they would "tend to show that a felony had been committed, or that a particular person committed a felony."

The cards certainly established that Teresa and Nick had been in an intimate relationship — something they both continued to deny ten months after Chuck's murder. If Pince and Downes had to get a search warrant to seize them as evidence, they would do that.

Brad Pince and Michael Downes wondered if Teresa was responsible for putting those cards in Nick's accordion file, knowing full well that Grace would find them when she worked on the books.

Grace told them that Nick was accusing her of trying to send him to prison for ten years with her stubborn snooping. And he'd brought in his big guns when he'd said that she could be "arrested as a conspirator, dragged to Washington State, and forced to leave my son behind.

"He told me that you destroyed evidence, Mr. Pince, that Chuck Leonard was a pornographer, and that the sheriff's office destroyed evidence proving that he was molesting his daughter, and that you ruined Teresa's alibi."

Grace Callas said that, above all, her husband had warned her not to talk to any detectives from Washington. That would be best for him, certainly. Grace was a loose cannon, highly suspicious, given to outbursts of emotion, and torn between getting revenge against him and Teresa and not wanting to let go of her marriage.

Few people are more dangerous than women scorned.

The two cards that someone had slipped into the financial records of Nick and Grace's corporation would have stunned any wife. The first one was all trees and hearts, drawn as simply as a child would, although the printed sentiments were written by an artist at the American Greetings card company:

I don't ever want
to take you for granted.
I don't ever want to forget
what it was like before you
or how it would be
without you.
I don't ever want to forget
our first kiss
or our last touch,
or let a day go by
without telling you
how much you mean to me,
how deeply I love you, and how much I
  need you.

*I don't ever want you to doubt
the way I feel or how much
happier I am because of you.
I love you.*

And in Teresa's own handwriting:

*With all My heart & Soul
Love,
Teresa
XXOOO*

The second card showed a bridal couple through a car's rear window. They were dressed in 1930s wedding clothes and kissing. The word "ALWAYS" was printed in capital letters beneath.

This card was written in Teresa's hand, and like the first, would give any wife pause.

*Nick,
    You give Me peace . . . that I've never had. . . . Thank you — for you.
    T*

"I love You so Much. . . . Your (sic) everything to Me. I thank you for being in my life, Standing by Me & Loving Me! You are Everything I could Want. . . . What everyone wants. . . . You are kind & knowing

. . . gentel (sic) & smart. . . . Your (sic) Just right! — I miss You Every Second & think about You Every Second. . . . I feel as if I've known You all My Life. . . . I know Your Love for Me . . . & I cannot tell You How Special It and You have Made me feel! . . . I know I have caused You pain & I cannot tell you how Sorry I am for that! The Outside World is Crazy for me & I am trying to find a way thru this. . . . You are the Most Wonderful!
Love You,
Teresa! OOXX

Teresa had many reasons to be thankful to Nick Callas. Were it not for him and the bail money he'd posted for her, she would probably still be sitting behind bars in the Snohomish County Jail. Instead, she was living in a nice apartment that her attorney, George Cody, was paying for, and she had at least $10,000 in cash to pay John Henry Browne. She wasn't working, and either Nick Callas or George Cody had given her Browne's fee.

They both trusted her.

Teresa's one regret was that she could not see Morgan, although she was still allowed monitored phone conversations with her. Without Morgan, she seemed devastated.

With the assistance of Detective Tim

Schennum of the Costa Mesa Police Department, Michael Downes and Brad Pince obtained a search warrant for Eleanor Stegmeier's office. To search an attorney's, physician's, or clergy person's office, California law demands that a "special master" (a state bar–appointed attorney) be present. Grace Callas's lawyer was not pleased to have a search warrant served on her at her office.

After an impasse, she agreed to talk with Detective Schennum. The original cards were delivered to Downes and Pince soon after. It would have been much easier and less costly if that had been done in the beginning, but Grace's attorney had wanted to protect her.

Browne and Downes jousted in their arguments. Browne pointed out that Teresa had been responsible and cooperative since she had bailed out from jail, and Downes voiced his concern that she was "an unpredictable person" whom he still considered a danger to the witnesses prepared to testify against her.

BUT I TRUSTED YOU

Chuck Leonard was a vital, popular middle-school counselor who helped scores of children through their tough teenage problems. He had a wide circle of friends and many women were attracted to him. (THERESA LEONARD COLLECTION)

Teresa Gaethe was a pretty blonde, always Chuck's preferred type, and they met romantically in New Orleans. They appeared to be genuinely in love.

Chuck and Teresa hit it off so well in New Orleans that he hated to leave her behind when his educational conference ended. He wrote to her constantly, sending loving cards and flowers from his garden in Washington State. And she wrote to him and called him. They seemed destined to be together.

An airplane view of Chuck Leonard's Lake Goodwin neighbor-hood. It was the ideal place to live. (POLICE AIR PHOTO)

Chuck Leonard's neighbors were also friends. His next-door neigh-bor, a doctor, lived in the house on the left, and the house that Chuck built is on the right. (POLICE AIR PHOTO)

The lake house that Chuck Leonard enlarged by digging out the foundation. His house, lawn, and garden were his pride and joy, and he even had a glass floor in his living room. He invited Teresa Gaethe to share it with him. (THERESA LEONARD COLLECTION)

Life was great at first for Chuck and Teresa, although he wasn't anxious to get married. She didn't bond nearly as well with his friends—especially his friends' wives and fiancées. (THERESA LEONARD COLLECTION)

Chuck Leonard smiles at his wedding reception in the lake house, but the celebration became a fiasco when Teresa asked her hired security guards to throw out one of his former girlfriends. Chuck had seen no need for the guards. (THERESA LEONARD COLLECTION)

Despite their disastrous wedding reception, Chuck and Teresa looked happy as they began their marriage, lounging on the beach. But Chuck had told one of his friends that he had made a "terrible mistake." He was determined to make his marriage last—if he could. (THERESA LEONARD COLLECTION)

Whatever problems they had in their marriage, both Chuck and Teresa loved their daughter, Morgan. Chuck was amazed by how much he loved the little girl, who came along when he was nearing fifty. He would do anything to see that she stayed in his life. They both loved the lake he lived on, and Chuck could not bear the thought that she would be taken far away from him. (THERESA LEONARD COLLECTION)

Teresa had a fairly successful consignment store in Marysville, selling high-end clothing and accessories. She painted it pink, and it attracted both new clients and her former customers from the Bon Marché department store. (POLICE PHOTO)

Teresa told her former husband that she owned an "exclusive boutique" in Washington State, a description that seems a bit grandiose for the tiny frame building. She also worked for a travel agency part-time. Later, most of her income came from her millionaire lover. (POLICE PHOTO)

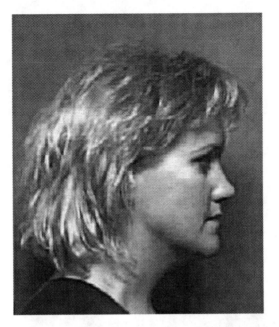

After Chuck's tragic death, Teresa was asked to give a statement to the Snohomish County Sheriff's detectives. She and Chuck had been separated for a few years, but they were not legally divorced. They also shared custody of Morgan. (POLICE PHOTO)

Teresa was fortunate to have one of Washington State's most successful criminal defense attorneys agree to defend her. John Henry Browne, however, found that his client's bizarre actions made his job difficult. (ANN RULE COLLECTION)

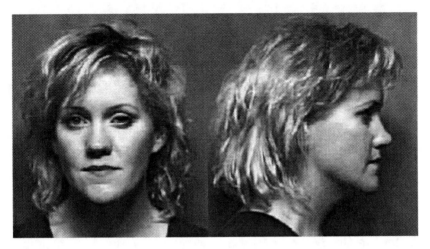

Teresa Gaethe-Leonard before she had plastic surgery.
(POLICE PHOTO)

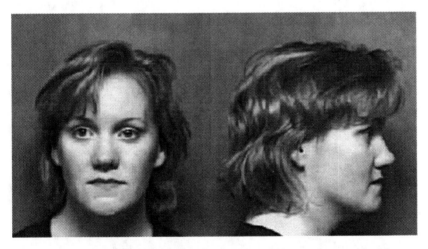

Teresa after plastic surgery—probably on her nose and chin.
If she had turned to surgery to change her look, it didn't work;
she looked almost the same afterward. (POLICE PHOTO)

Detective Brad Pince of the Snohomish County Sheriff's Office was in charge of the Chuck Leonard murder investigation. It took him to California, Hawaii, and even Puerto Rico, but he gathered enough evidence—both physical and circumstantial—to arrest the guilty person. It may well be the most memorable case in his long career. (ANN RULE COLLECTION)

Left to right: Snohomish County Detective Jim Scharf and Senior Deputy Prosecutor Michael Downes worked with Brad Pince and Detective John Padilla to prove that an almost unbelievable motive caused the murder of a good man. Downes helped in the entire investigative process. (ANN RULE COLLECTION)

Detective Brad Pince testifies in Teresa Gaethe-Leonard's trial as he opens sealed evidence packets. (THERESA LEONARD COLLECTION)

Teresa Gaethe-Leonard in a photo taken after being in the Washington State Women's Prison in Purdy for several years. Instead of designer clothes, she wears a blue denim uniform and a white T-shirt. She threw away what could have been a life most women would envy. She has not seen her daughter, Morgan, or a picture of her since Morgan was about seven. She faces many more years of prison, all lost because of her deluded scheme that she thought would let her marry a millionaire.

CHAPTER SEVEN

And unpredictable Teresa Gaethe-Leonard was. As Christmas decorations appeared in the first week of December 1997, law enforcement departments in Washington State were searching for her. She had disappeared.

She probably would not look like the Teresa in her earlier photographs. She had had plastic surgery in November. Teresa had a new nose, a forehead lift or Botox injections, and a modification of her prominent chin. If she had a new haircut, and changed the color of her hair she might be hard to recognize.

Wherever she was.

She had apparently paid for the surgery with the estimated $10,000 to $15,000 meant to retain John Henry Browne. Although Browne was a generous man who often represented clients pro bono (for free) when they had no means to pay, he wasn't pleased that she had simply run out on him without any warning. She had shown up for an appointment with him a few days earlier, and she was scheduled to be in his office again on December 3.

Teresa had missed her appointment with Browne, but she had been in touch with him as recently as the previous weekend. He was as baffled as Nick Callas and George Cody were that she would bolt and run, mostly because Browne felt her defense case had been getting stronger. He believed she had a good chance at acquittal. That chance would diminish markedly now if the detectives could prove Teresa had deliberately disappeared — and they probably could.

Browne walked into the Snohomish County Sheriff's Office to notify them that Teresa was missing.

According to Nick Callas, he had stopped sending Teresa money for living expenses in late spring 1997. He believed that George Cody was taking care of that.

Callas did admit, however, that beyond putting up her bail money, it was he who had furnished the check to pay John Henry Browne.

Cody hadn't spoken to Teresa for a few days, nor had he been able to reach her by phone after December 1. He went to the apartment he'd rented for her. The manager let him in, and there was the immediate sense that the rooms had been abandoned. It smelled empty. Dust had begun to settle on flat areas, and beyond some food spoiling in the refrigerator, there was no sign that anyone currently lived there. Most of Teresa's furniture was gone, along with her personal items.

Their footsteps echoed on bare floors.

Stunned, Cody gave notice on the apartment — he felt in his gut that Teresa didn't plan to come back here. Her car was parked nearby, however, and he had it towed to a safe place.

Now Teresa had betrayed three men who were trying to help her gain her freedom: Nick Callas, George Cody, and John Henry Browne. And aside from breaking promises to them, she had cost each of them financially — Nick the most. Browne was the only one without emotional ties to Teresa, but he was frustrated with himself that he hadn't seen it coming.

Nick was now holding the bag for $500,000 in bail money. His marriage had blown all to pieces, and for all her promises to him, her professions of love and her sentimental cards, he realized that Teresa had abandoned him.

Yes, she had been depressed because she

had little contact with Morgan, but that could change at any time. If she should be acquitted of murder charges, Morgan could live with her again, but for now, Morgan was on the State's witness list. And even if Teresa could somehow arrange to meet up with her young daughter, as a fugitive from justice, she would always be looking over her shoulder.

It had been only three months since Teresa's "accidental" overdose in Washington State. Had she gone off to some lonely place where she could commit suicide without being rescued? Michael Downes thought not. He cited signs that she had planned her escape. Her home in Everett had been emptied of almost everything of value. Eventually, the Snohomish County detectives would locate her belongings in storage at a female acquaintance's home.

Chuck's sister, Theresa Leonard, had taken custody of Morgan, and they were living in Portland, Oregon. Theresa was frightened when she heard that Teresa had fled. She worried that Morgan's mother might try to kidnap the five-year-old and take her with her in her flight to avoid prosecution. The Snohomish County investigators reassured Aunt Theresa that they had notified the Portland Police Department and Morgan's school that her mother did not have legal custody of her, and that it was possible she might attempt to abduct her.

Jan Jorgensen, spokeswoman for the Snohomish County Sheriff's Office, told reporters that they were receiving assistance from the FBI, the U.S. Marshal's Service, and the Washington State Attorney General's Office in an ever-spreading dragnet for Teresa.

Michael Downes stopped himself from saying "I told you so," but it was obvious that the "no bail" he'd requested three months earlier would have prevented her from running simply because she would have been jailed until her trial.

The Snohomish County detectives first thought that she had probably gone to Hawaii, and that she was being hidden by Callas. But he willingly cooperated with them, and they believed he hadn't heard from her. Some of his devotion to her had to have diminished since Teresa had just cost him $500,000. He assured the investigators that she hadn't contacted him at all and he had no idea where she was.

Nor did any of Teresa's girlfriends who considered themselves part of her inside circle or the psychologist whom the defense team had consulted, even though Teresa had had twenty-five sessions with her since May.

Teresa clearly knew when to keep herself to herself.

Witnesses came forward to say that Teresa appeared to have black eyes before Thanksgiving; many suspected she had either been in a brawl or, more likely, had had plastic surgery. What did she look like now? Detectives found the plastic surgeon who had operated on her. He verified that her face had changed after he had operated on her on November 11, modifying her chin and nose. With her blond hair dyed dark, and wearing sunglasses, it would be very hard to spot her, even if they knew where to look.

As the days passed, it seemed likely that Teresa had left the country, or at least the mainland. She could not have done that with her own ID, even though she had in her possession various credit cards using different names. She would need either a driver's license or a passport with a photo on it at some points in her journey — to get on a plane or to cash checks.

From the beginning, Brad Pince, John Padilla, and Jim Scharf had worked with various phone companies to have numbers that she might call monitored. Nick Callas had myriad phone numbers, set up under many names, some with special calling plans that would assure his wife would not know how often he'd talked to Teresa over the last few years. One was a "500" setup that seemed designed specifically so the two of them could send and receive calls to each other from anywhere in the world.

Even after she had sacrificed Nick's bail money when she fled, detectives had seen how addicted he was to her. Long after he had to have known that she was capable of murder he had remained steadfastly supportive of her; it apparently never occurred to him that Teresa would ever be dangerous to him or his family. He appeared to cling to his belief that Teresa was "ninety percent angel."

Pince and Padilla kept careful track of calls to Nick Callas's many numbers. And that paid off. Cell phone calls had come in to one of those phones from Puerto Rico. A cautious statement to the media said that someone close to Teresa had heard from her, although detectives would not reveal which of her friends or relatives had received the calls.

Two weeks later, the investigators said that the Puerto Rico cell phone calls had gone to Nick Callas. They still would not verify that the calls had come from Teresa Gaethe-Leonard. How she had made her way to Puerto Rico was anyone's guess — but she had evidently had money.

By checking flight manifests, detectives found the name of a thirty-five-year-old Snohomish County woman who had flown on American Airlines from Seattle to Chicago on December 2, 1997, and then to Puerto Rico on a one-way ticket. Her name was Carolyn Fabray.

Carolyn turned out to be another woman who had felt sorry for Teresa, and stayed a friend to her despite the murder charges against her. She admitted to detectives that she was storing several large furniture pieces — including a bed and a futon — because Teresa could no longer pay her apartment rent. She had even offered her pick-up truck to move the furniture.

Did she know where her driver's license, credit cards, and other pieces of ID were? When the investigators asked her that, she went to her bedroom and came back with the purse she kept them in. As she rifled through her purse and then dumped the contents on a table, she looked up, surprised.

"They're not here?" she said, surprised. "My ID is gone."

"All of it?" Detective Joe Ward asked.

"No — but my Washington State ID card is gone, and some of my kids' medical cards are missing."

"Did your state ID card have your photograph on it?" Brad Pince asked, already knowing the answer.

"Yes."

Carolyn Fabray bore a resemblance to Teresa Gaethe-Leonard: same age, same body type, and her features were similar. Without knowing it, she had provided Teresa with a way to pass airport security. It was 1997 — four years before 9/11, and few who staffed the airline ticket counters and gates took more than a cursory look at ID.

A federal warrant for Teresa Gaethe-Leonard's arrest on charges of fleeing to avoid prosecution was issued on December 11, 1997, nine days after she vanished. The FBI and the Fugitive Task Force in Puerto Rico were notified of the general location of the calls emanating from there.

Teresa was probably somewhere in San Juan, but they didn't know exactly where. And there was a good chance that she might be moving on to other countries, using Puerto Rico only as a jumping-off location. Nick Callas suggested that she might sign on to be a crew member on a boat.

But she hadn't.

Five days later, Teresa was arrested in yet another hospital room. She had been taken there after a suicide attempt, this one far more serious than the one in August. Had she meant to come so close to dying? Possibly not, but what could be more lonely than being far from home and the daughter she cherished as Christmas approached — not to mention being faced with murder charges in an upcoming trial? There was no cold weather, or snow, or evergreen trees in San Juan. There were poinsettias, but they were trees reaching rooftops, not plants wrapped in red-and-gold foil. The language she heard was Spanish.

Teresa was adrift and alone.

Probably Teresa loved Morgan as much as she was capable of loving anyone. The little girl was part of her, closer to her than the sisters and brother she had grown up with. Morgan was the one person in the world who had believed in her completely, and taken her every word as gospel. As one of Teresa's employees said once, "Teresa and Morgan were like two peas in a pod."

One has to wonder if Teresa pondered on what a stupid and cruel thing she had done when she shot Chuck. Perhaps she didn't care for anyone else — even Morgan. She had taken another human being's life, and that had ruined her own future. What did she have to look forward to as she sat alone in a hotel room, watching neon lights create flashing multicolored images on the shadowy walls of her room and hearing the constant rhythm of steel drums and the thrum of salsa, bomba, and reggae music instead of Christmas carols?

Even though she may not have been aware of it, those who hunted Teresa were closing in on her, and Nick, the man she'd counted on completely for years, was no longer in her corner. She had burned too many bridges behind her.

John Henry Browne explained to reporters how Teresa had been located in San Juan, Puerto Rico. He had received a call from her sister Lois with disturbing news about Teresa's condition and he had moved immediately to talk to the hospital where she'd reportedly been taken.

She'd been living in the Embassy Suites Hotel in San Juan under the name Sally Lopez. She might have been out of money or going back to her first apartment over a laundromat. She might have been planning to catch another plane, headed far away.

Or she may have finally decided to check out of her life.

Teresa's time at the Embassy Suites had run out, and she was due to leave the hotel on December 15 — but by 1:00 p.m., she failed to turn in her key and receive a copy of her bill.

The main desk gave her a few more hours, and then a staff member checked her room to see if she was still there. The door was bolted from the inside and they had to break in. When they did, they saw that she had wedged a chair against the door, too.

Teresa was inside, unconscious and cold to the touch. The hotel called an ambulance, and she was rushed to the Catalina Regional Hospital. She was placed under the care of Dr. Gootsman, who said that she had overdosed on prescription drugs and probably alcohol. Her condition was "serious but stable." She was admitted to the San Juan hospital as Sally Lopez. She also went by the name Sally Fabray in Puerto Rico.

Pince called the FBI office in San Juan and let Special Agent Louis Vega know that Teresa Gaethe-Leonard had been located. Even though it was almost midnight in Puerto Rico, Vega said he would contact another agent and they would go at once to the Catalina Hospital and see what they could find out.

Vega called Brad Pince back at 3:30 a.m. San Juan time with a report on Teresa. "She's in custody," Vega said. "She's been turned over to the San Juan Police Department, but she's not in any condition to leave the hospital. She's being guarded by the police until she's well enough to be released to jail."

Pince checked with hospital personnel, and they said Teresa would probably be able to leave in a day or two. That turned out to be an underestimate of her condition: She got worse before she got better and spent Christmas in a hospital bed.

It was probably better than being in jail.

Louis Vega checked her hotel suite on December 16. There were no suitcases in her room, but he took possession of some of Teresa's jewelry pieces. There was a box of brown hair dye, a long-distance telephone card, two airline luggage tags, and a pocket calendar. The hotel's security department had found $325 in cash, and had put it in their safe.

Where were her clothes? Had she thrown them away, given them away, or sent them on ahead to her next destination? If she had done that, her destination had changed, and she had become so morose that she drank and took pills until she became comatose. She seemed to have been serious — serious enough that she'd blocked the door to keep everyone out.

Until it didn't matter anymore.

Teresa's defense attorney and the Snohomish County detectives located Teresa at almost the same time.

"The major thing was that we wanted her alive," Browne said. "So obviously the best thing to do is keep her in custody and keep her alive."

It certainly seemed the wise choice. Teresa had imbibed so much alcohol and sleeping pills that she barely survived. Another hour or so, and she probably would have been dead.

Teresa had called Nick Callas from Puerto Rico and the Snohomish County investigators were only hours behind her when she was found comatose in the Embassy Suites. She remained hospitalized for two weeks, and when her condition was stable, and doctors thought she would survive, barring any unforeseen complications, she was moved to a women's prison north of San Juan.

Pale and thin, Teresa immediately made friends with the warden's wife, who felt sorry for her. Teresa wasn't like the other women at Vega Alta. She was genteel and had lovely manners. When she saw that Teresa couldn't stomach the food most prisoners ate, the warden's wife cooked special dishes for her and carried them into the prison, urging Teresa to eat because she was much too *delgada*.

As she always had, Teresa evoked sympathy in both men and women, and the warden's wife in Puerto Rico doubted that the charges against her back in Washington State could be as serious as the FBI said. She visited with Teresa and tried to keep her from being homesick. Teresa spoke of her little girl and of how much she missed her.

It was all very sad.

Deputy Prosecutor Michael Downes hoped that Teresa would waive extradition and return to Snohomish County without a morass of legal paperwork. John Henry Browne said he was sure that would not be a problem, and even if Teresa did initially refuse to come home, he would urge her to waive extradition.

"You can delay things for months," he said, "but my guess is that Teresa won't want to spend a lot of time in a Puerto Rican jail."

Some reporters wrote that John Henry Browne was no longer representing Teresa Gaethe-Leonard, in light of her escape. His office neither verified nor denied that.

Although it seems exotic, Puerto Rico is not a foreign country but a U.S. commonwealth. Extraditing Teresa to the continental United States would be almost automatic anyway. However, Snohomish County authorities had to prove that the person being held in the women's prison in Vega Alta north of San Juan really was Teresa Gaethe-Leonard. There was a good chance she might look entirely different than her picture on the Wanted bulletins, but it was unlikely that she had managed to change her fingerprints. A few years later, the advances in DNA matching would have simplified everything, but in 1998, it was not yet commonly used or accepted as irrefutable evidence.

Actually, Teresa was quite comfortable in her Puerto Rican prison, but she was thousands of miles away from Morgan. She put on some of the weight she'd lost, and she enjoyed visiting with the warden's wife. But Browne had said he believed she would come back to Snohomish County without a struggle. Those who knew how adept she was at escaping were apprehensive, especially when they heard how close she had grown to the warden's wife.

She might run again if she got the chance.

Michael Downes kept hearing conflicting information. Teresa was to have an extradition hearing at Hato Rey Superior Court near San Juan, but that didn't happen.

There was one good reason for Teresa to waive extradition — loyalty to Nick Callas. If she agreed to return to Washington State by February 4, 1998, which would be exactly sixty days since she hadn't shown up for her court hearing, and almost a year since Chuck Leonard died, there was a good chance that Nick could get most of his half-million-dollar bail money returned. The county would deduct the expenses it had in searching for Teresa, and for bringing her back, but that was surely better for Callas than losing the whole $500,000.

Even so, it would be expensive, and it might take a very long time for Callas's money to come back to him. The cost of tracking the bail jumper would probably be between $75,000 and $100,000.

Teresa's lover had cooperated with the Snohomish County authorities and helped them locate Teresa. How he felt about her was a moot question. Their relationship had lasted eleven years, even after she married Chuck. She had to have some kind of emotional hold over him.

Callas and his wife had finally separated. Any wife would have been displeased — if not furious — to have her husband pay a huge bail amount for his mistress, an accused murderess. And Grace Callas couldn't forgive Nick for his years of deception and for "giving away" half a million dollars of *their* money.

It was time for Teresa to come home. Brad Pince, and Detectives Sally Heth and Susie Johnson boarded an American Airlines flight at 7:30 a.m. on January 20, 1998, headed for Puerto Rico to pick up Teresa Gaethe-Leonard. The next morning, they talked to the owners of several small apartments located above a laundromat in San Juan — the last place Teresa had reportedly lived before she checked into the Embassy Suites.

They gave the detectives copies of a rental agreement signed by a woman named Carol. Pince showed them a booking photo of Teresa Gaethe-Leonard, and the landlords said that was the woman they knew as "Carol." The mystery of where her clothes and other belongings were was solved; her suitcases, some shoes, and some purses had been left at her first small apartment in San Juan. Her landlords had boxed up all of her personal possessions with the help of a local attorney who presented them with an official document giving him the right to take possession of her things. What part he played in Teresa's life was hard to determine. When she got back to the continental United States, Teresa would tell a cell mate that there was a man in Puerto Rico who was very interested

178

in helping her.

That could very well have been true, except that he spoke only Spanish — at least in front of laundromat/apartment owners. Otherwise, he fit the pattern of the older men who doted on her.

Finding some of Teresa's clothes solved one problem; they didn't know what she was going to wear on the plane to Seattle. She'd left the hospital in one of their gowns and had worn prison garb ever since.

The Snohomish County detectives then drove to the San Juan police station, where Teresa had been moved from the prison in Vega Alta. They planned to pick her up and leave as soon as possible to return to Everett. When they finally saw her in person, she did look different. Her plastic surgery was subtle, but her forehead was smoother, and her nose and chin appeared to have been altered. She insisted that she hadn't been trying to disguise herself, but had wanted only to look more attractive.

If that was her real reason, it hadn't worked; she looked much plainer than she did in most of her earlier photos. She had gained weight with the warden's wife's cooking, and her face showed the stress of her circumstances. But it was more than that. There was no question that she'd had work done on her face by a skilled surgeon.

Detective Susie Johnson took five photos of Teresa, three of them showing healed-over bedsores on her head and spine. It was clear she had been unconscious longer than any doctor had predicted.

"That happened when I lay in one position in the hospital for fourteen days," Teresa explained. "I got pneumonia, too."

After Teresa was thoroughly searched and the paperwork completed, an unmarked San Juan police car drove them to the airport where they waited to board a United Airlines flight back to Washington State. The Snohomish County detectives bought Teresa a sandwich and a soft drink from a vendor at the San Juan Airport.

On the plane, Susie Johnson and Sally Heth sat on either side of her, and Brad Pince sat across the aisle.

"She was very chatty in the airport and on the plane," Heth said, "both to me and Susie Johnson."

Teresa seemed familiar with the island of Puerto Rico, and said that Ponce was a much more pleasant city to visit than San Juan. Although it was "very corrupt," Teresa said that anyone with lots of money could get anything they wanted — and faster — in Ponce. "You can get your car fixed first," she said, "even if it was last in the line."

Teresa described Puerto Rico as "the trampoline between South America and North America for drug runners."

Sally Heth wondered if Teresa had been intending to bounce on that trampoline into some hiding place in South America.

Teresa was friendly enough on the long flight home. She helped her female captors as they worked over crossword puzzles to pass the time. She offered correct suggestions for words that fit into spaces. They could tell that she was an intelligent woman with a large vocabulary and excellent social skills. She seemed to accept her capture, although she was embarrassed to have to board the planes in handcuffs, and she tried to avoid the stares of other passengers.

After a few hours in flight, Heth escorted Teresa to the plane's bathroom. While they were there, Teresa confided that her brother was a detective somewhere in the Midwest. (It was unclear if she was talking about Frank Jones or Lois Jones's husband, although it was probably her brother-in-law.)

Heth hesitated for a moment, and then said, "May I ask you a personal question?"

"Sure."

"What does your brother think about your situation?"

Teresa answered somewhat obliquely, "They have it all wrong."

"Who are they?"

"The newspapers." Teresa was implying that her brother had read about her case in the newspapers. "They think that I wanted to run away and live with my boyfriend in Hawaii, and that is *not* true at all."

The two women — detective and prisoner — agreed that the media rarely report the news accurately. Heth didn't have to lie to Teresa to say that. The press can sometimes be the bane of police investigators' existence.

"I thought it was more of a domestic situation —" Heth said carefully, referring to what had happened between Teresa and Chuck.

"Yeah, John Henry's taking care of things," Teresa said, referring to her attorney, and then caught herself. "He would probably kill me if he knew I was talking to you — it's not like you're on my side."

The conversation then ended abruptly. When they returned to their seats, Teresa turned her back on Heth and begin to talk to Detective Johnson on subjects less fraught with pitfalls.

When they landed in Seattle, Pince drove them all to the Snohomish County Jail sixty miles north, where they booked Teresa.

They had journeyed to Puerto Rico and back in less than forty-eight hours.

There would be no reunion between Teresa and Morgan, who had turned six on December 30, 1997, just before the New Year. Morgan was now living with Chuck's sister, her aunt Theresa, and her two older cousins in Oregon. She had spent her first Christmas without her father or her mother. There was a strong possibility that she would be a witness in her mother's trial, and that made meetings between them doubtful.

If he could avoid it, John Henry Browne — who was still representing Teresa — didn't want to call Morgan to the witness stand. She had already been through enough.

Detectives had taken to calling Theresa Leonard the "good Theresa" and their prisoner the "bad Teresa." Chuck's sister loved Morgan dearly and was prepared to do anything she could to see that the child had a safe and happy life. Morgan and Theresa's daughter soon became closer than just cousins; despite the gap between their ages, they eventually thought of each other as sisters.

They were gradually achieving some degree of normalcy. Teresa had sent presents for Morgan before she fled; she complained that Morgan had never gotten them, but she had. Aunt Theresa was doing her best not to bad-mouth the woman whom she believed had murdered her brother — not for Teresa's sake but for Morgan's, and for Chuck's sake, too.

Because of her escape, Teresa Gaethe-Leonard had once again missed a trial date. A new date was set. She was scheduled to go on trial in two months. George Cody, the original lawyer who had been there for her right up until he discovered her empty apartment, withdrew from her case entirely. Cody had no choice; he was now on the State's witness list to testify against Teresa.

Teresa herself was back in the Snohomish County Jail, and not likely to be released; her bail was now $5 million, and she had no one left who would gamble anywhere near that much money on her. She steadfastly clung to her not-guilty plea in Chuck's death.

John Henry Browne was preparing a complicated defense, made more difficult for him when his client jumped bail and disappeared. Still, her behavior whenever she was free from a jail cell made his plea believable. Snohomish County Superior Court Judge Charles French accepted Browne's plea of "innocent by reason of insanity."

This was a woman who had twice attempted suicide with overdoses of drugs and alcohol. Browne had her examined by a forensic psychologist who was prepared to testify that Teresa was legally insane at the time she killed her estranged husband, according to the M'Naughten Rule. M'Naughten stipulates that the defendant must be incapable of discerning the difference between right and wrong at the time of his or her crime.

Usually, if a suspect plans and prepares for her crime, flees from the scene, and makes efforts to cover up evidence, she can be construed to be aware of the difference between right and wrong during that criminal act. Joyce Lilly's statements to detectives — four of them at this point — indicated that Teresa had planned Chuck's murder, even to the point of picking out her "disguise" clothes and entering his house on a dry run three months before she actually shot him.

And Teresa had covered up her crime afterward by insisting that Joyce hide the murder gun, her clothes and boots, and the key to Chuck's house. Teresa had even hidden her car in Joyce's garage.

She seemed to be in her right mind before, during, and after she shot Chuck.

But how does anyone know what is going on in someone else's mind at any time? Brains don't have picture windows.

At John Henry Browne's request, Teresa was transferred to Western State Hospital for a psychiatric evaluation.

Trial dates passed in March, April, and May 1998 and either the State or the Defense had reasons to seek delays. The prosecution added twenty-eight new witnesses, and John Henry Browne was defending another high-profile case in Seattle. He argued that he couldn't possible interview the latest witnesses before trial. If he could not get a continuance, he said he would seek a review by the state court of appeals.

At length, a fall date in 1998 was chosen for Teresa's trial. Chuck Leonard had been dead for seventeen months, and there had been no justice one way or the other stemming from his murder. Teresa's psyche was deemed so fragile that she had spent many weeks in late spring in Western State Hospital, a mental health treatment facility, where she was evaluated, tested, and counseled by psychologists and psychiatrists there.

She was given an IQ test, but the psychologist administrating the test noted that Teresa failed to expand on her answers, even when she was urged to do so. She hurried through questions, and by the end of the test had stopped writing down answers altogether. It wasn't surprising that her full-scale IQ was only 83. This put her in about the 15th percentile, meaning that about 85 percent of people who had taken the test scored higher than she did.

How could that be? A normal IQ (depending on the test given) is between 90 and 110. To finish a four-year college, most students need an IQ of at least 120. How could Teresa have managed a busy concierge desk at a large hotel, fielding calls and requests from guests, or taken care of all the banking and record keeping at The Consignment Shop if her IQ was only 83? For that matter, how could she have been so clever when she helped the female detectives fill in their crossword puzzle on the flight home from Puerto Rico?

Depression certainly can lower intelligence scores, but not to this extent. It seemed possible that Teresa was deliberately trying to appear a lot dumber than she really was.

With her trial looming in September, Teresa was sent once more to Western State Hospital to be sure she was capable of participating in her own defense. She would remain there until her trial began.

On September 8, 1998, the doctors at Western State Hospital determined that Teresa was competent to stand trial. Her day in court had been postponed six times, but now it was time. If she was found guilty, Teresa faced a minimum of twenty-five years in prison.

The Defense's original plan had been to show that she didn't really know what she was doing when she shot Chuck Leonard — that she was insane under the law. Gradually, it had shifted, and with her competency established, their new approach was to show a jury that she had cause to kill her estranged husband, that almost any mother would have done the same. Teresa, they would argue, had been protecting her little girl from a sexually abusive father. If so, she very likely had been suffering from post-traumatic stress disorder (PTSD).

Although PTSD had become the proper term for the stress reaction during the Gulf War, the concept has been around for decades, affecting those caught up in events "beyond normal human experience." War isn't normal for most young soldiers who never expected to shoot to kill. PTSD was called "shell shock" in World War I, and "battle fatigue" in World War II. It was probably called something else in the Civil War and the Revolutionary War.

There are other events that can be construed as beyond normal human experience, and Teresa's defense team believed she had suffered through many of them, enough to cause her mind to splinter into too many shards to count.

Teresa told some of her doctors that her father had spanked her so hard when she was a child that she had been knocked unconscious. She told others that she had only had the wind knocked out of her.

Her sisters agreed to come from Louisiana to testify about the sexual abuse in their home when they were young. Having endured sexual abuse herself, wouldn't Teresa Gaethe-Leonard have been even more horrified to believe that her own child was suffering as she had?

In similar cases across the United States, mothers who have shot sex offenders who molested their children have either been acquitted or given short sentences. And the public — including the jurors — had been pulling for them. Most would agree that a mother's love is probably the most protective and unselfish kind of love.

The Snohomish County investigators hadn't encountered acquaintances of Teresa's who recalled that she was concerned about Chuck molesting Morgan. They asked friends and relatives of the couple if they recalled any concern on her part about that.

Chuck's father and stepmother said that

Teresa had complained on occasion that she was worried because Chuck sometimes left Morgan alone in his house while he worked outside in the yard. But they'd never heard about any suspected sexual abuse.

Defense investigators found employees and friends of Teresa who recalled that there were times when Morgan didn't want to go to her father's house. She told Joyce Lilly once that she didn't like him to touch her. That had occurred when she wanted to call her mother and he wouldn't let her.

There was an occasion when she left The Consignment Shop with Chuck, but had come running back in, saying she didn't want to go. That was in one of Joyce's statements, and it was allegedly the reason Joyce and Teresa had given Morgan teddy bears with their phone numbers hidden in their pockets, a move instigated by Teresa.

A woman who had visited Teresa's shop had once seen Morgan, age three or four, climbing under clothing racks without underpants on.

Joyce Lilly's recall of Teresa and Chuck's marriage, and about the way they treated Morgan, was often one of confusion. Joyce, who was very modest, questioned Teresa about why Morgan was happier without a lot of clothing on; the four-year-old often emulated her father, dropping coats and shoes from the moment she walked through her own — or Joyce's — front door and dancing around happily. Teresa had pooh-poohed her concern.

"We're proud of our bodies in my family," Teresa said calmly. "We don't believe in false modesty."

On the other hand, Chuck was so paranoid that Teresa might accuse him of something that he had Morgan wear her bathing suit when he gave her a bath.

Chuck's friends were adamant that there were many times Morgan hadn't wanted to go to Teresa's house when her visit with her father was over. Chuck's own diaries had passages that mentioned days when Morgan had clung to him and refused to go with Teresa. Separation and divorce are hard on children, and both parents were known to indulge Morgan, possibly to make up for the chaos in her young life.

She was a very intelligent child and, like most children of divorce, Morgan caught on quickly that she could play one parent against another to get what she wanted.

Jan, Chuck's friend and neighbor down the block, was married by this time and he and his wife, Sandy, often babysat for Chuck. Sandy recalled years later, "There is no way that little girl was molested. We would have known because we spent so much time with her."

Brad Pince had worked for years investigating sex crimes against children, and he sincerely doubted that Morgan had suffered abuse. If Teresa had been so concerned about it, why hadn't she mentioned molestation in her divorce filings? Why hadn't she reported it to the authorities? And why had she been so casual about having at least one male neighbor in her apartment building — whom she didn't know well — babysit for Morgan? It didn't add up.

Moreover, Pince knew it was a favorite fall-back ploy that angry estranged wives used in custody wars: when all else failed, women were more likely to accuse their exes of abusing their children. Of course, it was sometimes true, but it was a fist in the belly, a horrible accusation, especially when it was made against a dead man who could no longer defend himself.

Now it suddenly popped up at her trial like an ugly toadstool. From what Pince and the other investigators had learned about Chuck Leonard, he had indeed had a lively sex life — but with adult women, who seemed to understand that he was not interested in long-term commitments.

Chuck idolized his little girl and saw himself as her protector. As Morgan grew, detectives had no doubt that Chuck would have been the kind of dad who scrutinized and intimidated any young suitor who wanted to date her.

But a child abuser? An incestuous father? Never.

Teresa's defense stance now was that Chuck was sitting up in bed, wide awake, on the night he died and they were arguing. She had gone to his house in the early hours of the morning, carrying a gun, but only to talk to him about her concerns, and he had taunted her about Morgan. Her reaction was to shoot him. *But all forensic evidence indicated he had been lying down, sound asleep, when the first bullet ripped into him.*

CHAPTER EIGHT

Teresa Gaethe-Leonard's trial before Superior Court Judge Gerald L. Knight promised to include a war of the psychiatrists and psychologists. Theirs was far from an exact science, and it would be up to the jury to decide who to believe. John Henry Browne maintained that Teresa's mental state had deteriorated markedly since Chuck Leonard was killed, and that she no longer had any clear memory of the shooting, and that she never planned it.

He did not dispute that she had, indeed, shot and killed Chuck Leonard, and there seemed to be no expectation that she could be found innocent — but she could be convicted of lesser offenses, like second-degree murder or manslaughter.

Browne was a master debater, and a genius at planning and carrying out defense strategy, but he faced an uphill battle. Michael Downes, prosecuting for the State, had an abundance of physical evidence to show that Teresa had very carefully planned Chuck's murder.

With a manslaughter conviction, Teresa wouldn't spend much time in prison. With premeditation and a first-degree conviction, she would be in prison until her hair turned gray and her face was lined with wrinkles.

An eleventh-hour request to postpone Teresa's trial once again came from Deputy Prosecutor Michael Downes. He and his team had been informed that John Henry Browne was prepared to argue an additional defense for Teresa — battered-woman syndrome.

Judge Gerald Knight ruled that the trial would go forward as planned on September 9 and warned Browne not to elicit testimony that Teresa was a battered woman. If he did, Knight said firmly that he might declare a mistrial.

Some in the courtroom wondered if Chuck Leonard might be considered a "battered man," but they didn't say it out loud.

By the time the State and the Defense teams agreed on twelve jurors and two alternate jurors who would step in if any of the original dozen should become ill or step down, there were eleven women and one man on the jury, with two male alternate jurors.

It was — and is — always difficult to say whether female jurors will empathize with a woman defendant. Would this jury, perhaps, judge Teresa Gaethe-Leonard more harshly because they knew how most normal women would react? Would the lone male see Teresa as a frightened, dependent woman in trouble? No one could say. The most important assets good jurors can have is the ability to listen carefully to witnesses from both sides, study the physical and circumstantial evidence, and eventually vote their consciences.

What would the eleven women on Teresa's jury think? Many of them had children and understood the power of mother love. Possibly some of them had had husbands who had strayed. There was no way of telling whether they would view Teresa as a victim and a heroine or as a husband-stealing plotter. Jurors' own life experiences and lessons learned cannot be excluded from their decision making.

That may well be a juror's strongest talent. That, and the ability to stay awake and listen carefully for six or seven hours a day. Trials can be exciting, but they can also be dry and repetitive. The hours after lunch in a stuffy courtroom have put many a juror to sleep. And not a few journalists.

One thing is true of any trial: neither the judge, the attorneys, the gallery, nor the defendant has ever been able to read a jury from the expression on their faces or their body language. They always surprise you when you talk to them after trial.

For the first time, almost all of the people who had passed through Teresa's life walked in and out of a single courtroom: her sisters Lois and Macie, but not her brother; Nick Callas, but not Gary Gaethe; Joyce Lilly, Rick Lilly, and George Bowden, Joyce's attorney; Teresa's employees at The Consignment Shop, women who had been her "best friends" for a while and then been dropped from her life; George Cody, Teresa's first attorney; Michelle Conley, Chuck's last lover; a dozen or more of Chuck's friends and former girlfriends; Theresa Leonard, Chuck's sister; his father and stepmother, Fred and Caroline Leonard; Doug Butler, Chuck's teacher friend who had found his body; his boyhood friend from Bremerton where he grew up; his friend who owned a video-rental store; and the detectives from Snohomish County who had helped bring Teresa to trial: Brad Pince, John Padilla, Jim Scharf, Joe Ward, and Rob Palmer.

The gallery in Judge Knight's courtroom

was packed almost every day in September and October as the weeks of trial unfolded. Teresa's story was like a teleplay script for a miniseries, only more shocking because it was real, and because it had happened in the town where many in the gallery lived. They had followed it during the nineteen months since Chuck Leonard was murdered, and wanted to know more about what had happened and why. Newspaper and television coverage had never told them enough.

That wasn't the reporters' fault; so many details had been kept under wraps. Now, the press bench held media reporters from all over Washington State.

It was still warm in mid-September and opening windows helped lower the stuffiness and heat in the courtroom, but that created another problem as street noise drifted in and made it difficult for the jurors to hear the witnesses and attorneys. Sirens from emergency vehicles often brought testimony to a halt.

Senior Deputy Prosecutor Michael Downes asked the jurors to raise their hands if they couldn't hear.

Downes then began his opening remarks, explaining the State's case: "The evidence the State will present to you will show that at approximately four or five in the morning of February 20, of 1997, the defendant drove twenty-five miles to her estranged husband's house, that she walked into his house, down to his bedroom, shot and killed him with a .45-caliber automatic handgun by shooting him three times in the chest area. The fatal wound entered his chest, went into one of his lungs, and he bled to death internally as a result. . . ."

Michael Downes knew this case so thoroughly that he probably could have made his opening statement in his sleep, but he glanced occasionally at his notes. The jury listened raptly as he described the Leonards' relationship at the time Chuck was killed, the "rehearsal" for murder in November 1996, and the actual fatal shooting three months later. Downes promised to present witnesses to Teresa's affair with Nick Callas, and to her plot to find a way to give him a baby, even though she knew she could not conceive herself.

"There was a divorce in this case," the prosecutor pointed out. "It was filed. The paperwork was filed by the defendant. She filled it out. There are various boxes that you can check off to indicate whether there are any particular problems. And one box of interest is whether there are any child abuse–type problems. That was not checked off. One box is whether there were physical abuse–type problems [against Teresa]. That box was not checked off."

But these were allegedly the two issues that had motivated Teresa to kill Chuck. And she hadn't even mentioned them when she filed for divorce!

Downes promised to call to the witness stand two men from Teresa's apartment building who would testify that she was looking for a .45-caliber handgun in early 1997.

He told the jurors about Teresa's Hawaiian lover, and the $500,000 bail money Nick Callas had wired to the Snohomish County Clerk's Office. "Part of the bail order says, 'Look, if you get released, you got to come back here for the hearings.' And the defendant was advised of that when the hearings were set — pretrial hearing, trial hearings, things like that. In September, she was advised that she had to be present at a pretrial hearing on December 4, 1997. And on December 4, everybody showed up for the hearing — except for the defendant. She had left the continental United States on an American Airlines flight, under a false name, having paid cash for the ticket, and flew to Puerto Rico."

Michael Downes told the jury about Teresa's second drug overdose in four months, and how Snohomish County detectives had gone to Puerto Rico to bring her back.

Downes said he was prepared to present physical evidence that would prove the bullets that killed Chuck Leonard had been fired by the gun that Teresa gave to her friend, Joyce Lilly, to hide a few hours after his murder. Teresa's sweatpants, also hidden by Joyce, had a splotch of blood that tested as being consistent with Chuck's blood, and, in the crotch, body fluids that matched Teresa's.

"You may, during the course of this case, hear evidence about a mental defense phrased two different ways. One is referred to as 'diminished capacity,' and the other is referred to as 'insanity.'"

Diminished capacity is often the defendant's personal choice — in taking drugs, drinking alcohol, or participating in other activities that render them temporarily incapable of employing their usual decision making. On occasion, it can be used when a defendant is developmentally disabled. Legal insanity can render them unable to tell the difference between right and wrong. But Teresa had planned Chuck's murder, and she had also planned her alibi and hidden any evidence that might tie her to the homicide.

She had to have known the difference between right and wrong, or she wouldn't have tried so hard to disassociate herself from Chuck's death.

Downes said that Joyce Lilly would testify that, on two occasions, Morgan had commented to her that she didn't "like the way Daddy touched me." But he also pointed out that both times were after Chuck had refused to let Morgan call her mother.

"Joyce Lilly did relate that to the defendant, and the defendant didn't have any particular reaction to it at the time; she didn't have any questions to ask Ms. Lilly."

If Teresa was so horrified at the possibility that her daughter had been molested by her ex-husband at that time, why hadn't she shown some emotion? Why didn't she pursue the subject and ask her friend Joyce exactly what Morgan had said? Why didn't she file for sole custody?

John Henry Browne spoke next, laying out the Defense approach. He unfolded his tall frame from his chair at the Defense table, and he smiled at the jurors. His approach to them was folksy, akin to "We're all in this together."

"This is not an argument," he began. "If anything I say sounds like an argument, I'm sure I'll get objected to."

202

Browne is very good with jurors, and occasionally an irritant to judges and opposing attorneys. He can be sentimental or a fierce fighter for his clients. He now began with the part of this tragic case that had affected him the most. He hoped that he wouldn't have to call Morgan Leonard as a witness.

So did deputy prosecutor Michael Downes. Everyone involved with this case felt the same way.

"This case is about 'Punky,'" Browne told the jury. "Punky is Morgan Leonard. She's almost seven years old. Shortly before Mr. Leonard's death, these two teddy bears [he held them up] were given to Punky by Joyce Lilly and Teresa Leonard, and inside each teddy bear was a telephone number — one for Teresa and one for Joyce."

Brown explained that Punky had told Joyce that she "didn't like the way her daddy touched her, didn't like sleeping in bed with Daddy and his girlfriend, didn't like sleeping next to the floor, and didn't like the fact that Daddy wouldn't let her call Mommy."

The foundation of the Defense case emerged early. Teresa Gaethe-Leonard was portrayed by her attorney as a woman who had survived a brutal childhood with sexual, physical, and emotional abuse. To deal with that, Browne suggested that Teresa had learned to compartmentalize her memories, feelings, and events.

"Your life is so difficult that you shut it off," he said. "You put it into a little box, you put it on the wall, you close the door. And unless you get treatment, which Teresa did not, it stays in the boxes and it's very hard for it to come out."

Teresa had, Browne said, grown up to marry first to get out of her family home, was divorced from her first husband, and then met Chuck Leonard. Now, the dead victim in this case emerged looking like the villain — a cheating husband, wife abuser, child abuser, a man who had wanted his wife to abort her pregnancy, and as Teresa's attorney described him, almost deserving of death.

Teresa had told John Henry Browne that when she confronted Chuck in the wee hours of February 20 Chuck was awake and sitting up in bed when she arrived. She had accused him of sexually touching his daughter. Teresa had decided that she wasn't going to let what happened to her happen to her daughter. Although she couldn't really recall what happened that night, she knew she had gone to Chuck's house to confront him — to say: "I know what's going on, and she [Morgan] was never coming back to his house."

"That," Browne said, "was the last thing she remembers."

He had failed to add something important, and now he added it. Teresa had recalled something more. "By the way, Chuck Leonard said to Teresa, 'I'm sorry, I'm sorry, I'm sorry.'"

Browne assured the jurors in his opening remarks that he would produce psychiatrists and psychologists who would testify that Teresa met the criteria of both legal insanity and diminished capacity.

And he ended with a description of a woman who no longer wanted to live. "Teresa doesn't want to be here. Teresa wants to be dead. She's tried that twice now. She doesn't want to be here because she views, in her mind — the only thing that matters to her in her whole life is Morgan. And when Teresa talks to you and when she talks to me, it's: 'Morgan's dead in my mind. She has to be dead. Therefore, I don't want to be alive.'

"I have faith that the system will work. I have faith that you'll — with everything you see and hear — come to the right result."

The jurors filed out for a break. Brad Pince noticed how emotional and despondent Teresa seemed when they were present, but, when they left, she immediately sat up straight, and when she turned to smile at her sisters in the gallery, there were no tears in her eyes.

And so it began. Teresa Gaethe-Leonard might be cold-hearted, scheming, money-hungry, a duplicitous woman who really hated the men she had professed to love and used them only as stepping-stones on her way up. There would be witnesses to describe her intricate plans to kill Chuck Leonard, to obtain a high-caliber weapon and a disguise, and to draw in her best friend to help cover for her.

And there would be others who saw her as an ultimate victim who had done what she believed she had to do to save her child, and done so when she wasn't in her right mind. They believed that Teresa had a mission in life, and that was to protect Morgan.

Teresa Gaethe-Leonard was a highly emotional defendant, often breaking into sobs. She'd been found competent to participate in her own defense and to stand trial, but she had spent the weeks before trial at Western State Hospital, because the Defense team felt she'd had "a very tough time" in the Snohomish County Jail.

On the fifth day of testimony — September 15 — she was more upset than usual.

Considering the witnesses, that wasn't surprising. On that morning, Michelle Conley — Chuck Leonard's last serious lover — took the stand to describe the night in November 1996 when someone crept into his bedroom.

That part of Michelle's testimony didn't bother Teresa too much, but when John Henry Browne cross-examined her, Teresa's whole body tensed.

"Did you ever see photographs in the house of — naked photographs of Chuck and Morgan?"

"No."

"Did you see some adult video tapes in the house?"

"Yes."

"Approximately how many?"

"There were several."

"And you," Browne asked, "as I understand it, just saw snippets of one?"

"Correct."

"There were times when Morgan spent the night at Chuck's house and you were there, right? And you spent the night with them, and all three of you slept in the bed together?"

"Yes."

"And you told us that you might have had just T-shirts on when that happened?"

"No, we had [all our] clothes on."

Michelle could not say that she saw Teresa in the car she followed that creepy night in November — but she recognized the car.

"When's the last time you saw Morgan?" Browne asked suddenly.

"Day before yesterday."

Teresa's tormented wail echoed off the courtroom walls. She hadn't had any contact with her daughter for more than a year. She began crying softly.

Browne pushed ahead. "You remain close to Morgan, don't you?"

"Yes."

"In fact, Morgan refers to you as her other mommy, right?"

"Yes."

Judge Knight called a recess. Teresa seemed too upset to continue. Her daughter had two mother figures, and neither one was her. But Teresa Gaethe-Leonard was an accomplished actress who was chameleonlike when she dealt with lovers, friends, and sometimes strangers.

The irony was apparent. Teresa still had a living child, and there was always the possibility that she would one day regain custody of her. If she were found insane at the time of Chuck's murder, she wasn't likely to go to prison; she would be sent to Western State

Hospital for treatment, and it was possible she would be released when she was deemed to be in her right mind.

Michelle Conley had lost the man she loved. Forever. But Michelle had always cared about Morgan, and even though Chuck was gone, she never thought of abandoning his little girl.

Teresa's life — the life she could have had — was passing before her eyes. She may well have been crying for herself and no one else.

That Tuesday in September was going to get harder. Nick Callas was scheduled to testify in the State's case against his former mistress.

But it was obvious from the way he looked at Teresa that he still cared about her. Romantics might call them star-crossed lovers; realists would say their affair was built on deceit and lies and was bound to disintegrate into dust. Even though Nick's marriage had ended, and Teresa had cost him tens of thousands of dollars while they were lovers, and, technically, $500,000 when she ran to Puerto Rico, she still seemed to have a hold over him.

Answering Michael Downes's questions, the handsome Greek real estate entrepreneur said he'd first met Teresa eleven years earlier — in 1987 — when she'd come to his office on Maui looking for a rental property with a girlfriend.

"Do you see her present?"

Callas looked at the Defense table, his eyes meeting Teresa's.

"She's sitting right there."

They sat a dozen feet apart, but it was like a thousand miles. Callas said the relationship that began in a businesslike manner had soon become romantic, and, in 1987, they were together as lovers for a little less than six months.

"Was there something that caused it to end for that time?" Downes asked.

"Yes . . . Teresa left the island."

That seemed to be the end of that, although Callas said they had occasionally talked on the phone, and Teresa had sent him cards. He could not recall writing to her. He had heard from her again after she moved from New Orleans to Washington State in 1989 or 1990.

"Did you and Teresa Leonard resume your romantic relationship at some point?"

"Yes — in March of 1995."

Teresa had written to Callas even before she moved out of Chuck's house; they were still married. She had obviously wanted another man to jump to before she cut her ties with Chuck.

Even though Callas was married in 1989 and had an adopted son, he could not resist seeing Teresa again. He sent tickets for both herself and Joyce Lilly, and Joyce had watched them kiss within moments after Nick came to the condo that first night. It had been eight years since they had seen each other.

Callas testified that after that first meeting, Teresa flew to Maui regularly every few months. By June 1995, he had begun to send her money — between $1,000 and $1,500 a month; he managed that by writing checks on his many different condo accounts, staggering them so that there were never too many checks from any particular account.

"Did you and she go other places together?" Downes asked.

"We had three trips together. One was to Jackson Hole, Wyoming; one was to Whistler in Canada; and the third was to Campbell River, British Columbia."

They had gone to ski, and their trips lasted six to nine days.

"Who paid for all these trips?"

"I did."

Callas estimated his net worth as $2 million, and he testified that he had no annual income because everything he made was plowed back into his business.

"Okay," Downes said. "Was it a struggle for you to pay for the defendant's trip to Hawaii. . . . Was it a struggle for you to allow her to use a condominium rent-free?"

"No . . . no."

Beyond all the perks Teresa was already receiving from Nick, there was one he didn't know about.

"Are you aware that the defendant had an American Express card for her consignment shop with the name 'Nick Callas' on it?"

"I wasn't then; I am now."

Painstakingly, Michael Downes went over a long list of checks sent to Teresa by the witness and a list of payments made to various American Express cards that Teresa was using. Callas estimated that he had talked to Teresa up to ten times a day during the two years their affair had burned most intensely. Asked by Downes to come up with the total number of phone calls the two of them had shared over two years, Callas guessed it would be seven thousand or more.

It was time for the noon break, and Nick Callas appeared relieved to step down from the stand. Still, he would have to continue in the afternoon.

Although his phone records indicated that

there had been up to five phone calls from Teresa to Callas or from him to her on February 20, 1997, Nick Callas didn't remember them. At some point that day or during the next few days, Teresa told him that Chuck had died of "profound trauma," but she didn't go into detail.

"I interpreted [that] as if there was a collision with a tree." Callas testified. "That was my mental image."

Teresa had told him that Chuck had died suddenly, but he had to look on the Internet to find out he had been murdered, shot three times. When he learned that Chuck had been murdered and Teresa had been arrested, Callas had begun to pay legal expenses for his mistress. He thought the initial costs were about $22,000.

The strain was beginning to show on Nick Callas's face, and it was about to become more intense. State's Exhibits No. 115 and No. 116 were the two cards Teresa had given to him in midsummer 1997.

Although they weren't dated, Callas thought Teresa had handed them to him in her apartment in Lynnwood, Washington. These were the cards his wife had found among his business papers. But Downes didn't ask Callas about the cards — not yet.

"Would you say that you were the defendant's best friend?" he asked instead.

"I was certainly one of her best friends, or I felt I was one of her best friends, yes."

"Prior to the time of Chuck Leonard's demise," Michael Downes asked, "did the defendant ever tell you that he had been physically or sexually abusive to Morgan?"

"No."

Odd. If Nick was Teresa's lover and probably her "best friend," and she was desperately worried about Morgan's safety, why hadn't she confided in him?

There were so many people she could have told — if it was true. But the subject of abuse to Morgan hadn't really come up, except obliquely to Joyce Lilly, until Teresa needed a good defense.

Callas answered Downes's queries about when and how he had learned that Teresa had fled in December 1997.

"I called her cell phone number and received a Spanish-speaking default message, and found a cell phone technological person who researched it for me. He told me that the cell phone had been turned on in Puerto Rico."

"Had you had some concerns for some time prior to this Spanish-speaking message that you might have a problem on your hands as it related to your $500,000?"

Downes asked.

"Yes. . . . It was the end of November — I don't recall any specific day — when the communication between Teresa and me broke down, and I was no longer able to speak with her when I wanted to, nor was she calling me frequently. That wasn't normal. It also wasn't the arrangement or agreement [between us]. At that point, I became concerned."

Nick Callas testified that he hired an attorney to represent his interests regarding the bail money after someone told him Teresa had had plastic surgery and her eyes were black postoperatively. Teresa's younger sister, Macie, was visiting Teresa's home in Everett that November. Nick Callas had called her to see how Teresa was, and she mentioned then that Teresa had cut her hair.

Callas had even contacted George Cody, Teresa's first attorney, and asked him if she'd changed her features with plastic surgery. Cody was noncommittal. He said he hadn't seen Teresa since early November 1997.

Nor had Nick.

And then he had tracked her to Puerto Rico, finally realizing that she had broken her promises to him and left him responsible for the huge bail she forfeited.

John Henry Browne began his cross-examination by asking Nick Callas to read aloud portions of the sentimental cards Teresa had given him. The witness began, his voice filled with emotion:

"'Nick, you give me peace that I've never had. Thank you for you.'"

Callas looked up, tears glistening in his eyes, and with his voice breaking he said, "I don't know if I can do this."

"Well," Browne said, "take a minute. Wait a minute, Nick. Why don't you just read it over to yourself. Is there something in that card that indicates —"

"I haven't finished yet. I'm sorry," Callas said. Tears now spilled from his eyes and ran down his cheeks. He took a deep breath and started the next sentence: "'I know I have caused you pain, and I cannot tell you how sorry I am for that. The outside world —'"

Nick Callas could not continue, and asked if he could leave the courtroom to gather his emotions. Judge Knight nodded. When he returned, he was able to get through the words that Teresa had written, private and personal words his wife had read, that now a gallery full of strangers and court personnel listened to. He had been touched by those two cards and believed that Teresa really was grateful for everything he'd done for her — before and after Chuck's murder.

Reading them again tore him up emotionally.

John Henry Browne asked him about Teresa's overdose in August 1997, and Callas recalled that it had happened shortly after she was told she could no longer have her weekly phone calls to her daughter: "She was expecting to, and excited to speak with Morgan on that Wednesday and getting prepared for it, and either she made a call to set it up or they called her and said she wouldn't be allowed to speak with Morgan again."

"Can you tell the . . . jury your understanding of Teresa's relationship with Morgan?" Browne probed.

Nick Callas nodded. Even though he had never laid eyes on Morgan himself, or, for that matter, seen Teresa interact with her child, he had observed Teresa's feelings for her.

"All mothers love their children," he began, "love their children, but Teresa loved Morgan in a different way. I really don't know how to describe it. It's hard to say that one parent can love their daughter or son more than another parent, but Teresa's life was dedicated to Morgan . . . one hundred percent of the time Teresa does something for Morgan without doing something for herself. I know that's why I sent money to her."

"Were there ever any discussions between you and Teresa about getting married?" Browne asked.

"No."

"Did you have any feeling that Teresa was unhappy with the relationship the way it was?"

"No."

"Were there any plans for Teresa and Morgan to move to Hawaii?"

"No."

"Did you have any plans to divorce Grace?"

"No."

Callas seemed to have been completely unaware of Teresa's plans to come to Hawaii, marry him, arrange to give him his own child — even if it took a surrogate mother to carry it. With questioning from both Michael Downes and John Henry Browne, Nick Callas's male parts were discussed in open court. He explained why he was completely unable to provide healthy sperm to his wife or to any other woman. It was obvious that this was information Teresa was hearing for the first time. Shock washed across her face, although she quickly masked it.

Teresa's pie-in-the-sky plans had been just that. There was no way she could have had a child with Nick — none at all. He believed she was a wonderful, unselfish mother, but he had never met Morgan, never seen her beyond a photograph. He hadn't known that Teresa was determined to marry him. There were so many things he hadn't known about her.

Finally, after hours of torturous testimony, Nick Callas was allowed to step down.

Joyce Lilly testified about the early morning hours of February 20. The jury listened avidly as she told them what Teresa had said about "whacking" Chuck, her "murder costume," and how she — Joyce — had been stuck with the physical evidence of the murder, right down to the .45 automatic, the bullets, and the key to Chuck's house.

She was an emotional witness. It was plain that she would rather have been anywhere but in the witness chair, still half guilty about betraying her old friend. Even so, Joyce had no other choice.

The question that hung in the air concerned two possible witnesses — Teresa Gaethe-Leonard, herself, and Morgan "Punky" Leonard. It is almost always unwise for murder defendants to take the witness stand. In doing so, they open themselves up to cross-examination by the State with questions they might not care to answer.

Although she was a very intelligent little girl, Morgan was only six. She had been through so much, and neither Michael Downes nor John Henry Browne wanted to bring her into this trial. Downes weighed whether he would have to do it to assure that Morgan's father received the justice he deserved.

Teresa sobbed at the thought of Morgan testifying, and said she would plead guilty before she let that happen.

In the end, neither mother nor daughter testified.

There was much discussion about a film Chuck Leonard had taken with frames that showed his daughter. When it finally was shown, it was anticlimactic; it turned out to be a long, boring home movie with nothing more salacious than a tiny girl in a play pool.

Teresa — along with her sisters who were there to support her — cried periodically throughout her three-week trial, giving some credence to the Defense contention that she was mentally ill and had been insane at the time she shot Chuck Leonard.

Now came the battle of the psychologists and psychiatrists. Listening to and evaluating testimony by mental health professionals is often supremely frustrating, generally because they tend to use terms unfamiliar to laymen and even to those with quite a bit of knowledge about mental illness and personality disorders. Moreover, they often waffle and seem unable to give a straight-out diagnosis. That was certainly true of those who testified at Teresa's trial.

None of them appeared to have brought their records on Teresa Gaethe-Leonard to court with them. They often couldn't recall dates or seemed surprised when they learned that some of the things Teresa had told them weren't true.

One psychiatrist estimated that the defendant had undergone about fifty emotional, intelligence, and sanity tests, and seen more psychiatric experts than anyone could count.

Some who testified hadn't seen Teresa in a year or more. The trial transcripts show that none of these witnesses would say definitively that Teresa had a low IQ or an average IQ — even though her test results indicated her score was only 83. Nor would any experts say absolutely that she was malingering or suffering from real post-traumatic stress disorder, or even if her "hallucinations" were actual or contrived.

One psychiatrist — who had seen Teresa for approximately six two-hour sessions —

testified that she had become depressed when her marriage faltered in 1991, and that depression reached "clinical proportions" by the fall of 1996 — approximately when Teresa did her dry-run with a borrowed gun.

As this doctor spoke, Teresa bowed her head and rocked slightly in her chair. She turned often to look back at her sisters in the gallery; they, too, were tearful.

She had told this psychiatrist that she finally became depressed enough to fly off to Puerto Rico because she'd received a box containing all the cards and presents — still unwrapped — that she'd sent to Morgan at her aunt Theresa's address. But that wasn't true; Theresa testified that Morgan had opened all the presents and cards, and that she still had them and knew her mother had sent them.

This psychiatrist for the defense said that Teresa had only sparse memories of driving to Chuck's house on the night he died or of what had happened while she was there. He testified that he believed Teresa was psychotic at the time she shot Chuck and suffering from acute stress.

That diagnosis, however, seemed at war with Teresa's November late-night visit to Chuck's bedroom when she was armed with a borrowed gun. One had to wonder if she had been insane then, too, regained her sanity, and then lost contact with reality once more three months later. Both forays had required considerable planning, enough to make her low scores on IQ tests and her confused, "psychotic" state questionable.

After final arguments on Tuesday, September 29, 1998, where Michael Downes described Teresa as a calculating killer who shot Chuck Leonard so she could marry her wealthy lover, and John Henry Browne called her a fragile, abused woman who was desperately trying to protect her daughter, it was almost time for Teresa's jury to retire to deliberate.

Neither the State nor the Defense spared the details of Chuck Leonard's gruesome and bloody death. He had lived long enough to chase Teresa up the ship staircase and even managed to grab her ankle with his last ounce of strength.

John Henry Browne pointed out that the evidence wasn't in the three bullets Teresa had fired nineteen months before, but in the four she didn't fire. He suggested that if Teresa had truly intended to kill Chuck, she would have shot at him again at that time.

But she didn't.

Chuck was already a dead man walking, but Browne didn't say that.

Had Teresa planned the murder of her estranged husband and her escape to Puerto Rico methodically — right down to her plastic surgery? She'd told her attorney that she had facial surgery not so she would look different but because she didn't want to look like her mother, who had caused her much pain when she was a child. This was the same mother she once said she loved dearly and joined in Texas for a vacation every year.

Prosecutor Michael Downes reminded jurors that Teresa had been consumed by her desire to move to Hawaii to marry Nick Callas, and that Chuck Leonard was in her way. She had planned her crime, even to the point that she told Joyce Lilly "that she was going to 'whack Chuck tonight.'"

The Defense position that Chuck was molesting their daughter hadn't come up until a very long time — months — later.

The jurors wouldn't hear of all the lies and variations of the truth that Teresa had practiced in her life; it would be impossible to take all the little threads left dangling and crochet them into a recognizable pattern. Indeed, no one really knew how many lies, con games, and self-serving statements Teresa might have employed for years. It would be akin to counting pennies in a gallon jar.

As Browne finished his final arguments,

he looked at Teresa, who sat with her head bowed, staring at a small picture of Morgan, which was propped against a box of tissues out of the jury's view.

In a bit of courtroom drama, he glanced at her and said, "Teresa, Morgan knows. She knows what you did and why you did it. Do you understand that?"

Teresa didn't look up.

The rule of thumb in trials is generally that the longer the jury stays out deliberating, the more likely they are to acquit. A rapid decision usually means a guilty verdict. But it isn't carved in stone. Teresa was charged with both first-degree murder and bail jumping.

In less than three hours, the foreman signaled that the jury had a verdict. When the principals and the gallery had all gathered in the courtroom, the jury foreman handed the verdict to the bailiff.

There was a hush in the room, as the bailiff unfolded the paper with the jury's decision on it.

"We, the jury, find Teresa Gaethe Leonard . . . guilty of murder in the first degree."

They had also found her guilty on the second, lesser charge of bail jumping.

One of Chuck's friends let out a muffled sigh of relief. Theresa Leonard, his sister, began to cry quietly. Teresa Gaethe-Leonard herself sat still as a stone, her spine straight, and then dabbed at her eyes with a tissue. Her attorneys seemed more shaken than she was.

And so did the jurors who filed out rapidly, waving away reporters. Some stopped to light cigarettes. Others hurried to their cars.

Sentencing was set for October 16, but that would be postponed until Wednesday, November 25. Once again, the holiday season was bleak for Teresa, all because of her own doing. In November 1996, Teresa had put on her "camouflage" clothing and gone to Chuck's house to shoot him, but been put off because Michelle Conley was with him. In November 1997, she underwent plastic surgery and stole her friend's ID as she prepared to fly to Puerto Rico, and now, as Thanksgiving and Christmas decorations appeared in the Snohomish County Courthouse, she would hear her sentence as a convicted murderess.

Teresa had walked into the courtroom between her two tall attorneys, and that made her seem even more frail and diminutive. She had always hated to wear handcuffs, and she asked to have them removed before she entered the room, but her guards refused. She was both an escape and a suicide risk. The gallery was full to bursting as curious onlookers made room for just one more person on the long benches.

Several of the people impacted by Chuck's death would probably speak; the attorneys would speak, and perhaps even Teresa would make a statement before Judge Gerald Knight handed down the sentence.

According to Washington State statute, Teresa's sentencing range would be between twenty-six and thirty-four years in prison. Prosecutor Michael Downes requested that she receive a sentence at the high end of the range, and her defense attorney, John Henry Browne, asked for a twenty-five-year term, saying, "Truth generally lies between the extremes."

Theresa Leonard, who now had permanent custody of Morgan, attempted to explain the tremendous loss her brother's murder was for her family. Most of all, it was difficult to explain to six-year-old Morgan.

"She's grieving the loss of both her father and her mother," Theresa said. "Chuck was many things to many people. He drove fast, played hard, and loved many. No doubt he loved blondes. [But] he never pulled any punches with kids. He was direct and honest with them. He loved Morgan without reservation."

Teresa stood before Judge Knight, speaking in his courtroom for the first time.

"I wrote this probably fifty-five times, trying to make it short so you would listen," she began, but as she went on she became increasingly emotional. "A mother's basic instinct is to protect her child, which was my motivating action. . . . Punky, I kept my promise to you that you would not suffer through a family life like my own."

It was time for Judge Knight to pronounce sentence and to make any remarks he might have. During a trial, no one knows what the judge is thinking any more than he or she can read jurors' minds. This was the moment when Judge Gerald Knight could voice his opinion.

"I do not believe that Mr. Leonard abused his daughter," Judge Knight said firmly. He told Teresa that it didn't matter what she might have believed about that, her decision to act as "judge, jury, and executioner" had ended in miserable tragedy for many people. She had left her child a virtual orphan without either parent.

Judge Knight then sentenced Teresa Gaethe-Leonard to thirty years in prison.

On December 3, 1998, Teresa entered the

Washington State prison system. She was incarcerated at the Washington Corrections Center for Women in Purdy. She joined a roster of infamous female felons, such as Diane Downs, Mary Kay Letourneau, and Christine Marler. Teresa's earliest release date is July 29, 2023, and her maximum expiration of sentence is November 11, 2027. In either case, she will be over sixty when she walks out of prison. Even then, she will have to have two years of monitored community placement before she is completely free.

Teresa's plan is to move back to New Orleans and join her sister Lois.

Teresa has been a relatively cooperative prisoner, although she was reported for having intimate contact with another female prisoner when correction officers found them kissing.

Teresa's sisters have stood by her, sending her mail-order items of clothing, underwear, makeup, and magazines. She has been assigned to work with guide and service dogs, and that has brought her some serenity.

Does Nick Callas write to Teresa while she is in prison? I honestly don't know. His real estate business is booming and he is doing well. As for his personal life, that has faded from the public eye.

Teresa has no contact at all with her daughter, Morgan, who is now seventeen and just graduated from high school. She has never asked to see photographs of Morgan, although she could have if she had gone through Morgan's counselor.

Morgan had three years of therapy right after Chuck's death to help her deal with her losses. She was very fragile and had nightmares, mostly about her mother. It took her nearly a year to begin to accept that "my mommy killed my daddy." Sometimes she had good dreams where she woke up saying she felt "Daddy hugging me."

Today, Morgan is a bright, talented teenager who shares a special bond with her aunt Theresa, and Theresa's daughter, her "sister." She has also met her older half-sister and has a warm secure family to replace the one she lost.

When asked if she wanted to have a different name in this book to protect her privacy, she said no. She wants the truth to be told, and that includes her name. Soon, she will be on her way to college.

Morgan, like Chuck, loves kittens and cats. She still has the cat her dad gave her in October 1996, and the Leonards have four more cats, bringing the number of feline pets to the same number Chuck had. They talk about Chuck openly and tell funny stories. Morgan wears his old sweaters around the house and keeps his photographs prominent in her life.

Throughout high school, Morgan has played varsity lacrosse, and was one of their star players.

Her father would be proud of Morgan. Just as she is proud of him.

■ ■ ■ ■

DEATH IN PARADISE: THE HAUNTING VOYAGE OF THE *SPELLBOUND*

■ ■ ■ ■

The sea is a cruel mistress. From time immemorial, men have tried to tame her, believing that their strength and intelligence can fool her capriciousness. There is a fascination — even a mystique — inherent in the endless miles of water one envisions when the last harbor is left behind. Our oceans are both beautiful and deadly, as heedless as any woman who alternately beckons and taunts a man. Although we can chart her tides to the moment and the fathom, no human can ever know when wild winds will whip the oceans of the world into a froth of fury.

Women waiting for their seagoing men to come home once paced the widow's walks atop their Victorian mansions, praying that their husbands and lovers would return safely to them. The more fortunate of those women would have them in their arms and beds again, but some inexplicable things can happen to a man at sea. He may disappear or go mad, or change in ways that no one could predict.

Many modern women choose not to wait; they go along on the wide-water journeys, experienced and proficient in handling the wheel and adjusting mainsails, jibs, and spinnakers. Jody Edwards was one of these modern women. Where her husband, Loren, went, Jody went, too. They were a love match, perfectly suited to one another.

They were not each other's first loves — but they were their last. Jody was about five feet, three inches tall, a bouncy brunette. Loren was tall and spare, but tightly muscled. Although his hair would turn iron gray, he continued to wear it in a crew cut. His skin was usually suntanned to a dark toast color.

Loren was handsome in a Gary Cooper/ John Wayne kind of way, masculine but not a pretty boy. He was born on November 24, 1927, in Tekoa, Whitman County, close to the Idaho state line on the sunny side of Washington. He was the youngest of three children. His parents — Ira and Ruby — struggled to wrest a living out of the community that counted on its wheat fields and pine forests, but by 1934, the Great Depression was at its lowest ebb. Loren was seven when Ira moved his family to Seattle, where there were more jobs than in Tekoa or Pine City. Not many, and the pay wasn't good — but it was an improvement.

The Second World War brought an end to the depression, but it also cost many young Americans' lives. Loren graduated from Roosevelt High School in Seattle in 1946, and he was safe from the war, which had ended the prior August. He joined the army and worked in the Signal Corps in Alaska. When he was mustered out, he entered the University of Washington's School of Forestry under the GI Bill.

He tried to get his bachelor's degree, but he had a wife by then and two young sons. With working and studying and spending time with his family, Loren couldn't keep up and he dropped out before graduating.

He followed his interest and his talents and became a master carpenter and then a contractor, a profession he would work in for a quarter of a century.

Loren Edwards, who grew up in the rolling hills of the Palouse where thousands of acres of golden wheat thrived in the heat, had always been fascinated with boats of all kinds. When he was nine, he built a seaworthy kayak in the family garage. His dream was always to have his own boat, and when he got that, to have a larger craft.

Jody Peet grew up on the rainy side of the Cascade Mountain Range in the tiny hamlet of Preston. Preston is little more than a wide spot in the road just off I-90 as that freeway traverses the foothills of Snoqualmie Pass. Even those who regularly cross the steadily steeper pass on their way to Spokane and other eastern cities of Washington State are often unfamiliar with Preston. Unless they have business there, they are more likely to stop for lunch in Issaquah or North Bend.

Jody attended her lower grades in the small school in Preston and, later on, rode the school bus to Issaquah High School. With her dark hair and dimples, she was very pretty.

As young marrieds, Loren and Jody had known each other when they were part of the same loosely connected social group. Jody was married to Bob Peet then, and pregnant with her second child at the age of nineteen. The Peets' future stretched out ahead with no real problems in sight.

That all ended tragically when Bob Peet died in an automobile accident in 1954. Her family feared for Jody, but she struggled to overcome her loss and provide a home for her children.

And then Loren Edwards and his first wife divorced. He became reacquainted with Jody

Peet, and to everyone's delighted surprise, they fell in love. They were married in 1956. Jody stayed home with their blended family, and Loren's career as a contractor continued to succeed. He built a home for Jody's parents, and she volunteered for the Red Cross and for support groups that helped handicapped children.

Both Jody and Loren were devoted to their parents — and to each other's. Loren was particularly close to his father, Ira. Ira had gotten his family through hard times in a government job, and he wasn't nearly ready to retire, not even when he was seventy-four. He simply started a new career in real estate.

Jody and Loren's marriage was one of deep love and many shared interests. Jody loved boating almost as much as Loren did, and they graduated from kayaks and canoes to small powerboats. They joined a platoon of people with outboard cruisers who responded to a Seattle radio station's promotion and traveled to Alaska and back. It wasn't luxurious onboard living, but they had a great time.

Seattle seems to drift in the middle of water, and there are probably more boat owners there than in almost any other city in America. Some feel adventurous just to cast off their anchors in Lake Washington, while others venture out into Elliott Bay and Puget Sound and head to the San Juan Islands to the north or to the Pacific Ocean. Simply finding a place to dock a boat in the winter months is daunting; there is a long waiting list for every slip along every dock.

Jody and Loren Edwards shared a very ambitious dream: they wanted to build a magnificent sailboat, one they could sail on the high seas, a craft so powerful and perfect that it would be almost impervious to storms with driving winds. It was the midseventies, and their children were grown and doing well. They had saved their money and built up equity in a series of boats, so they finally felt ready to build a fifty-four-foot ketch. It would take years, and intensive labor on their part, but they were prepared to sacrifice whatever luxury they needed to.

The Edwardses weren't rich, and this was a rich man's boat. In the seventies, even with their doing much of the work themselves, it would cost well over $100,000. Today, it would be a million-dollar craft. They lived in a modest home in Preston, but that didn't matter to them. Their ultimate home would be at sea.

They named their ketch before it ever existed. The perfect name — *Spellbound*

— was magical, mysterious, and what they considered the best appellation for the craft that was to be the result of their consuming passion.

Because they were confident in their ability to create the *Spellbound,* the Edwardses quickly signed up for a slip on the waiting list of the Kirkland municipal dock in the Marina Park there. They knew it would take a year or more before their names came up.

Peyton Whitely worked as a popular reporter at the *Seattle Times* for forty-one years, often covering criminal cases. He was a superb researcher and a gifted writer. He was also a boat fancier, and he docked his boat at the Marina Park in Kirkland. He met Loren and Jody Edwards when they became his neighbors on the dock. They weren't close friends, but they nodded and waved, and he admired their yellow-hulled fiberglass ketch. Loren's skill and experience as a builder were evident. The Edwardses had lovingly varnished and rubbed the wooden parts of the boat, and every mitered corner was precise. The lamps and compass were gimbaled so that they would remain upright no matter how waves might toss and turn the craft. There was a ship-to-shore radio system.

Many people dream of an exotic cruise in

a flawless sailboat, but the couple with the yellow-hulled ketch were actually going to do it. They were more than halfway there as they christened the *Spellbound*. She would soon be able to carry a good-size crew and a number of passengers.

It was August 1977 when Loren and Jody embarked on their extended cruise to the South Pacific. They had a crew that was mostly "homegrown": their daughter, Kerry, twenty, and her friend Lori Huey, twenty-one, and they planned to pick up Loren's son Gary — one of his sons from his first marriage — in Southern California.

This was meant to be a voyage to paradise, and it was. . . for a while. The *Spellbound* was seaworthy and proud, and they encountered no problems as they sailed a leisurely course off the coasts of Washington, Oregon, and then California, bound for San Diego. The winds grew warmer and every day was a vacation, with the four on board taking turns at the wheel.

It was September 16 when Gary Edwards, twenty-seven, prepared to leave for San Diego and meet up with his stepmother, father, stepsister, and her friend Lori. Gary was very strong and familiar with sailing, and he would be an asset to help crew the ketch.

Gary worried his California girlfriend when he told her of the danger of pirates and smugglers off the Mexican coast. She had been concerned about storms at sea and shipwrecks, but she thought pirates had been gone for a hundred years.

Still, Gary Edwards was right about that danger. Although foreign waters weren't as bristling with pirates and smugglers in the seventies as they would be in the first decade of the current century, they were something to consider. Gary Edwards felt there had to be some basis to the rumors he had heard.

Gary showed his girlfriend a handgun he had purchased to afford his family extra protection if they were attacked at sea. It was a menacing-looking weapon — a Walther PPK/S .380-caliber automatic pistol. The gun held seven rounds, Gary explained, and it was very accurate. It was heavy — weighing almost a pound and a half.

He tucked it into his seabag, confident that he could fight off pirates if they should attack his father's boat.

The magnificent journey began with a jubilant crew. They planned to be at sea for three years, with stopovers at exotic ports of call. They sailed serenely through Mexican waters without ever meeting pirate ships and were soon in the Pacific Ocean. The Edwardses had planned their journey carefully and thoroughly, with long-lasting provisions stored away. They could catch fish and buy fresh local produce and groceries whenever they landed somewhere big enough to have a store.

The Edwards family headed out to one of the most tantalizing and enchanting ports of call: Tahiti. There are thirty-five islands and eighty-three coral atolls in French Polynesia, but the total land there is only about 3,500 square kilometers. Located midway between Australia and South America, these South Pacific islands seem almost as mythical as Brigadoon. There are volcanoes, silky sand, and aqua lagoons, and the air smells of tropical flowers: bougainvillea, frangipani, ginger, jasmine, Chinese and Polynesian hibiscus, and the national flower *tiare Tahiti,* a type of gardenia.

The first Polynesians had arrived on the islands by 800 A.D. Many, many famous visitors came later. In the late 1880s, the Tahitians accepted the offer to be a protectorate of France. The islands were a natural draw for writers and artists, the perfect ambiance where one could escape from the world and create a masterpiece.

French artist Paul Gauguin settled on the island of Hiva Oa in the Marquesas in 1891, and in the dozen years before his death there, his brightly hued paintings of sultry, dark-eyed native women and the flora and fauna in Tahiti made that far-off paradise familiar to people all over the world.

Sometimes, the Edwards family had to pinch themselves when they realized that they would actually arrive in Papeete soon. They planned to shop at the morning market on the territory's largest island and drive the 117-kilometer road that circled Tahiti, where visitors could view monuments and museums, beaches, waterfalls, cliffs, and temple ruins.

Seattle was so far away. Another world.

One day, they would go home, filled with enough memories to last a lifetime. They didn't even think about the more mundane practices that separated the Emerald City in Washington State and the lushly beautiful tropical islands. The islands' legal system alone was quite different. Whatever crimes that might occur in Tahiti would be handled by French law enforcement officers, and the law itself was different in Tahiti, and in France.

But the Edwardses had no reason to expect anything bad to happen to them. Aside from a little seasickness, and the kind of minor arguments all families have when they are together in a small space for too long, the voyage had been everything they could have hoped for.

Loren had charted the weather carefully, so they were aware that they wouldn't be docking in the best of weather. Summer in Tahiti runs from November to April, and the air is hot and cloying, heavy with humidity. And then the trade winds blow from May to August.

The Edwardses would be landing six weeks into the hurricane season, but Loren assured them the *Spellbound* could take hurricane-force winds and blinding rain. He had designed the craft to withstand such storms.

By the middle of February 1978, the *Spellbound* was within a few hundred miles of Tahiti. It had been a wonderful trip so far.

And then, suddenly, the Edwardses' fortunes changed.

They received an emergency message patched forward by several ham-radio operators. Loren's beloved father, Ira, seventy-nine, was in a Seattle hospital in critical condition. He had been fine when they left Seattle, but now he had been diagnosed with terminal cancer in its very late stages. He might survive for a few months, weeks, or just days.

Any thought of continuing on their cruise as planned was abandoned. They had to get to Papeete. With its population of 70,000, it had an airport. Loren would disembark there and catch the first plane for the United States that he could. The rest of the crew would stay in Papeete until they could head for home, or until Loren rejoined them. Gary could sail the *Spellbound,* and Jody, Kerry, and Lori would be enough crew.

Fortunately, the weather was good, and there were no reports of hurricanes in the area. They kept a constant pace toward Papeete. The wind blew five to seven knots, and they agreed not to sink the anchor at all. Each crew member would have two hours at the helm, eight hours off. They were racing against death. They could not make the wind blow harder, but they were making steady progress.

No one heard from the Edwards crew for almost ten days. Then, on February 25, the captain of a charter boat moored on the island of Rangiroa in French Polynesia monitored a weak emergency radio signal. He finally determined it concerned a sailing ship called the *Spellbound* somewhere near Rangiroa. It was coming through a ham-radio operator in Los Angeles. The charter-boat captain could not determine exactly what was wrong, only that the ship was in trouble of some kind.

The charter boat notified authorities and set out to find the mysterious boat in distress. After several hours, they came upon a yellow-hulled sailboat drifting aimlessly sixty miles out at sea.

Four rescuers climbed aboard. They had been told that a captain and four crew members were supposed to be on board. But that was no longer true.

There were only three people on the sailboat — all of whom appeared to be in shock. The lone man identified himself as Gary Edwards and said the two women were his stepsister, Kerry, and her friend Lori.

One of Gary Edwards's wrists was grotesquely swollen and looked to be broken. Kerry Edwards appeared to have a severe head injury. She had deep cuts over her right eye, which was blackened. Lori Huey said she wasn't injured.

And yet no one knew exactly what had happened to them. Was it possible that Gary Edwards's fear of pirates had come true? And where were his parents?

"They're dead," Gary said. "We buried them at sea — somewhere off Rangiroa."

Asked how the couple had died, the three

survivors all seemed confused. That was, perhaps, to be expected. Adrift at sea in a strange place, losing the two people who knew the most about how the ship ran and who were the parents of two of the survivors, it was no wonder they were stunned and bewildered.

The first order of business for the rescuers was to find medical treatment for the injured. The chance of locating the elder Edwardses' bodies in the deep ocean was minuscule. There were sharks in the water, which brought horrible images to mind. That would all have to be sorted out later, if it was even possible.

The *Spellbound,* completely undamaged, was sailed into Rangiroa. Kerry was found to have a fractured skull, and Gary had his broken wrist set and cast in plaster. Lori hovered close by her friend, while the three who had emerged alive from the death ship waited to talk to authorities.

It would be difficult to say who had jurisdiction over the investigation. Coverage overlapped, and several agencies might step in. The French police were in Papeete, 300 miles away. The U.S. Coast Guard might be involved, and perhaps the FBI. As a rule, a criminal offense on the high seas is not under any U.S. jurisdiction. Despite the number of bizarre deaths that have proliferated on cruise ships at sea in the last few years, not many mysteries have been solved.

As I write this, a television news broadcast headlines the story of a thirty-nine-year-old man who either leapt — or was pushed — from a Norwegian luxury cruise liner in the Bahamas. The captain ordered a 590-square-mile search of the rough water, but they gave up when they found no sign of him at all.

A few years ago, an elderly man was reported by his wife to have left the ship; a bridegroom vanished — with a pool of blood on the deck beneath his porthole; and his bride was strangely unemotional. A beautiful young woman, whose parents were frantic when she didn't come back to their quarters after a night of dancing, never returned.

These stories were all in the top of the news for a few weeks, and then they disappeared, explained away by drunkenness, suicide, accidental falls from upper decks.

The public looks at the most likely suspects in cases of shipboard disappearance and violent death with misgivings, but any arrest is extremely rare. For some reason, unexplained deaths at sea don't get the attention that stateside crimes do. At least not until the recent U.S. hostages taken by pirates in the Indian Ocean when the whole nation watched, breath held, as the captain of the container ship — the *Maersk Alabama,* with twenty Americans on board — was finally rescued, his captors killed instantly by American sharpshooters. Pirate attacks on Norwegian and Canadian ships followed within a week.

As for crimes in the sea off the South Pacific islands in the late seventies, U.S. authorities agreed to step in in only three instances: when arrests had been made; when the home residences of those involved were in the United States; or on direct orders to intervene from Washington, D.C.

Because Loren and Jody Edwards were American citizens whose usual residence was in Washington State, FBI special agents would ask some penetrating questions. But would they go further than that?

What could have happened?

And why had both Loren and Jody perished at sea? The first reports that seemed to have any substance, after being filtered through the morass of rumors, came from the ham-radio operator in Los Angeles who had picked up the *Spellbound*'s distress call and sent rescuers to the ship. He was thousands of miles away, but somehow the cry for help had come to him, rather than to anyone in the South Seas. He had taken a personal interest in the crew, and he met Kerry Edwards and Lori Huey on March 1 when they came through the LAX airport to change planes for Seattle. He saw them safely through the bustling airport to the correct departure gate, and talked with them until they boarded.

Kerry told him that she and her father had been in the cockpit of the ship at about four in the morning on February 24. "We were working there," she said, "and suddenly the boom came loose."

(The boom is an extremely heavy horizontal pole along the bottom of both a fore and aft rigged sail. It helps to control the angle and shape of the sails, and serves as an attachment point for more complicated control lines. During some sailing maneuvers, the boom swings rapidly from one side of a boat to the other, and sailors have to be extremely careful that their heads are out of its path. If they don't duck, the boom's impact is always dangerous.)

"Somehow, it got loose," Kerry said faintly, "but I don't remember much else."

She was quite sure that she had been struck on her head, and that the boom had dealt her father a fatal blow when it hit him. Although her memory was fuzzy, she believed that her mother, Gary, and Lori were below decks at the time. She didn't think they had witnessed the fatal accident.

When Jody Edwards learned that her husband had died from being hit by the out-of-control boom, she was wild with grief. Loren was her world, and he had been her beloved companion for twenty-two years. She couldn't believe he was gone.

Since Kerry was so badly injured, and Gary had to be at the wheel, Lori Huey stayed up all that endless Friday night, trying in vain to comfort Jody. Jody couldn't understand why someone with Loren's skill as a sailor would ever get in the way of a swinging boom.

The next morning, Jody finally fell into a fitful sleep. The others hoped she could stay asleep for hours because she was totally exhausted and in deep shock.

But that didn't happen. While they thought Jody was sleeping, Kerry, Lori, and Gary were working in another location on the ship. Suddenly, they heard a single shot sound belowdecks.

They rushed to Jody's bunk, meeting there at the same time.

They were horrified to find that Jody had

taken her own life. Kerry trembled as she described to the Los Angeles radio operator the shock at finding her mother shot to death.

The three survivors talked for hours about what they should do. Should they keep the elder Edwardses' bodies on board, hoping they would be able to land soon? Or should they let the sea embrace them? The weather was warm, and they had to face the fact that their remains would begin to decompose.

Finally, they voted to bury them at sea. They wrapped Loren and Jody in heavy chains, and committed them to the ocean that both of them had loved.

Kerry told the man who had saved them from so many miles away that she and Lori had sensed that the police in Papeete suspected them of foul play. Interrogated through a French-English interpreter, she recalled at least seven detectives asking questions.

In extreme pain from her fractured skull and cuts, and in shock, Kerry had been through a tremendous ordeal. She and Lori wanted only to go home to America. Gary Edwards volunteered to stay with the *Spellbound* in Papeete to keep it from being vandalized.

Finally, on February 28, four days after

the double tragedy, the young women were allowed to leave and fly out of Tahiti.

Two and a half hours after their short stopover at LAX, Lori and Kerry arrived in Seattle. They were met by a phalanx of relatives and friends. Port Authority police whisked them through a crowd of reporters and curious bystanders at SeaTac Airport into a secluded area.

At first glance, Kerry and Lori appeared to be ordinary tourists returning from a tropical vacation. They were tan, and they wore brightly colored skirts with Tahitian prints, and strands of island beads, but the girls' faces were strained and hollow, there was terror in their gaze, and Kerry had a deep cut over one eye.

They insisted they had nothing to say to the reporters who were anxious to hear what had happened in Rangiroa. Soon, Lori and Kerry retained attorneys to represent them, and the lawyers advised them not to give *any* media interviews.

Of the five people who left San Diego on the *Spellbound,* only Lori Huey was uninjured. On March 3, Kerry Edwards was admitted to Overlake Hospital in Bellevue and underwent surgery to repair her fractured skull. She, too, had come close to dying of her injuries — but physicians felt she would survive.

Larry Edwards, Gary's elder brother, flew to Tahiti to join Gary in protecting the magnificent sailing ship that now had no destination and was only a sad reminder of a trip to paradise that never happened, at least not in the way the Edwardses had planned. The ship was now worth almost $200,000, and one man couldn't stay awake twenty-four hours a day to patrol it.

The Edwards family was being torn apart, all within a period of nine days, as if some evil presence stalked them. On March 5, Ira Edwards, the beloved patriarch of their family, died of cancer.

Jody, Loren, and now Ira were gone. Their family had been blessed, and it seemed as if a curse had fallen upon them.

Early in April, six weeks after the tragedy, a federal grand jury met in Seattle to begin a closed-door investigation into Loren and Jody's deaths. Kerry Edwards and Lori Huey testified at the secret hearing, but they continued to decline to comment publicly on what had occurred in the sea off Rangiroa. Gary remained far away on board the ill-fated ship.

Peyton Whitely, the *Seattle Times* reporter who had once shared a dock with the Edwardses, was more curious than most about what had happened to his friends, casual acquaintances though they were. He knew they had been inordinately proud of the yellow-hulled sailboat that had once dwarfed most of the other boats at the Marina Park in Kirkland. Most of the details of the deadly twenty-four hours on board that boat were still hidden. That was, of course, tantalizing to an investigative reporter.

Whitely pitched the story to his editor and said he was ready to travel to Tahiti to see what he could find out. His concept of the coverage was right on target, but his timing was off. As it happened, another *Times* reporter was already scheduled to go to Papeete for a different kind of assignment. Her editor figured Eloise Schumacher could do double duty and see what she could find out about the crew of the *Spellbound*. Whitely told Schumacher everything he had found out about the Edwardses, even though he was frustrated that he wouldn't be making the trip himself.

Eloise located the *Spellbound* and Gary Edwards. And he agreed to an interview. Later, she would admit to being somewhat leery of being alone on the death ship with Gary, probably because no one knew what had really happened in February. She shivered involuntarily as she saw what looked like dried bloodstains on the deck.

The tall, tanned son of the deceased couple wore sunglasses, and it was impossible to read his feelings when she couldn't see his eyes.

Gary Edwards was a handsome man who had both a mustache and a beard and apparently hadn't cut his hair for months. He posed for a photograph to accompany her article — leaning against the mast, wearing cutoff jean shorts and without a shirt. He looked half hippie and half Indiana Jones.

Probably she couldn't have read his feelings even if she looked deep into his eyes. In the four-hour interview aboard the sailboat, Gary spoke volubly as his mood changed with mercurial speed. One moment he laughed, and the next he was choking back tears. He said he was anxious to correct some erroneous reports about the time frame in which his father and stepmother perished.

First of all, he said, his wrist wasn't injured at the same time the boom hit his father. "I hurt it four days earlier," he pointed out. "On February 20. A winch handle hit it. I didn't think it was broken, but the winch tore some ligaments, and that injury prevented me from doing a lot of things on the boat."

Gary Edwards said that another misstatement revolved around Kerry and the comments the ham-radio operator in Los Angeles had passed on.

"Kerry wasn't hurt when my dad was killed. It was four a.m., *before* my dad died, and I was in the cockpit at the wheel. I heard her moaning and screaming from her bunk — that's three steps down from the cockpit."

Gary said he had gone to Kerry and found her with a pillow over her head. "She kept saying her head hurt. She had been asleep and she had no idea how she got hurt. I think she might have gotten up, fallen, and hit her head on the corner of the bunk."

Having Kerry injured had further upset the carefully planned schedule they were trying to adhere to to traverse as many miles as possible to Papeete so that Loren could catch a plane to see his dying father.

"So you were injured first — four days before your father and Kerry were?" Eloise Schumacher asked.

"Yes. First me. Then Kerry, and then my dad."

Gary explained that his stepmother — Jody — had come up from the master cabin before dawn on February 24 so she could take care of Kerry.

"My dad took over the helm," Gary went

on. "We were just disoriented then, because it was night and dark, and we weren't keeping track of where we were going."

Gary Edwards drew a deep breath as he continued to recall the events of the early morning hours of February 24. "Two hours after Kerry's mishap — whatever happened to her — I was steering in the cockpit and I thought I saw an atoll. I climbed up on the bow to see better. I called to my father — who was inside — to climb up on the stern to see if he could see the atoll.

"All of a sudden, the boat jerked. I turned around and saw my father lying in the cockpit."

For just a moment or two, Gary took off his sunglasses, and Eloise Schumacher saw that his eyes brimmed with tears. Still, he kept on talking, remembering that bleak dawn as if he could actually see it play out before him. He explained that the sailboat was running with only two sails, and the mainsail hadn't been unfurled at the time of the accident.

"He was either hit by the main boom, and then fell backward into the cockpit, hitting his head on the steering wheels — or he lost his balance and fell," Gary speculated.

He recalled that his father had been suffering with dizziness almost from the beginning of their voyage. Loren Edwards was planning to see a doctor about this when he got back to the States.

With a three-year voyage planned, that would be delaying treatment for a very long time. There were many things that could cause a sense of imbalance, some dangerous and some transient. He might have had high blood pressure, Ménière's syndrome, or a middle-ear infection. He might even have had a brain tumor. And maybe he was only suffering from sporadic seasickness.

Gary continued his recall of the morning of February 24. Loren Edwards was lying on the cockpit floor, bleeding heavily. Jody had rushed up from tending to Kerry, to kneel beside her husband. While Gary and Jody tried to help Loren, Lori Huey had taken over the helm.

"We tried to stop the bleeding," Gary continued, although he didn't specify where the blood was coming from. "I gave him artificial respiration while my mother did a chest massage."

But nothing helped, and Loren died soon after.

"After that, my stepmother sat in the cockpit all day Friday with Lori, just staring and talking. She was in shock, of course," Gary said. "She would say, 'Why me?' or

'Not again . . .'"

Still, Gary told Eloise Schumacher that none of them ever thought that Jody might be suicidal. She had always been a strong woman — both physically and emotionally. Jody stayed with Lori almost all the time, leaving only to check on Kerry, get a blanket, or go to the head.

The long day and night passed, and Lori and Gary kept sending out distress signals on the radio. Kerry wasn't able to do much because of her head injury.

And then, almost exactly twenty-four hours after her husband died, Jody Edwards was gone, too. "I heard a shot and I ran across the deck," Gary said. "Jody had shot herself with my pistol.

"I'd been setting a sail, Lori had gone to the head, and Kerry was lying in her bunk when it happened."

In shock, with the South Pacific sun beating down on them, they drifted, becalmed, in the heedless ocean. Except for Lori Huey, they were all injured, and Lori couldn't stay at the helm all the time.

Gary Edwards said he didn't know where they were. "My injured hand was so swollen that I couldn't adjust the sextant properly."

Gary and the two girls talked over what they should do. They didn't want to bury

Loren and Jody at sea so far from home, but they didn't know how long it would be until they were able to reach shore — some kind of shore. They didn't even know how far away they were from land, and the sun grew hotter. And so, just as Kerry had told the ham-radio operator at the LAX airport, Gary, Kerry, and Lori had wrapped the couple in their sleeping bags and then bound the cocoonlike "coffins" with heavy chains. They said a prayer and watched the bodies slip silently into the sea.

"All I can tell you," Gary told Eloise Schumacher, "is they're buried at sea someplace north of Rangiroa."

Kerry Edwards and her half brother both appeared to be telling believable, straightforward stories — and yet they differed in many instances. Kerry believed that she and her father had been struck at the same time by the wildly swinging boom, but Gary said she was mistaken. "Kerry was in her bunk asleep when she got hurt — and I don't know how she got hurt. She doesn't remember, really."

In another interview, Kerry agreed that her father had been "dizzy" during the trip, but she felt she knew why. Before they hit the open sea, he had stepped from his boat to another and injured his shin. It had become infected, and she thought that had probably caused him to have an ear infection, too.

That was highly unlikely, but it seemed apparent that Loren's balance had been compromised. There was no longer any way to determine whether he suffered from an ear infection, soaring blood pressure, or other ailments. There could be no autopsy. His body drifted in the sea, lost forever.

And Kerry's own skull fracture could have clouded her judgment. She had admitted that she slept through most of the vital period after she and her father were injured.

It's almost impossible to put oneself in the place of the three shocked and frightened survivors of the *Spellbound*'s tragic voyage. To be adrift at sea, not knowing where you were, and faced with one calamity after another, would leave almost anyone with post-traumatic shock.

Gary Edwards was adamant that he wasn't anxious to return to the United States. "I won't leave Tahiti until I'm ready to," he said flatly. "I don't think about leaving. It could be two days or two years before I take off."

Eloise Schumacher was puzzled. She thought he would have been eager to get away from the far-from-home spot where his family had virtually disintegrated. He pointed out that there were several practical reasons why he could not leave what he called his "tropical prison."

The search party on the charter boat, and the search plane that had been called in, still had to be paid for their time, fuel, and expertise. That would cost $3,500. Gary said he didn't have that at the moment. Moreover, his visa had expired, and the French police were withholding his passport until he could pay the debt.

The *Seattle Times* reporter asked Gary about the investigation of his parents' deaths that was currently being carried on by a federal grand jury, the FBI, and the Coast Guard.

"They know I'm here. What can they do to me?" Gary answered angrily. "If they want me, they can come down here and get me. I'm not going anywhere. I'm in no hurry to argue with anybody at home. I don't care what's going on there. I don't want to go argue with a grand jury which has no idea what it is like to be in the middle of the ocean with two bodies in the hot sun all day. My going back and debating won't solve a thing.

"They can believe whatever they damn well want."

It was hard for Eloise Schumacher to judge

the man. He was certainly bitter, and perhaps he felt guilty because he hadn't been able to save his father or perceive his stepmother's suicidal state. He knew that he was under suspicion; he'd been questioned enough by French police. He had suffered great personal losses, too.

Gary Edwards admitted that remaining in Papeete was an escape of sorts, a way to postpone his grief about his parents. Once he was back in the States, the awful reality of the tragedy couldn't be denied.

And still, living on the sailboat gave him an eerie feeling, especially when night settled. "I walk through the places where my mother and father lay. I see the bloodstains on the floor and on the deck. I see the places where the FBI and the Coast Guard drove holes to get blood samples . . ."

In essence, Gary felt he was trapped in paradise, bound by his burden to protect the *Spellbound,* which had meant so much to his parents. The ketch had been a shining dream, but now it was an albatross.

"Do you feel ostracized?" Eloise Schumacher asked. "The *Tahiti Bulletin* seems to have a story about your family's loss in their paper almost every day."

He shook his head. "No, I don't feel unwelcome or ostracized. People here are kind."

Gary wasn't alone. An old friend of his from Canada had come over to live aboard with him, and he had a French girlfriend he'd met in Tahiti.

"I'm not worried about running out of money. It only costs about $3.60 a day to moor my ship at the quay, along the main road."

Ironically, Gary Edwards had found work as an extra in a TV movie being filmed in Tahiti: *Overboard.* It was based on a book about a sailboat that had met with a disaster at sea.

Like his father, Gary Edwards was a skilled carpenter, and he worked other jobs painting and repairing boats. When he wasn't working, he spent his time swimming, visiting the colorful native markets, and working on the *Spellbound.* Except for his injured wrist, which he said was healing rapidly, he was in excellent physical shape.

Even so, he dreaded the thought of sailing his parents' sailboat again. Papeete and Rangiroa were so far from American territory. Sailing to Hawaii would require a month or more.

"I can't face the ocean again so soon. The trip from here to there [Hawaii] would kill me."

Gary wanted to sell the *Spellbound.* He

couldn't visualize himself ever sailing her again. "It will always be my parents' boat, and it will always have their bloodstains. The only way to get rid of them is to replace the boat."

He sounded like Lady MacBeth saying "Out, damned spot!" as she tried to scrub the imagined blood from her hands. If he had to, he could live for a year in Tahiti for a thousand dollars, but he would have to live on what had become a ghost boat, surrounded by gruesome reminders of two incomprehensible deaths. And money to pay off the search parties and to sail the ship away wasn't that easy to come by. In the initial frantic days after they landed in Rangiroa, he had requested funds from home, and he'd received $2,500 from his parents' estate.

The elder Edwardses' bank in Kirkland had called Papeete and asked that that money be returned because it was part of their estate. No one had been able to find a will. Gary said Loren had told him once that he'd written a will, and built a secret compartment in the fifty-four-foot sailboat for important papers.

"I would almost have to destroy the boat to find that compartment," Gary sighed. "I have looked in all the obvious places and I haven't found it."

A long time later, that will and insurance papers were located back in Seattle, but it would be years before the probate case could be closed.

One thing investigators discovered was that there had been several guns on board the *Spellbound*. None of them had been declared to customs for fear that they would be seized. Jody Edwards had known where they were. Beyond the Walther automatic handgun that Gary brought in his seabag, there were two rifles and a shotgun.

"My father made the decision not to declare our guns when we went through customs in the Marquesas Islands," Gary recalled.

When he was asked if he knew how long the survivors had drifted at sea after Jody Edwards died on February 25, he felt it had been only about fourteen hours before the rescuing chartered boat found them, and that they made port in Rangiroa by 10:30 that Saturday night. His father had been dead for forty hours then, and his mother only since the wee hours of Saturday morning.

"The girls were very messed up mentally," Gary recalled. They had been flown to Papeete the next day — Sunday — where they were questioned by French detectives. Gary had arrived on Monday. When the police saw how seriously Kerry was injured, she was hospitalized.

"Lori and I were kept separated, and questioned for hours."

Gary adamantly denied that the rumors and innuendos that were floating around Tahiti and beginning to appear in the local paper bothered him. The reason was simple: the gossip wasn't true.

"Let everyone talk," he said. "I know what I did was right, and I'm not ashamed of it. I don't care what happens now. When I decide to come back to Seattle, I will. But I may sail around the world first. You never know."

Back home in Washington State, Lori Huey and Kerry Edwards struggled to pick up the ragged threads of their lives. They knew that relatives and friends were baffled over discrepancies in their recall and Gary's. But shock, severe injury, grief, panic, and being viewed as murder suspects in a foreign country would certainly unhinge anyone. One moment, they had almost reached their exotic destination, and the next blood ran on the decks of the *Spellbound*.

Kerry told reporters that the FBI special agents had warned her against making statements on the tragedy. She would say only that she was feeling a great deal better, and was well enough to start working part-time in a pizza parlor.

Lori sought a peaceful escape from her memories of horror by taking a hiking and camping trip high in the Cascade Mountains. It was a totally different ambiance there from the tropical islands of the South Pacific. The wind in the Cascades smelled of fir, spruce, and pine, and the soft patter of raindrops on her tent helped to erase her memory of the relentless heat off Rangiroa.

Lori's attorney had told her she didn't have to talk to reporters, and even though she had no guilty knowledge of what happened on the *Spellbound,* he said it would be better to avoid talking to the media.

She hoped to find a job when she climbed on down the mountain pass, and somehow get on with her life.

Lori's friends, however, told the *Seattle Times* that Lori had described the events of February 24 and 25 just as Gary had. Loren had died almost instantly when struck by the boom, and Jody had committed suicide in her overwhelming sorrow. There had been nothing any of them could do.

For those who found truth in the paranormal, it was easy to believe that the *Spellbound* was under an evil spell, covered with a suffocating blanket of bad luck.

■ ■ ■ ■

There were so many questions left unanswered. Why would Jody Edwards have chosen to commit suicide, leaving her children adrift in the open sea? Most mothers will overlook even the most intense pain and grief to be sure their children get to safe harbor. Kerry needed her on that dread dawn of February 25; her twenty-year-old daughter was critically injured, and no one on board seemed to know what had happened to her. Perhaps Jody believed they were all lost anyway, perishing from disorganization and panic without Loren there to calm them with his strength and common sense.

With Jody dead, there would be only Gary (with one useless hand) and petite Lori to bring their boat safely into harbor, where Kerry could get medical care. Wouldn't Jody have chosen to stay with them — at least until they were all safe?

Again, it's almost impossible to judge the state of mind of someone suddenly plunged into disaster.

There was also the puzzle of Kerry's memory. She was sure she'd been with her father when he was struck in the head, and that she had been struck, too. But Gary contradicted her and insisted she had suffered her skull fracture when she was sleeping below deck in her bunk. When the sailboat lurched with sudden wave action, she could have been going to the head, or getting a drink of water, and fallen, striking her brow on something hard and sharp. But Gary insisted she was in her bed when he first heard her whimpering in pain. How had she managed to crawl back into her bunk?

As always, when witnesses refuse to talk publicly, there was suspicion. Grand jury hearings are secret, held behind closed doors, but most laymen weren't aware of that. They wondered if the Edwardses had family skeletons or volatile relationships that had exploded into violence. That was the romantic notion of true gothic tradition and soap operas, but if there was any substance behind the whispered questions, the grand jury would surely have returned indictments against someone.

And they did not.

A few people who were not on the *Spellbound* that night wondered aloud if it was possible for pirates to have killed Loren and injured Kerry, strangers bent on robbery who had glided silently up to the sailboat in the dark and crept aboard, unseen.

If so, why hadn't they attacked the other three people on board, too? That explanation was a long shot — but possible.

One couple who lived on Papeete had known Loren and Jody and their family well, after they went on several cruises with a platoon of sailboats in American waters. They didn't know what to think about the Edwardses' deaths. They had heard the rumors that said Gary had killed them, but they tried to be fair with him and often invited him over to supper. He was always polite and grateful for a home-cooked meal.

On one of those nights, their daughter, Gwen,* who was in her early twenties, was visiting them.

"I didn't approve of their associating with him, because I thought he might be dangerous," Gwen recalled. "I think he sensed that."

According to Gwen, when her parents invited Gary over for supper, he had glared at her throughout the meal. After he finally left, she made her parents promise never to ask him again.

"He scared me," she said. "I felt as though he hated me — or maybe he just hated women in general."

Several months later, Gwen was in Hawaii when Gary and two men he'd hired to help him bring the *Spellbound* there showed up. The two crewmen were pleasant enough, and they didn't seem to have any alliance with Gary Edwards beyond being hired for a pickup job.

"It was the oddest thing," Gwen explained in 2009. "I was walking up the dock, talking to the two guys, and I saw Gary coming toward us. He looked surly, as usual, but he didn't say anything. When he came abreast of us, he picked me up by my wrists — with just one hand — and dangled me over the edge of the dock, banging me into the logs and concrete there.

"I was afraid he was going to drop me, but he was so strong. He pulled me back up and dropped me on the dock. I was bruised and hurt, but he just walked away."

Gary Edwards's crewmen were shocked by what their captain had just done. They helped Gwen up and dusted her off, and walked her to a safe place.

"They quit crewing for him right then," Gwen recalled. "They didn't want to get back on the boat with him.

"I never saw him again, and that was fine with me."

In the fall of 1978, Gary sailed the *Spellbound* into Richmond, California. He had taken care of his visa difficulties and was finally free to head for the United States, where the ketch would undergo repairs.

Gary stayed with the boat.

He hoped to sell it. It had been a millstone around his neck for eight months, a constant reminder of what happened in those ghastly predawn hours in February.

Two years after the tragedy occurred, Larry Edwards signed an affidavit accusing his brother of being "the slayer" of their parents. The motive was rumored to be for financial profit, and to cover up an attempted sexual attack on Kerry Edwards as she slept. Because of her fractured skull, she didn't remember what had happened.

If Loren and Jody's deaths were engineered by their son, how could it be proven? There were no witnesses — at least none who cared to talk about it. There were no bodies to be autopsied for cause or time of death.

The elder Edwardses' estate consisted mainly of their modest home and their magnificent sailing craft, which was dry-docked in California. There was a good chance that it would always be considered a "bad-luck" boat, and sailors are notoriously superstitious. Would anyone risk sailing it?

The *Spellbound*'s value had plummeted, but it was probably still worth over $100,000. Despite its original $200,000 value, the ship was not insured. Gary Edwards said his parents had decided against buying insurance when they learned it would cost 20 percent of the boat's value in premiums each year. Only very wealthy boat owners could afford $40,000 a year for insurance. And while they were sailing around the world, Loren's income would have been much reduced.

The *Spellbound* was sold in the summer of 1979 for $110,000. And that amount was, according to Loren and Jody's wills, to be divided equally five ways — to their children.

Faced with his brother's accusations, Gary Edwards renounced any claim to his share of that money on Friday, December 21, 1980.

"I already know I am innocent," he said. "Whatever share of the estate I might receive would probably be exhausted in a long and bitter legal battle. To fight this selfish battle for the sake of convincing others is not worth it. I will not be a part of a ghoulish rehashing of details for the sake of blood money."

For five years, Jody and Loren Edwards had worked on the *Spellbound*. They built it, outfitted it, sanded and varnished it again and again, laid out its huge sails, always dreaming of the day they would sail into the balmy breezes of the South Pacific — even while Northwest rain pounded down on them.

Had they had any way of knowing how it would all end, they surely would never have laid the keel. All the sanding and varnishing of the deck of the ship that languished in Papeete for so long could never quite erase the blood shed there.

No one was ever arrested, and the investigation into Loren and Jody's deaths sank into oblivion decades ago. Gary, Kerry, and Lori have slipped into obscurity — as they wanted to. He would be almost sixty now, and the two young women in their fifties. I've tried, but I cannot find them. Even the *Seattle Times* reporters who came as close to unraveling the secrets of the *Spellbound* as anyone — Eloise Schumacher and Peyton Whitely — had to take a few beats to remember the story because they wrote it so many years ago.

Whitely said he was startled a few years ago to walk down the dock where he had once known Loren and Jody as neighbors.

And there it was: the *Spellbound*. It had a different name, but he recognized the yellow fiberglass hull. There was no question that it was the same ketch. The people working on it were unfamiliar to him, but Whitely introduced himself and asked the man if he was the owner. He nodded.

"Do you know the history of this boat?" the longtime reporter asked.

"Can't say I do."

But the current owner was curious to know more about the thirty-year-old sailboat. Whitely hesitated, wondering if he should tell what he knew.

The man listened avidly, but when he learned of the Edwardses' fatal cruise, it didn't alarm him. Indeed, he found it intriguing.

Where the *Spellbound* is today I don't know. But I will always think of her as the symbol of a lost dream.

SHARPER THAN A SERPENT'S TOOTH

I've probably mentioned this before, but it's worth repeating. After several decades as a true-crime writer, I still find myself stumped by legal terms from time to time. We all do. Most laymen still believe that the term "corpus delicti" refers to the body of a murder victim. It doesn't. This misconception has been perpetuated by the fact that *corpus* is the Latin root word for "corpse." But, in correct usage, corpus delicti doesn't mean a victim's body at all. Instead, it refers to the body of a crime — all the elements that indicate a crime has been committed. Detectives and prosecutors have to prove to judges and juries that they have enough evidence — both physical and circumstantial — to show that a crime has been committed.

An actual corpse may or may not be part of the corpus delicti. If an adult disappears, he or she may have left of their own accord, and they are free to do that. But if there are eyewitnesses to violence to tell their stories, or a purse or keys left behind, or traces or even puddles of blood evident at a possible crime scene, then a rational person would tend to believe that that missing person did not choose to step out of his life. Probably the most telling evidence is the fingerprint of a victim or a suspect left in dried blood. One or both of them were there when that blood was wet.

Did someone have a motive for the absent person to come to harm? There are myriad variables that can prove a homicide has been committed: Has the suspected target for violence been seen anywhere? Has he cashed a check, drawn money out of a bank, used a credit card, made calls on a cell phone, or attempted to collect Social Security? We all leave paper trails that we are unaware of. If there is no trail at all, investigators begin to believe the person who has vanished is no longer alive.

They don't have to find a body to prove murder, and more and more homicide cases have been solved in recent years without any part of the victim's body being found.

There are other ways.

Even so, it takes a prosecutor with a lot of guts to file murder charges against a suspect when the corpse of an alleged victim is missing, hidden under water, in the ground, or beneath cement.

There is always the chance that the victim may show up, alive and healthy, or that he has simply chosen to disappear for his own obscure reasons.

Convictions in homicides in which no body was discovered and identified are still rare, but the advent of DNA as an investigative tool has made identification much easier than it was before the eighties and nineties. Perhaps I've written about a dozen "no body" cases in my career. Not that many out of the hundreds I've researched.

Columbia County, Oregon, District Attorney Marty Sells did obtain a successful conviction in the case of school bus driver Vicki Brown in the midseventies, although her corpse is still missing today. That defendant was the first to be found guilty of murder in Oregon — though no body was found — in eighty years.

One conviction in the state of Washington where no body was ever found occurred in 1965 in Snohomish County, when Joel A. Lung was found guilty of murder in the death of his estranged wife.

When Lung appealed, State Supreme Court Justice Matthew W. Hill wrote: "The production of the body or parts thereof is not essential to establish that a homicide has been committed. All that is required is circumstantial evidence sufficient to convince the minds of reasonable men to a moral certainty of the fact of death to the exclusion of every other reasonable hypothesis."

Anne Marie Fahey, who lived in Wilmington, Delaware, literally disappeared from the face of the earth — but Tom Capano, a major political figure in the area, was convicted of her murder, and of wedging her body into a Styrofoam cooler, which he tossed into shark-filled waters. Anne Marie never surfaced, but the telltale cooler did.

Steven Sherer went to prison for killing his wife, Jamie, in Redmond, Washington, even though no one found her remains. A forensic anthropologist testified in Sherer's trial that a grave didn't have to be a six-foot-deep rectangular space; a petite woman like Jamie could be hidden forever in a relatively small hole dug on wild land.

The grisly case that faced King County, Washington, sheriff's investigators and prosecuting attorneys in November 1978 certainly had all the earmarks of a bloody murder. Yet they had no body. They did have highly suspicious — and bizarre — circumstances, and enough blood to convince them that no one could have lost so much and remained alive.

When Lorraine Curtis Millroy* and her husband moved into their spacious tri-level home in the Eastgate area near Bellevue in 1954, they looked forward to years of happiness. This was true of many young couples who'd been torn apart by World War II. Millroy had a good job at the Boeing Airplane Company, and Lorraine also qualified for skilled positions during most of their marriage, taking time off to raise a family.

In September of 1955, they welcomed their first child, a red-headed boy they named Dustin Lex.* Three years later, they had a little girl, Amy.* As the youngsters grew up, the family made many close friends in the tightly knit neighborhood. Millroy rose to higher levels at Boeing, and their marriage was sound.

It was a good time in America then — a peaceful period between wars. The Korean War was far away. Families barbecued in their backyards, kids had sandboxes and wading pools. It was safe for Girl Scouts to sell cookies door-to-door.

But the Millroys fell victim to a changing world, a world where family solidarity evaporated when teenagers became part of a heretofore unknown drug culture. Their cozy brown-and-white brick home was torn with dissension, and all their hopes for the future disappeared.

Thanksgiving 1978 was a bleak holiday for the Millroys. Lorraine's husband wasn't at the head of the table; he was working for Boeing in Kansas, but they were separated by more than miles, and he had filed for divorce.

Dustin Millroy had changed so much that neighbors and even his longtime high school and college friends were stunned by his appearance and his state of mind. The guy who'd always been "mellow" had changed radically. At twenty-three, Dusty was reclusive, erratic, and paranoid. He was convinced that the CIA was out to get him.

Lorraine had done her best to make the holiday calm and happy, but she was fighting overwhelming odds. Her daughter was home from Bellingham, where she attended Western Washington University. She had brought her boyfriend with her, and they tried to help calm things down. Lorraine cooked a turkey and made pumpkin pies as she always had, and tried to make the day appear to be a regular Thanksgiving.

But the atmosphere was strained. Dusty remained in his basement bedroom most of the time, refusing to join the group. His sister saw that he had descended further into his weird fantasy life.

Lorraine confided to her daughter that Dusty's behavior was getting stranger and stranger. "I'm actually afraid of him," she said with desperation in her voice. "I want him out of the house. But I don't know whom to call. I couldn't do it last time."

Dusty had recently had a psychotic episode, bursting from their house and running naked through the streets. His mother had tried to have him committed then, but a law passed in Washington a few years before made it impossible to commit an individual unless he could be declared dangerous to himself or others.

No one felt that Dusty was that dangerous. Not his physician or the authorities or even his mother. But, on this Thanksgiving Day, Lorraine believed he was dangerous to himself — and she feared he was a threat to others, too.

The Millroy family managed to get through the holiday without a major scene, Dusty's sister and her boyfriend headed back to college, and once again, Lorraine was alone with the son she scarcely recognized anymore.

On Monday, November 27, Lorraine Millroy's neighbors were startled when they received a call from her supervisor at the research lab where she worked as a secretary. Lorraine hadn't come to work that morning. She was an extremely punctual member of the staff, and she had never before failed to show up for work without calling to say she was ill or that she had family problems. *She always called.*

Several times during that Monday, Lorraine's neighbors attempted to reach her by telephone, but it rang endlessly and no one picked it up. Then they had gone over to knock on her door. There was no response at all.

When both Lorraine and Dusty were home, her friends were used to seeing four vehicles parked in the driveway next to their house: two Volkswagen "bugs," an orange and white Chevy van, and an old Buick that belonged to Dusty. Lorraine was the only one who drove the van; she never allowed Dusty to borrow it.

Now, it was gone. The beat-up Buick sedan was still there.

Lorraine's closest neighbor's husband came home from work around 4:30. None of the women had been able to locate Lorraine, and they were afraid to go inside. While they held back, Jim Breakey* went next door to try to raise someone at the Millroy residence. He pounded on the door again, and then waited, listening for some response from inside. But, again, no one answered.

He was worried, too. Everyone who lived nearby knew how deeply Dusty was involved with drugs. They also knew that Lorraine was depressed and concerned about her son — and that she was, as she said, "scared to death of him."

It was getting harder and harder to remember the cute little red-haired kid who had once been part of the happy group of children who grew up together. Dusty had lost his way and couldn't seem to find a path back to sanity — nor did he appear to want to.

It had been dark for almost three hours, and it was suppertime. At 6:15, Lorraine's van pulled into her driveway. Peeking through their curtained windows, her anxious neighbors recognized Dusty Millroy in the driver's seat. They watched him as he walked into the house — alone. And then they walked over and knocked on the Millroys' front door again. No one answered, so they called his name, trying to persuade him to let them in. They knew he was inside, but he refused to respond to their knocks and calls — nor would he answer the phone when they dialed the Millroys' number.

The neighbors felt a cold chill that had

nothing to do with the wintry weather. Something was terribly wrong at the Millroy house.

Realizing they had to do something, they called the King County Sheriff's Office at 6:39, reporting "suspicious circumstances." No one knew if Lorraine had left of her own volition, if she was hiding in some part of her home, if she was injured, or, worse, was no longer alive. None of them wanted to speculate aloud on that possibility. Somehow if they said it, that might make it true.

Deputies Ray Green, J. J. Chilstrom, and Leo Hursh responded, and, after listening to the neighbors' fears, the officers agreed that they had had good reason to call in.

The deputies attempted to get an answer to their knocks at the Millroy home, but they had no more response than Lorraine's neighbors had.

The Millroy house was blazing with lights on inside, but most of the drapes were pulled. Chilstrom peered into the living room where the curtains didn't quite close, and he could see two women's purses and some papers sitting on the grate inside the fireplace. They didn't appear to be burned, and it looked as if there hadn't been a real fire there for a long time. He could also see a sleeping bag on the floor of the room.

Deputy Leo Hursh walked around the perimeter of the house, aiming his flashlight along the ground and toward doors and windows, not even sure what he was looking for. What he found didn't ease anyone's mind. On the south side of the house near the carport area, Hursh found dark red stains on the basement doorknob. It could be paint, but it would take a true optimist to believe that.

The three deputies looked through the windows of the orange van parked in the driveway. There were more red splotches on the van's interior and on rags and a sheet of three-quarter-inch plywood inside. An ax lay on the rear seat of the van, its blade covered with a rug.

Supervising Sergeant Mike Connally and Detective John Tolton joined the deputies outside the Millroy home. The circumstances were no longer only suspicious; they were ominous.

Periodically, the sheriff's men banged on the front door, but if anyone was inside, they didn't answer. Dusty could have slipped out another door while worried neighbors waited for police.

None of Lorraine's friends had a key to her house to use in case of an emergency. They could break a window or force a door, but the deputies didn't want to do that if they didn't have to. Connally and Hursh noticed that the front-door lock was the same make as the locks on their own homes. It was a long shot, but it was worth a try.

Connally's house key went in, but it wouldn't turn. Leo Hursh's turned, clicked, and the front door swung open.

"Police!" they called out, entering the home. There was no reply. With their hands on their guns, the officers moved cautiously through the silent house.

When they got to the kitchen, they stopped, appalled. The room looked like an abattoir. There was no question at all what the red stains were. Blood was splashed on the stove and on brightly polished pots and pans hanging above it. A mahogany trail snaked across the kitchen floor, ending at the top of the basement stairway. They followed it down the steps. There, they found great quantities of blood on the basement floor and on the carport door. Whoever had bled this profusely had to be either dead or critically injured.

They peered into a bedroom in the basement. The unmade bed was piled deep with all kinds of junk — clothes, books, remains of food. There were bloody tissues on the nightstand, and the room was generally in disarray.

Lorraine's friends told them that this would be Dusty Millroy's room. She had complained to them that Dusty's room was as jumbled and full of trash as his mind had become.

In stark comparison, the tastefully decorated basement recreation room was neat — with one major exception. Someone had piled cushions from the van on top of the couch. They wondered if that person had needed to make room in the van for a large object, a human-sized object?

It wasn't cold in the Millroy home, but the searchers felt a chill, feeling as though they were in a horror movie, not a pleasant house in the suburbs of Bellevue. They had found only bloodstains, but that was more than enough. They expected to find the source of those stains in each room they entered.

But they had yet to find anything — or anyone.

They came to a locked door: the basement bathroom. It could be locked only from the inside, and they knew someone was in there. Again, they called out: "King County Sheriff — come out."

Only dead silence answered them.

Sergeant Connally and Deputy Hursh

picked the lock with a nail, and turned the knob.

Dusty Millroy was inside. He was seated on the floor facing the door, and he held a small-caliber pistol, aimed right at them.

"Put the gun down," Leo Hursh said.

Dusty stared back at him, his eyes wild — but Hursh could tell he was debating with himself about what he was going to do.

"Put it someplace where you can't reach it," Connally said firmly. "I'm going to count to five."

Finally, Dusty tossed the gun behind the vanity sink.

With his scraggly beard and mustache and his long red hair falling to his waist, Dusty Millroy looked like a crazed mountain man. He wore only a pair of stained trousers.

The King County officers took him upstairs to the living room and read him his Miranda rights. He said he understood, and initialed the card. He complained of being cold, and he told Hursh where to find his boots and brown corduroy jacket. The boots were muddy, and the jacket had dark blotches on it.

"Are those bloodstains?" Detective Tolton asked.

"Naw — they're just grease spots."

Millroy's explanation for the condition of

the home he shared with his mother was vague, if not downright peculiar. He didn't really know what had happened or where his mother was. He said he'd taken her van and driven east, heading up toward Snoqualmie Pass because he "felt like getting away."

"Why did you take the van?" Deputy Hursh asked. "We understand that isn't your vehicle."

"Well, it was raining for one thing and the rear window's broken out of my car."

"Where did you go — exactly?" Tolton asked.

"To Cle Elum [a small town about forty miles east of the Snoqualmie Pass summit]. I wanted to get out of the city. Besides, I was scared and I felt really weird."

"Do you know where your mother is?" Hursh asked. They would phrase this question a dozen different ways, and their suspect always shook his head.

He continued to deny that he had any idea where his mother might be. It was a mystery to him.

There was clearly no point in pursuing this line of questioning. If Dusty knew, he wasn't going to tell them. They arrested him for investigation of murder and transported him to the King County Sheriff's Office in Seattle.

■ ■ ■ ■

Back at the crime scene, the sheriff's investigators took statements from neighbors. One woman recalled seeing Dusty arrive at the Millroy home that morning about 9:00. "He was driving his old Buick. He pulled into the driveway, and then pulled it forward. I said hello to him, and he just stared at me, but that wasn't unusual for him.

"I went bowling then, and when I got back at eleven I got a call from another neighbor who said no one could find Lorraine. I walked over to her house and saw that Lorraine's van was gone. Then the van pulled in around six and I sent my teenage son over to see who was driving it. He came back and said, 'You're not going to like it, but Dusty was driving it.'

"My son said that Dusty was staggering as he walked from the van to the house. That wasn't unusual, either."

"What was he wearing at that time?"

"Jeans, his sheepskin jacket — and cowboy boots."

Her neighbors all agreed that the missing woman — whom they'd last talked to on Saturday, November 25 — had been in a good mood then. They had the impression that she'd made a major decision in her life and was about to carry out her decision.

"I think it had to do with Dusty," the woman who lived directly across the street said. "We all knew he needed to be locked up and have some treatment, but she had a hard time coming to terms with that. She just seemed kind of relieved the last time I talked to her."

All of the people who were interviewed — most of whom had known Lorraine Millroy for twenty-five years — were aware that Dusty had had psychiatric problems and that his mother had been terribly worried about him, even to the point of being afraid of him. None of them had heard from her, or had any idea where she was, but as the days went by, they feared for her life.

A recent photograph of Lorraine Millroy appeared in several papers in Bellevue, Seattle, and other parts of King County, with an accompanying article that asked for any information on her the public might know. She was fifty-one, with reddish blond hair, blue eyes, and she weighed 130 pounds, perfect for her height of five feet five.

No one came forward.

At 12:30 on the afternoon of Tuesday, November 28, Lieutenant Frank Chase interviewed Dusty Millroy in his office at the

King County Courthouse. Detective Sam Hicks witnessed the interview, which elicited statements that were peculiar, to say the least.

Dusty said his sister and her boyfriend had stayed with him and his mother all through the four-day Thanksgiving holiday. He had said good-bye to them as they were about to leave to return to Bellingham on Sunday night, November 26.

"I went down to my room about eight and locked my door," he recalled. "I ate some popcorn and fell asleep. When I woke up this morning — yesterday morning now, I guess — I walked into the kitchen. There was a mess on the floor."

"What did the mess look like?" Lieutenant Chase asked.

"Goop — a lot of goop."

"Goop?"

"Blood — kind of like blood. But it could have been chicken grease. I thought maybe my mother had killed a chicken in there. I took some rags and tried to clean it up. My mother gets mad at me if I leave a mess — she fines me two dollars — so I cleaned it the best I could."

Asked if he ever had arguments with his mother, Millroy said that they'd argued about two weeks before because he hadn't paid his rent, and he'd been overdue. "She nagged me about it and we did have a fight then."

"Did you have another argument yesterday morning?"

Dusty shook his head. "No — when I got up, she was gone. I figured her boyfriend had given her a ride to work, because all our cars were still there."

"How about the night before? Did you argue then?"

"No, like I said, my sister was there and her boyfriend — we made popcorn, and I went down to my room and didn't come up all night."

"But you took a trip over the mountains, you say. Why was that again?"

"I guess when I saw all that stuff on the kitchen floor, I assumed my mother was dead, and that didn't make me very happy. I had to get out. I was afraid of being killed myself."

Dusty Millroy admitted that he'd taken his mother's purses and, after removing the credit cards, had placed them on the fireplace grate.

"Why did you do that?"

"I don't know. I really don't know."

Chase saw that Millroy was searching for answers. Possibly he didn't know why he'd done whatever he had done. Or maybe he was being deliberately vague. They still hadn't found his mother.

Dusty Millroy also admitted he'd had the .22-caliber gun, the one he pointed at the sheriff's men, for some time.

"I got it for protection," he said, but didn't say who he was afraid of.

"Did you ever fire it in the house?"

"There would have been bullet holes and cartridges in the kitchen if I'd fired it."

Frank Chase didn't ask him why he had said "kitchen," when he'd been asked about firing his gun in the whole house.

The investigators at the Millroy home had found all manner of incriminating evidence in Lorraine Millroy's orange van: bloody rags, blood, a shovel, and the sheet of plywood. That was the most telling physical evidence they'd ever seen. There was a portrait in blood etched into the grain of the plywood sheet; dried now, it formed a grotesque and telling pattern. The outline of a body was as clear as if it had been deliberately drawn with dark red paint. Even the pelvic girdle was perfectly outlined.

When Lieutenant Chase asked Millroy about the items in the van, he had a ready answer. "I found all that stuff there when I got into the van to take my drive into the mountains. I had a feeling that if I went for that ride across Snoqualmie Pass, it would lead me to my mother."

Asked why he had begun to clean up the house where he and his mother lived, Dusty seemed angry. "I shouldn't have cleaned up anything," he blurted. "I always get stuck with things."

He insisted that he hadn't dragged anything around through the house — as the trail of blood suggested.

"Why was the green plastic tarp in the back of your mother's van?"

"That was what I used to cover the broken window in my car."

Chase drew a sketch of the bloody outline on the plywood panel, but Dusty Millroy had no explanation for that either. "I didn't see any blood on the panel when I looked into the van. I don't know how it got there."

"Dusty, do you know where your mother is?" Chase asked quietly.

"No."

Dusty's rambling statements didn't make sense at all, and they contradicted each other. He alluded to "vibes" he'd received that told him to drive to Cle Elum, thinking he might find his mother there. The vibes had told him that his mother might be near Peoh Point Road, where he had once ridden trail bikes.

"What else did the vibes tell you?" Chase asked.

"That she would not be too far off the road."

"On top of the ground or in a grave?"

"It wouldn't be deep — with rocks on top."

"Did you leave anything in Cle Elum?"

"Nothing. I got stuck twice in the snow up there. Once some guys from Puget Power pulled me out, and the second time, some forest rangers pulled me out."

This was true. Detectives had already talked with the crews, who remembered the strange young man with the long red hair who had been silent and truculent as they helped to dig his orange van out of the snow in the wilderness areas near Cle Elum.

As the lengthy interview continued, Dusty Millroy acknowledged that his mother was probably dead. He said he figured that someone had killed her and taken her away.

"I was saved only because I was locked in my basement room with my gun for protection all night." He seemed oblivious to the impression he was making on the detectives. He was young, strong, and if there had, indeed, been a killer in the house, most sons would have protected their mothers. Yet he had saved himself.

The chance that his story was true was slight, but it was clear he was either lying or was psychotic enough that he believed what he was saying.

Lieutenant Chase left the interview room; he had been playing the role of the "good cop," in the time-honored interview technique of good cop/bad cop. While Chase had pretended to be understanding, Hicks had watched him with suspicious eyes.

Now, Sam Hicks confronted Dusty Millroy, mincing no words. He looked at Dusty with distaste, and the tension in the room was palpable.

"We believe that you found your mother in the kitchen of your house early Monday morning," the tall, dark-haired detective said. "You killed her and you drove her body away in her van —"

Dusty denied everything, but Hicks kept on talking.

"You dumped her body somewhere in the woods near Snoqualmie Pass — maybe near Peoh Point Road."

Millroy fidgeted and finally said, "I may have carried her out — but I didn't . . ."

He stopped before he said the words "kill her."

"Why would you 'carry her out'?" Hicks asked.

Dusty clamped his mouth shut and refused to say more. Nor would he allow hair samples to be taken from his body. They would have to get a search warrant to do that. They could, but it would take more time.

At 5:10 p.m., Dusty Millroy was booked into the King County Jail on suspicion of homicide.

On November 29, Detective Frank Tennison and Sergeant Dave Urban searched the canyon behind the Millroys' house for hours. They found no sign whatsoever of Lorraine's body.

A search warrant was obtained for the orange van, which had been sealed since the first night deputies were summoned to the Millroys' house. It had been transported to covered storage on a flatbed truck so that any bits of brush or soil caught underneath wouldn't be lost.

Tolton and Hursh processed the van, going through it inch by inch. They found two strands of hair caught in the rear doors. The blood inside the van was type A, but, at this point, no one knew what the missing woman's blood type was. And, in 1978, DNA identification was years in the future.

The chances that Lorraine Millroy was going to show up alive and well were almost nil. But where was she? And what had happened through the years to Dusty Millroy that had left him in this rambling, disoriented state?

Lorraine's estranged husband was on his way back from Wichita, Kansas, and their daughter was coming from Bellingham to talk to detectives. Hopefully, they could fill in some of the gaps in the macabre story. Amy Millroy talked with investigators Sam Hicks and Frank Tennison. She verified that she and her boyfriend had been home for the Thanksgiving holiday, leaving Sunday night. At that time, her mother had been in a "cheerful" frame of mind, and Dusty had locked himself in his room, a scenario that had become "almost normal" for their home.

"But it was very difficult for my mother to feel positive about her life," she added.

Amy recalled that her mother had tried in the past to get Dusty to move out and start a life of his own. She wanted him to take care of his financial responsibilities. But Dusty hadn't been able to make it on his own, and he'd soon ended up living in his car.

Worried about him, Lorraine Millroy had always relented, and allowed him to move back in. Her mother had also tried — in vain — to get Dusty into psychiatric treatment. But he was adamant that he wouldn't go.

"My brother has caused so much upheaval in our family," Amy sighed. She said she blamed him for their father opting out of the whole situation, filing for divorce and accepting a job in Boeing's Wichita division. "My mom's been on her own, trying to deal with Dusty."

Amy said that Dusty had last worked as a mechanic for a business that maintained fleet automobiles for corporate use. Although he had been talented in many areas and highly intelligent, all that changed when her brother had gotten heavily into LSD about a year before.

"He uses it regularly on weekends."

In the sixties, Timothy Leary and actor Cary Grant, along with many other celebrities, praised the hallucinogenic as a miraculous breakthrough to expand the mind. Lysergic acid stimulated the brain to see fantastic colors and remarkable scenes, along with terrifying delusions. Those who touted it were sure that it was the panacea for all manner of ills in the body and mind. Of course it wasn't, and Dusty's brain was only one of thousands that had been overwhelmed by the visions and out-of-body sensations the drug produced.

"I believe he also tried PCP," Amy said. "They call it 'Angel Dust,' I think."

The detectives knew about PCP, which surfaced in the midseventies. It was considered an "elephant tranquilizer" — an extremely powerful drug that gave those who ingested it superhuman strength and badly mangled brains.

Amy said that Dusty and his roommate at Evergreen State College in Olympia, Washington, had been so entrenched in the drug world that they were barely attending classes, and they had failed to finish the quarter there. Their experiences were only two among thousands of tragedies that were facing parents all over America. It seemed that Lorraine Millroy's awful fate might be one of the worst.

The King County detectives learned the names of several of Dusty's friends who had ridden trail bikes with him and had a list of possible spots where Dusty might have abandoned his mother's body. A concentrated grid search with sheriff's personnel, volunteers, and necrosearch dogs went on for days — netting nothing.

Sergeant Hicks and Detective Tolton interviewed Dusty Millroy again. Vaguely, Dusty said he thought he had traveled between ten and twenty miles from the area where he had first been stuck in the snow on Snoqualmie Pass, and the second time the van foundered, when he'd been dug out by forest rangers. Even though I-90 cut a fairly narrow path between rock outcroppings that rose steeply on both sides of the freeway, that would be an almost impossibly large area to search for a body in the snow.

"Tell me again why you left your house on Monday morning?" Hicks asked.

"How would you feel if your mother had just been murdered in the house? I was afraid," Dusty said morosely.

Lorraine's employer told detectives that Lorraine had been a close friend as well as an employee, and they had shared confidences. "She was afraid of Dusty. She wanted him out of the house."

The hunt for Lorraine Millroy's body now extended into adjacent Kittitas County, east of the King County line. A crew from that sheriff's office reported that they had found nothing at all in any of the spots Dusty Millroy had been known to frequent in the past. Nor were there any indications that Lorraine's body had been in either of the locations where the orange van had been stuck.

Sergeant Sam Hicks's search for Lorraine's blood type was just as frustrating. He checked back through all her places of employment, all her health insurance companies, physicians, dentists, and hospitals, but he found that, for one reason or another, either her blood type had never been recorded or some of her files had been lost.

Lorraine's health was good; her biggest problem was the agony she suffered emotionally as she tried to deal with Dusty. Her most recent doctor verified that she had asked for help in getting Dusty to a psychiatrist and that a referral had been made.

But Dusty never went.

Hicks received a phone call from Amy Millroy. She and her father had returned to the Eastgate home and found several items that disturbed them. Lorraine's bedroom slippers were there, and as far as they could determine, so were all her other clothes.

Amy believed that her mother had probably tinted her hair sometime after Amy and her boyfriend left the Sunday night after Thanksgiving to return to college.

"She usually did that in the morning. We found the shower cap she used for that in Dusty's room."

They had also found some clothing — Dusty's — that had been washed and left to molder in the washing machine. Faint reddish stains were still apparent on the sleeve of one shirt.

It was now the first week in December, and every possible area where Lorraine Millroy's body might be hidden had been searched by the King and Kittitas County detectives and volunteers.

She was simply gone.

She could be buried under the deep snow that began in the foothills a few miles east of her home or perhaps somewhere farther up on Snoqualmie Pass. If this was true, it would be spring before the great snowbanks began to thaw and slough off. Until then, no one would be able to find her body.

Lieutenant Chase and his investigators conferred with the King County prosecutor's senior trial deputy, Lee Yates, and Yates agreed that there was enough evidence to go ahead with a formal charge of second-degree murder against Dusty Millroy. In his affidavit to the court, Yates stated, "Despite the lack of a body, the evidence is consistent solely with the fact that Millroy killed his mother and disposed of her body."

To substantiate his argument, Yates cited the voluminous blood that had been found in at least six different locations in the Millroy home. Although they had yet to establish Lorraine Millroy's blood type, the blood in her van and the blood in her house were both type A. Yates referred to the body shape imprinted in dried blood on the plywood sheet in the van, the bloody plastic tarp, and ropes and rags found in the van. He was fully prepared to pursue the state's case — even if Lorraine Millroy was never found.

"No one has seen Lorraine Millroy since the night of November 26," Lee Yates told Superior Court Judge Frank Roberts, "nor has any paper trail turned up."

Roberts agreed with Yates's assertions. Dustin Lex Millroy, twenty-three, was charged with second-degree murder on December 6. Christmas trees and bright lights adorned the courthouse, while office holiday parties spilled the sound of laughter into the marble corridors.

But not at the empty house in Eastgate. Thanksgiving, however awkward it had been, had undoubtedly been the last family celebration for the Millroys.

On December 18, two elk hunters were slogging through the snow near the Taylor River Road east of North Bend, Washington. It wasn't far from where I-90 begins its climb to the summit of Snoqualmie Pass, and close to the road — just as Dusty Millroy had once visualized where his mother's body was, according to his account of nightmares.

The hunters recognized coyote tracks and followed them to what at first appeared to be the carcass of a deer.

But as they peered closer, they saw that it wasn't a deer or any other wild animal.

Lorraine Millroy had been found.

Sickened, the two men rushed to the CB radio in their truck and called the King County Sheriff's Office. It was 3:15 in the afternoon when Detective Tolton arrived, followed shortly by Sergeant Roy Weaver, Detective Frank Atchley, and several deputies.

It was close to the shortest day of the year, and the sun was already descending at a little after three o'clock. The sheriff's men raced against time as they examined the ruined remains of what had probably once been an attractive woman. Her body was nude, save for a bra and a turquoise robe partially wrapped around her head. Her hair was freshly colored a light red and it spread out brightly over the snow.

Wild animals had savaged the body, stripping the flesh completely away from the right arm. Many internal organs were missing from her right side. At this point, cause of death would be impossible to determine, although it looked as if she had suffered at

314

least one severe stab wound to her neck. Animal scavengers tend to enter a body at points of injury.

By 4:30, those at the crime scene had completed triangulation measurements, from where the woman's corpse lay, to trees, rocks, and other permanent markers. They could always return here and pinpoint where the victim was found. When they were finished, the corpse was placed in a body bag for transfer to the King County Medical Examiner's Office.

The next morning, Dr. John Eisele performed the postmortem exam on the body found in the lonely woods. She had not suffered only a single wound; she had been stabbed again and again in the neck and chest area, and animals had carried off her right lung, heart, liver, gall bladder, esophagus, and stomach. Consequently, there was no way of knowing how much damage those organs had suffered in the attack. There was, however, evidence of severe hemorrhaging in the jugular vein. Although Eisele wouldn't be able to state the exact cause of death, he estimated that Lorraine Millroy probably had died quickly of internal bleeding after a savage attack.

Looking at her hands, Dr. Eisele opined that she probably had had little, if any, warning. "See," he said to detectives. "Only her left hand bears any sign of a defensive wound."

Her blood type was A — as expected. And her fingerprints matched samplers of Lorraine Millroy's.

With her daughter's assistance, it was possible to reconstruct Lorraine Millroy's last day on earth. She had probably risen early on Monday morning — November 27 — so she could dye her hair before going into the kitchen to fix breakfast. She must have been in the kitchen in her robe when an argument with Dusty began. And it had proved to be the last argument for a woman who had done her best to find help for a son whose brain was so seared by drugs that he exhibited classic signs of paranoia.

Lorraine's husband and daughter had found a knife in her dishwasher, a knife that Lorraine always washed by hand to preserve the wooden handle. The knife's measurements were consistent with the depth and width of the wounds Lorraine Millroy had suffered. There was human blood on the knife — but not enough to determine the blood type, since her killer had run it through the steaming hot dishwasher cycle.

Dusty Millroy's story was like that of many

of his peers. He had been raised strictly and rebelled. As a teenager, he wasn't allowed to wear his hair long or have it cut like the Beatles' hair, the way some of his classmates wore theirs. Now it hung almost to his waist.

In high school, Dusty got drunk on beer and smoked marijuana. Still, he'd always had an even temper then, and he'd never been given to rages.

Dusty went on to Bellevue Community College, earning an associate degree in music and poetry — not a curriculum that would prepare him to make a living, unless he went on to get higher degrees.

His teenage friends had considered him "an ordinary, average guy" until 1975, when he went to Evergreen State College. There, everything changed. Evergreen was an avant garde college that fit with the seventies, a school oriented to "doing your own thing," and where personal growth was equally as important as something so prosaic as grades. This approach worked extremely well for highly intelligent students who were self-starters and could manage their own lives, but it wasn't the best college for others, and drugs weren't rare on its campus.

And it was a beautiful woodsy campus

where there was no dress code, but many brilliant educators.

Dusty Millroy was one of those who gravitated to hard drugs. As he took more and more, he began to be afraid, convinced that CIA spies were watching him constantly. At the same time, he refused to believe that his constant ingestion of LSD had anything to do with his paranoia and delusions.

By 1976, his condition grew worse. His old friends were shocked to see how much weight he'd lost, and the ugly open sores on his face and hands.

One friend recalled to detectives, "He was really paranoid, talked about 'losing the CIA.' He took off for Ankara, Turkey, and he was really doing LSD. I never dropped him, but his attitude about government spies following him was totally weird."

Dusty's family confirmed this. They had heard through the U.S. embassy in Turkey that Dusty was panhandling and was about to be arrested if someone didn't send him enough money to leave the country. They forwarded funds, and he was sent first to Germany and then home, where he moved in with his mother.

LSD — and probably other drugs — had burned out the mind of a "brilliant, quiet child who had never before shown a sign

318

of violence."

The constant stress that Lorraine Millroy had endured can only be imagined; she was in the middle of a divorce, striving to earn a living, and at her wits' end trying to find help for her son. The explosions between the two were to be expected. She never knew what he might do, and she was afraid — and yet she had attempted to keep some semblance of normalcy in the house. Dusty was still her son, and she couldn't bear to think of him living, cold and hungry, in his battered old car with its broken window, with rags stuffed in to keep out the freezing temperatures.

And Lorraine had taken him back home again and again, a home that was immaculate except for his rat's nest of a room. Only another mother would understand why she couldn't just give up on her son.

Still, she was full of fear. Her neighbors were afraid for her. But there had seemed no way to stop the inexorable path of tragedy that lay ahead.

With the discovery of Lorraine's body, prosecutor Lee Yates entered another charge; Dusty Millroy was now charged with first-degree murder. Before a trial, however, he would undergo ninety days of observation by psychiatrists at Western

State Hospital to see if he was competent to participate in his own defense.

There is, of course, a vast difference under the law between clinical insanity and legal insanity. Prosecutor Lee Yates and Rebecca Roe, the deputy prosecutor who would assist in the State's case, felt that, under the M'Naughton Rule, Millroy was not legally insane. He must have known that what he did was wrong: he had denied his crime, made efforts to cover it up, hidden the body — all acts of a man who realized the difference between right and wrong as he committed murder.

Sergeant Sam Hicks had felt that Millroy was "playing games" with him when Hicks interrogated him after his arrest. And Officer Hursh, who had talked to Millroy in his home about the blood spatters on the wall, felt the same way. When Hursh had asked him about the blood, Millroy had bristled, "What are you trying to do — nail me with a homicide beef?"

Millroy had then tried to explain away the blood by saying he'd had a severe nosebleed and that his forehead had then broken into a rash and had begun "dripping blood."

When he was first institutionalized, Dusty Millroy seemed quite withdrawn and disoriented. However, on February 15, he called Yates and said he wanted to talk about obtaining a reduced charge of second-degree murder. After advising him of his rights under Miranda once more, Lee Yates and Sam Hicks had an extended phone conversation with the suspect. Hicks asked Dusty to explain the difference between first- and second-degree murder in his own words, and Dusty responded, "Well, first degree is premeditated and second degree is spur of the moment."

His grasp of the fine points of the law didn't seem to be the words of a man who was legally insane.

Finally, Dusty Millroy was ready to tell them for the first time what had happened on the morning of November 27:

"Okay. After I woke up, I killed her, okay?" Millroy began.

"How did this happen?" Sergeant Hicks asked.

"It was just spur of the moment. It was no argument or anything. I just killed her."

Millroy said he'd awakened about eight or nine and found his mother in the kitchen, wearing the blue bathrobe and the shower cap. He said he'd glimpsed the knife on the counter.

"Did she make you mad or something?"

Hicks asked.

"No, she didn't."

"She was just standing there and you got mad and stabbed her?"

"Yeah."

Millroy said his mother had been facing him, had said nothing, and that he really had no idea why he had killed her.

"What did you do with the knife?" Hicks asked.

"I stabbed her in the neck."

"Did you stab her more than once?"

"Yes, I did."

"Where?"

"Around the neck and — and once or twice in the chest."

"But you don't know why you did it?"

"No."

"Did you have bad feelings about her before?"

"Yes — uh, being tossed out of the house and stuff like that."

In response to Hicks's questions, Millroy said he had wrapped his mother's body in the plastic tarp, dragged it downstairs, and then placed it on the plywood sheet in the van. "Then I drove to Cle Elum, but I changed my mind and turned around with her body still in the van."

Hicks asked Dusty if the Puget Power crew

or the forest rangers had seen her body when they were digging him out of the snow.

"I already got rid of it by then."

"You positive you didn't argue with your mother that morning?"

Sighing, Dusty Millroy admitted that there had been a discussion that morning. His mother told him that he would have to start thinking about moving out of the house, but she hadn't given him a specific time when he had to go.

Even so, her comments had angered him, and he had attacked his mother so unexpectedly that she had no time to resist the plunging knife.

"I knew I was in trouble then," he said. "That's why I had to hide her body. I tried to clean up the house and wash the clothes I wore."

This statement indicated that Millroy had indeed realized the difference between right and wrong at the time he killed his mother.

Despite his earlier admissions, when Dusty Millroy went to trial in early May 1979, however, it was a different man who took the stand.

Superior Court Judge Warren Chan was hearing the case without a jury. He entered a plea of innocence by reason of insanity for the defendant, in addition to the defendant's own plea of innocent.

But Dusty Millroy refused to entertain any arguments at all that he was insane, nor would he admit to his mother's murder — even though he'd already told Yates and Hicks that he had done it.

Two psychiatrists and a psychologist testified that Dusty was criminally insane — testimony that enraged the rail-thin defendant, who had insisted on making his own plea of innocent.

The defendant's father, referring to the recent mass suicide (by cyanide-laced Kool-Aid) of the Reverend Jim Jones's devout followers, described his son as a "Jonestown type — the sort of person who would have followed the Reverend Jim Jones."

"Jonestown follower?" Dusty blurted out, his eyes glinting with anger.

"What do you mean by that?" defense attorney Rich Brothers asked.

"That he would have been susceptible —"

"That's ridiculous!" Dusty exclaimed loudly, shaking his head.

When he took the stand — against his attorneys' advice — Dusty Millroy continued to disagree with any testimony that he was insane. "I never wanted the insanity plea in the first place. I am a pacifist. I don't believe in killing — even insects."

"Did you kill your mother?" defense attorney Brothers asked.

"No. I did not."

Dusty's mind circled once more around his main delusion. He testified that he felt the CIA was possibly responsible for his mother's murder.

"While I was at Evergreen State College, it became apparent that somebody had laced the well that supplied water to the college with some kind of chemical or drug," he said with his own crazy conviction. "The chemical caused men to become drowsy and women to become sexually productive [*sic*]."

The defendant explained to Judge Chan that strange people had begun showing up on campus and that he felt they were sent by some government organization.

"It looked like we were under observation of some kind. The government was using the students as guinea pigs, and about seventy percent of the students dropped out without finishing the year."

Millroy told the court that he was sure the CIA was to blame and that spies from that agency had followed him to California, and then to Turkey. "They tapped my phone," he said, "and they fired a shot at me."

325

Asked to describe his recall of November 27, he said he'd awakened, walked into the kitchen, and found "a mess on the floor. I thought it might be the remains of a chicken. I tried to clean it up, but I just tried that briefly. Then I suddenly noticed something was wrong. There was too much blood for any chicken."

He testified that he began to worry that his mother had been hurt. "I felt my mother had been injured because she was nowhere to be seen. I think the CIA killed her, because they were the only ones who had animosity to me. They are, of course, capable of such activities."

Dusty Millroy's mind was either churning with delusions and ugly fantasies, or he was trying very hard to appear insane.

He testified that he'd driven his mother's van to Cle Elum to look for her.

"Why did you do that?" his attorney asked.

"I did that because I'd heard a voice during the night — when I was half asleep — and it mentioned 'the highway east.'"

Millroy's courtroom statements certainly smacked of a man in the grip of psychosis. But prosecutor Yates had introduced the quite rational admission to his mother's murder that Dusty had given freely in February, just a few months earlier.

Dusty Millroy's affect was flat throughout his trial, with the worst emotional outbursts evident during the twelve minutes when Lee Yates cross-examined him. He was extremely annoyed when Yates suggested curtly that the defendant was playing games with the judge.

Yates wondered why the defendant had driven east up the mountain, searching for his mother.

"You're saying you thought you would just come upon [your mother] in the wilderness?"

"I thought maybe I could spot blood in the snow . . ."

"Oh, come on," Yates said, derision in his voice. "You don't expect us to believe that!"

"I don't care whether you believe it or not," Millroy spat out. "It's the truth."

Dusty quickly recovered the stoic attitude he'd exhibited through most of his trial.

There seemed to be no doubt in Judge Chan's mind that Dusty Millroy had been the immediate instrument of his mother's death. No one else had a motive to kill Lorraine Millroy, and all physical and circumstantial evidence pointed to her firstborn, her own son. She had coddled him, spoiled him, and forgiven his outrageous and bizarre behavior time and again. And she had finally had all she could bear and ordered him out of her home.

Had he used drugs the morning she was killed? Probably — but diminished responsibility brought about through the use of mind-altering substances or liquor is not a defense. Dusty had decided of his own free will to ingest LSD, and perhaps other drugs.

Judge Chan returned a verdict of guilty of first-degree murder, which carried with it a mandatory life sentence (which meant, actually, thirteen years and four months), with a consecutive five-year sentence for the use of a deadly weapon — his mother's favorite cooking knife — while committing her murder.

Lorraine Millroy had lived on the edge of disaster. The Washington State law — passed to protect the rights of the individual — that forbade committing an individual to an institution unless he was patently and demonstrably dangerous to himself or others was soon modified. For Lorraine Millroy, the new law came too late.

Prosecutor Lee Yates never denied that the entire case wasn't marked by pathos and tragedy, yet he stressed that under the M'Naughton Rule, Dusty Millroy had indeed known the difference between right and wrong at the moment he plunged a kitchen knife again and again into the neck and breast of the one person in the world who had tried desperately to save him.

Lee Yates went on to prosecute a number of homicide cases successfully, and then he went to work at the Public Defender's Office, helping accused people who had no funds to hire defense attorneys. He also became a stock car racing driver.

Sam Hicks and Leo Hursh worked closely together in solving Lorraine Millroy's murder, and they would investigate many other cases in the next three and a half years. Hicks was a tall, broad-shouldered man, whose desk sat in the middle of many desks in the Major Crimes Unit of the King County Sheriff's Office. He was usually smiling. I remember taking photographs of him with a Rollei camera, one that was guaranteed never to shoot double exposures.

And yet, when I had them developed, in three of the frames, there were two images of Sam, a transparent image superimposed on a more solid picture. No camera expert could explain that to me. They had never seen it before with a Rollei.

Perhaps it was an omen.

A few weeks later — in June 1982 — Sam Hicks and Leo Hursh went to a farmhouse in Black Diamond, the ghost of a one-time booming coal mining town. The rickety building sat back from the road, isolated from other dwellings. The two detectives wanted only to question a thirty-one-year-old man about the homicide death of a Seattle rock musician.

They didn't expect trouble.

But, as they left their police unit, shots rang out. They had no other choice than to crouch down in the open, perfect targets for someone who was firing a rifle at them from the barn.

Sam Hicks was killed instantly, and Leo Hursh injured. I went to Sam's funeral and then joined the miles-long cortege to the cemetery.

It was one of the saddest good-byes I've ever seen, with thousands of citizens standing along the route in honor of a good cop.

Where is Dusty Millroy now? I'm not sure. He is not in prison, he's not listed in death records, but someone with his name is listed in the phone book of a small town in Washington State. Not to protect him, but to protect the privacy of his sister and his father, I have chosen to use pseudonyms for this family, a family who sadly mirrored an upheaval in America that changed our world as we knew it.

DEATH IN PARADISE: THE HAUNTING VOYAGE OF THE *SPELLBOUND*

Gary Edwards on the sailing ship the Spellbound. *Gary joined his father, stepmother, half sister, and a friend on a dream trip to Papeete. What happened on that cruise is horrifying beyond belief.*

Friends and relatives greet the survivors of the Spellbound *disaster as they fly into Seattle. Lori Huey is second from left; she was the only sailor to escape uninjured. Kerry Edwards is third from left. The slash over her eye is evident, and later she would be diagnosed with a skull fracture. Port of Seattle police officers whisked them to a private area so they could escape from media cameras, and a curious crowd.*

SHARPER THAN
A SERPENT'S TOOTH

When King County sheriff's deputies saw Lorraine Millroy's purses partially burned in her fireplace, they feared for her safety. (POLICE PHOTO)

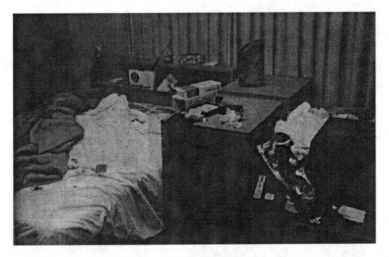

Lorraine's son's bedroom was cluttered, and detectives found bloodied tissues there. (POLICE PHOTO)

King County major crimes detective Sam Hicks was one of the first investigators at the empty house where Lorraine Millroy had once lived, and Hicks stayed with the dark mystery until the end. Sadly, Sergeant Hicks was killed in the line of duty a few years later when he was shot by a fugitive.
(ANN RULE COLLECTION)

Lieutenant Frank Chase brought forth some bizarre admissions when he interviewed Dusty Millroy. Even so, it took a long time to find out what had become of Lorraine Millroy. (ANN RULE COLLECTION)

When hunters stumbled upon what they thought was a deer carcass, they were shocked. They called King County Police, and the frigid scene in the mountain foothills was soon alive with investigators. (POLICE PHOTO)

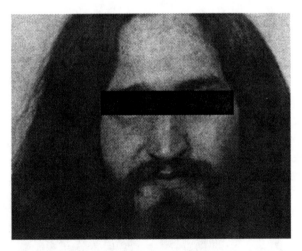

Dusty Millroy had plunged so deeply into drugs that changed his reality that nothing made sense to him. He was afraid of intruders, and upset because he had finally been barred from his childhood home. Although his family loved him, they didn't know what else to do. (POLICE PHOTO)

Monohan's Last Date

Frank Monohan believed he was headed for a date with an attractive and willing woman when he joined acquaintances he trusted on a trip over a Washington mountain pass. He was actually headed into oblivion. (POLICE PHOTO)

Don Majors was active in the "swingers" lifestyle. He was a consummate con man and as cold-blooded as they come. Women were drawn to his six-foot-five frame and his ice blue eyes. Frank Monohan believed in him completely, and didn't realize he was only a vulnerable patsy for the cross-country truck driver. (POLICE PHOTO)

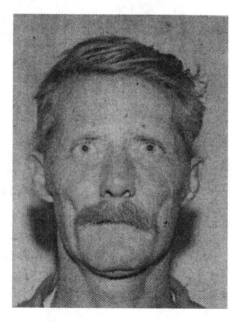

Seattle police detective Bud Jelberg worked missing persons cases for many years. He'd been searching, without success, for wealthy Frank Monohan, who had been missing for months. (ANN RULE COLLECTION)

Chelan County chief of detectives Bill Patterson was trying to identify a frozen body on Blewett Pass in his county. When Patterson and Jelberg compared notes, they realized that their unfinished puzzles could be completed. (ANN RULE COLLECTION)

RUN AS FAST AS YOU CAN

Seward Park has three hundred acres of jogging trails, forest, and waterfront. So many people flock there in the summer that there is a sense of safety in numbers, even along the trails that wind through the isolated forest sections.

Penny DeLeo usually ran the two-mile trail in Seward Park every morning. On her last run, she didn't come back.

Seward Park offered a swimming beach, too, and police officers chased a suspect to the water's edge before he surrendered.

Penny DeLeo's killer's motive for murder wasn't robbery. The young housewife and mother still wore an expensive watch and a large diamond ring when her body was discovered in Seward Park. (POLICE PHOTO)

Joyce Gaunt was in trouble at her foster home for staying out too late. She promised to come home, but she didn't. Her body was found in Seward Park, and Seattle police detectives thought about her unsolved case as they worked the crime scene where Penny DeLeo died. The two cases had several commonalities. (POLICE PHOTO)

Seattle homicide detective Wayne Dorman and his partner that summer morning, Ted Fonis, were the first investigators at the body site in Seward Park. The victim's family had already filed a missing report, so Dorman and Fonis were quite sure the dead woman was Penny DeLeo. (ANN RULE COLLECTION)

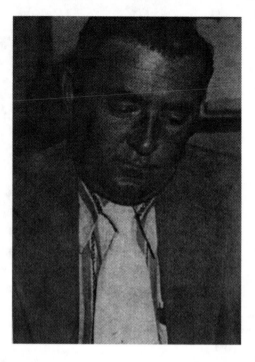

Ted "Teddy Bear" Fonis agreed with Dorman that someone had probably watched Penny DeLeo as she jogged daily in the park, someone who waited for a time when she was alone on the path. (ANN RULE COLLECTION)

Homicide detective Billy Baughman. Baughman, along with detective John Boatman, took statements from a most unlikely suspect in the murder of Penny DeLeo. (ANN RULE COLLECTION)

Detective Dick Reed executed a search warrant on the suspect's bedroom and took photographs that showed their quarry had everything he might want—from clothes to "toys." It was disastrous for his innocent victims that none of these things staved off his sexual compulsions about women. Reed found clothes that matched witnesses' description of the killer in the park.

THE DEADLY VOYEUR

Keith Person, fifteen, had tried to protect his friend Camilla Hutcheson, but their abductor shot him in the spine. Had he survived, he would have been paralyzed. His body lies next to Scatter Creek. Camilla jumped into the creek to escape the man with the gun and to get help for Keith. But it was too late. (POLICE PHOTO)

King County Sheriff's Office major crimes detective Ted Forrester had worked most of the complicated murder cases in his department. A soft-hearted man, Forrester was horrified when he heard what had happened to Keith and Camilla. He was assigned to their case from the beginning—when he responded to a call for help at Scatter Creek. Even Forrester, who had questioned numerous sadistic sociopaths, had trouble finding a motive for the attack on the unlucky teenagers. (ANN RULE COLLECTION)

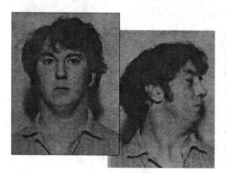

Vietnam veteran Jerry Lee Ross terrorized two high school students who were simply taking a walk in the small town where they lived. He had a wife and two little girls, and he was proud that he had once been a marine. Why did he kill? (POLICE PHOTO)

Dark Forest: Deep Danger

Belinda and Richard Cowden at an anniversary celebration. Their marriage was good, they lived in their own home, and they had a little boy, a new baby girl, and a close extended family. They went into the woods to celebrate Labor Day with a campout trip—but they never came home. What happened to them was almost unbelievable.

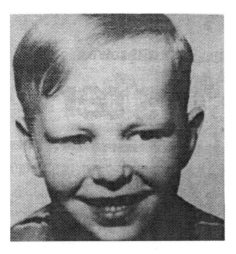

Five-year-old David Cowden walked a mile to the general store with his father on Sunday of the Labor Day weekend. They bought milk and with their dog, "Droopy," headed back for their camp where Belinda and five-month-old Melissa waited.

Wes Cowden, sole survivor of the three tightly bonded Cowden brothers, holds photographs of his brother Richard and his family, as he talks to reporters from the Eugene Register-Guard *on the sixteenth anniversary of their disappearance. The whole family was still haunted by the loss, and needed closure.* (EUGENE REGISTER-GUARD)

In this faded photograph, baby-faced Dwain Lee Little is only sixteen. His story made headlines because he was the youngest convict ever to be sent to the Oregon State Penitentiary in Salem. Authorities did their best to rehabilitate Dwain, guards and older prisoners looked out for him, and his education was probably better than he would have received on the outside. None of his supporters expected him to re-offend after he was paroled, but Warden Hoyt Cupp and forensic psychiatrists weren't so sure.

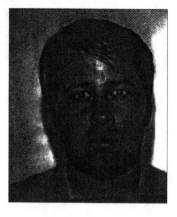

Dwain Lee Little's mug shot at his re-arrest for carrying a deadly weapon in 1975. At twenty-seven, he was quite handsome, and a jealous girlfriend reported him to police.

Dwain Little in about 1977, when he was paroled from the Oregon State Penitentiary once again. He moved to the Beaverton area, got married, and seemed to be adhering to his parole stipulations carefully.

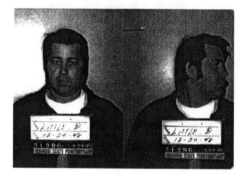

Dwain Little after his arrest near Portland in 1980 for yet another violent crime. He was soon headed back to the penitentiary.

Dwain Little at the age of sixty in 2008, still locked behind bars in the Oregon State Penitentiary. He is determined to be paroled again, but that isn't likely. He has allegedly confessed the worst of his crimes to a fellow inmate, but he will not talk to detectives.

■ ■ ■ ■

MONOHAN'S LAST DATE

■ ■ ■ ■

The seventies were, indeed, a strange decade. All manner of people were attempting to break free of the constraints put upon them by society and religion. "Swinging" was in, with many married couples switching partners and previously staid, new experimenters being drawn into "orgies." In 2007, an hour-long television series traced the fictional lives of thirtyish suburban residents in the seventies who changed partners as if they were at a square dance. It didn't last for a second season; there was something distasteful and even base about it. Despite some shocking aspects of the new millennium, swinging has never returned in the epidemic sweep that it once had. It seems crass, contrived, and sordid.

The puzzling death of a Northwest man who was leading two lives — until he came to the end of both of them — occupied investigators from three police agencies for three years, and in the unfolding of this amoral case, even experienced detectives were shocked at the sadism and perversion of the man who would emerge as a killer.

If there is evil in man — and there must be — Franklin Monohan's murderer had to be the living embodiment of all the greed, viciousness, and ugliness imaginable.

The first report came in to the Chelan County sheriff's dispatcher as an "unattended death." Chelan County, Washington, is on the eastern side of the vast Cascade Mountain range that bisects Washington and Oregon. In spring, summer, and part of fall, it is apple-growing country, where the best Delicious apples in the country ripen. In winter, it is very cold, and the edges along the shore of Lake Chelan, one of the largest lakes in America, sparkle with ice.

You can get to Chelan County by choosing one of three passes, although sometimes two of them are closed because of avalanches and icy roads. It was spring when a young couple traveled from Seattle along I-90, turning just beyond Roslyn and Cle Elum to take the scenic Blewett Pass approach toward the city of Wenatchee. Blewett's summit is at 4,102 feet, eleven hundred feet higher than Snoqualmie Pass. There are precious few stops as the road up to the summit climbs higher and higher, so the driver pulled over to the side of the road to relieve himself in one of the thick stands of evergreens.

It was sixteen minutes after eight in the morning on the fine spring day of May 28, 1975.

The man walked off the roadway, almost unerringly to the one spot where he viewed a silent tableau that would stay with him, hauntingly, for years. Had he moved even a few feet to the right or left, the corpse would have been hidden by the firs and budding cottonwood trees. He didn't see it at first because he was intent on the urgency of his mission. But then he turned.

It was not a pretty sight, and the man ran to the car where his wife waited, scarcely saying a word to her. They drove farther on, looking for a public phone but there weren't any, so he stood beside the roadway, waving frantically at passing cars. Fortunately, a Washington State Patrol trooper was also headed for Wenatchee that morning, and he skidded to a stop on the roadside gravel when he saw the man flagging him down.

"There's something back there . . ." he gasped. "It's exactly two and a half miles north of the summit."

His shocked state of mind said more than his words, and the trooper picked up his radio. The Washington State Patrol deals principally with traffic problems. Today, they run a very sophisticated crime laboratory — but in 1975, they were not geared for homicide investigations. As the trooper learned more details, he gave information that was relayed to chief criminal deputy Bill Patterson at the Chelan County Sheriff's headquarters in Wenatchee.

Patterson and Detective Jerry Monroe responded to the body site, which was nearly forty miles from their office. They realized at once that they would have to follow a trail that stretched back for months. All they found was a frozen and decomposing corpse that had been tossed into a snowbank, one that was now melting.

As they left their office, Patterson and Monroe had had the foresight to alert Dr. Robert Bonafaci, the Chelan County medical examiner, that a body had apparently been found. They requested that the skilled pathologist join them atop the pass.

It was approximately ten a.m. when the investigators began their probe. Patterson, who would live, eat, and sleep with the case for the next two years, had no warning that the body discovery would be the opening of a Pandora's box of intrigue.

They stared at the corpse that rested

twenty-two feet from the edge of the road. It wasn't visible to cars driving by. Until recently, it would have been buried under many feet of snow, but the spring thaw had begun to expose it. The dead man wasn't a hunter; his clothes were all wrong for that. The man was fairly tall, and he was dressed in expensive clothing.

That was about all they could be sure of at this point. Skin slippage and decomposition had made his facial features unrecognizable.

Dr. Bonafaci commented that the man still had his own teeth, which had a noticeable overbite. There was no jewelry or other identification on the body, and fingerprinting would be useless now. The body wore a long-sleeved beige sweater over a white shirt, dark blue double-knit trousers, and laced-up black oxfords. Except where it had been chewed by animals, the clothing was in excellent condition.

Monroe and Bonafaci took pictures of the scene prior to the body's removal for postmortem examination. If he had any money when he died, he had scarcely any now. The detectives found only a comb, a handkerchief, a quarter, a nickel, and three dimes. These items were bagged and marked for evidence.

Bonafaci said it might be impossible to tell how long the body had lain beside the lonely mountain pass road. The deep snow had frozen the corpse. "He could have been dumped as far back as October of 1974."

The dead man certainly wasn't dressed like the thousands of migrant workers who pour into Chelan County each spring and stay until the harvest is over. They are the most frequent homicide victims for whom the sheriff's men try to bring some justice. Inevitably, many of them are killed in fights over liquor or women or frustration at their lot in life and dumped unceremoniously in secluded spots. The harvest workers move on to the next crop, often in some far-off place, and the victims are forgotten.

But this man didn't appear to be one of that great traveling class. This man's clothing spoke of taste and money, although he certainly didn't have any cash left on him now.

Besides snow, the body was covered with sand and gravel. "That means he's been here through the winter," Patterson commented. "The snowplows would have showered the gravel over the bank during the winter."

As the body was lifted by the deputies, its nether side came into view. Neither Patterson, Monroe, nor Dr. Bonafaci could find any obvious exterior wounds that would account for the death.

"I may be able to tell more tomorrow," Bonafaci said, "after I've completed the autopsy."

The labels from the victim's clothing were cut off and retained, but they wouldn't help a great deal; although it was high-end stuff, the labels were from clothing lines that were produced by companies with hundreds of outlets.

News of the body discovery was published in local papers and on the evening news, and citizens began to respond by the next morning. A Wenatchee man called Chief Patterson to say that he had driven across Blewett Pass on November 1, 1974, in a snowstorm. "Me and my wife thought we heard a man calling for help around where they found the body. It was kind of scary. We stopped, turned the car around, and went back, turned the radio off, held our breaths even and listened, but we never saw anything. We finally decided it must have been the wind in the trees or something on the car radio. Never thought about it again 'til I read the paper."

That was possible. Winter comes early to the summit of Blewett Pass, and according to Bonafaci the body could conceivably have been there that long.

The medical examiner performed the post-mortem exam of the still-unidentified body while Patterson observed. Bonafaci located a small metal fragment between the dead man's tongue and right mandible (jawbone). It appeared to be part of a shattered bullet. Probing further, he found more pieces of lead in the soft tissue as he removed the jawbone. The skull itself was not fractured, nor was the brain damaged. Due to the advanced state of decomposition, the skull was retained for X-rays.

Blood typing wouldn't help. DNA hadn't been discovered yet. Putrefaction had destroyed all typing factors. Had there been any alcohol present in the blood, it had long since dissipated.

The dead man had been five feet eleven inches tall and had probably weighed about 180 pounds. Although Dr. Bonafaci suspected the cause of death had been a penetrating bullet wound, it would take more tests to verify that.

X-rays did show scattered metal fragments. Bonafaci interpreted the films as showing that the victim had been shot high in the back of the neck, and that the bullet had traveled forward and ended up, spent, in the oral cavity.

French fried potatoes were still discernible

in the stomach, indicating that the victim had eaten them shortly before he died.

"These hemorrhagic lungs — without free blood in the stomach — point to instant death," Bonafaci explained. "The wound track undoubtedly severed or at least severely damaged the cervical spinal cord."

Any call for help from the unknown victim could not have been heard by anyone — unless he realized that he was in danger just before the fatal shot.

After the first flurry of calls, the response from Wenatchee-area citizens was sparse, and Patterson sent out bulletins to law enforcement agencies around the state asking if they had any currently missing men who met the description of his "John Doe" body. The Chelan County investigators believed the mystery man had been between thirty-five and forty-five, but they couldn't be sure.

Bill Patterson also checked with local garages to see if there were any unclaimed abandoned cars that might have belonged to the dead man. Again, he found nothing that fit.

The victim couldn't have walked up the mountain pass and down the other side, and he didn't look like a hitchhiker. It was more likely that he'd had a car and that it had been stolen, or possibly he was riding with someone he knew and trusted and there'd been an argument.

"We just don't know," Patterson admitted. "We have no idea what happened."

He and Deputy Whaley drove back up to the summit of Blewett Pass and spent hours with a metal detector searching for a gun that might have been the fatal weapon. All they found among the sword ferns, wild huckleberries, and meadow daisies were beer cans and junk metal, plus some liquor and beer bottles. The victim could have been killed anywhere; the route via Snoqualmie Pass and then Blewett to Wenatchee and further east is the most popular choice of travelers in the summer and fall.

This was a likely spot to get rid of excess baggage.

The Kittitas County Sheriff's Office — whose jurisdiction adjoined Chelan County to the south — notified Patterson that they, too, had found a body of a middle-aged man who was initially unidentified.

"He was alongside a county road with a .22 bullet in his head," the Kittitas detective said. "We got a report on the body on the fifth of March. We found out who he was, though."

"Who was he?" Patterson asked wearily.

"Kind of a character. He was running for president on a kooky campaign, asking people to write his name in. He was his own main supporter."

The flamboyant victim in the Kittitas County case had planned to run in 1976 on a platform of minimal taxes and maximum benefits for "the little man."

His platform included a man-made bridge from Alaska to Russia, a new monetary system, taxation for all churches, return of all service people abroad, and complete amnesty for Vietnam defectors.

The would-be president's murder remained unsolved. His peculiar philosophies might have been enough to annoy his killer, but there seemed to be little to link him to the body in Chelan County except for body location, age, and manner of death.

The metal fragments removed from the Blewett Pass victim were weighed in an attempt to determine the caliber of the bullet that had killed him. The largest fragment weighed 28.6 grams, the smaller piece 1.7, for a combined total of 30.3 grams. Ballistics experts said that a .22-caliber long rifle slug, when whole, weighed 40 grams, leading investigators to believe the gun they were looking for was probably a .22-caliber rifle. Allowing for some of the fragments that had scattered, the weight was close.

At this point, however, the rifle didn't seem as important as finding the identity of the dead man, who remained nameless for almost a week.

That mystery, at least, would be solved in the weeks ahead.

More than 150 miles away from Blewett Pass — in Seattle — Detective Bud Jelberg, who handled missing persons and psychiatric cases for the Seattle Police Department, read the bulletin sent out by Bill Patterson. Jelberg had had a missing person file open on his desk for almost six months on a man named Franklin Lee Monohan. Monohan, forty-nine, had been missing since mid-December 1974 under circumstances that were most peculiar.

Frank Monohan had been reported missing by his estranged wife on January 8, 1975. The couple had been separated since early November 1974, and Monohan had moved into an apartment fashioned from a loft in his office. He ran a successful engineering business in the area near SeaTac airport. Despite the recent marital split, his wife said it was extremely unusual for him to let Christmas pass without making any effort to get in touch with his family.

Monohan was not a graduate engineer but a self-taught genius. His mastery in designing machine parts to specification had built the foundation of his highly lucrative business. He owned his own plane — one that still sat at a British Columbia airport, where it had seemingly been abandoned sometime in early December.

Monohan's checking account had a balance of well over $5,000, and it hadn't been touched since December.

Bud Jelberg understood the family's concern for the missing man. If Monohan had decided to disappear into greener pastures, he certainly would have cleared out his bank accounts and taken his money with him. He probably would have chosen to fly his own plane.

Jelberg had studied the pictures of the friendly-looking man, and set out to find him in early 1975. He'd found many people who left fewer signs behind, but the Seattle police's missing-persons expert discovered Monohan's vanishing was one of the most difficult cases in his career.

First, he'd contacted a former business partner, Tom Greco,* who was used to seeing Monohan almost daily. Greco said he'd been concerned about his friend. He hadn't seen Frank, nor had any of the other friends

Greco had questioned.

"I traced back, and realized the last time I saw him was on December 12," Greco told Jelberg. "If he leaves town on business, he always calls me after a couple of days, and he never leaves his plane at the airport for so long."

Jelberg checked traffic tickets, vehicle registrations, hospitals around the state, and found nothing indicating Monohan had been in an accident. There had been no activity in his personal checking account since the first of December. The last activity in his commercial account was on December 12. The most recent hits on the Standard Oil computer for credit card use were also noted as having been on December 12.

Accompanied by the missing man's estranged wife, Detective Jelberg went to Monohan's office. As she turned her key, they saw that everything was covered with dust — motes floating eerily in the air where light beams cut through the dimness. Still, there was no indication that a struggle had taken place there. Whatever had been there before seemed to remain, all neatly in place.

In the loft apartment, the pair found the missing man's clothes, food-stocked cupboards, and the other things a newly single man would choose to furnish a temporary home.

It looked as if Frank Monohan had stepped out to go to lunch and never returned. His wife said he'd always carried an American Express card. Reaching into the incoming mail drop in his office, Jelberg pulled out a number of envelopes that had been delivered since December 1974. One of them was an unopened bill from American Express. Finally, he had found evidence that someone had made purchases on Monohan's corporate card. There were many receipt slips for charges made after December 12.

Jelberg handed them to Mrs. Monohan, and she studied the signatures.

"These weren't signed by Frank," she gasped. "These on the fourteenth and fifteenth of December. His normal signature is 'F. L. Monohan,' and these are signed 'Frank' and 'Franklyn,' and they definitely aren't in his handwriting."

They found more charges from American Express for Monohan's card, most of them from the sprawling Southcenter Mall where Frank had his office. They were from toy stores, women's intimate apparel stores, a men's clothing store, and several others. Someone had gone on a spending spree with the missing man's charge card.

After they locked up, Jelberg and Monohan's estranged wife looked for his pickup with its canopy, half expecting to find it parked nearby. But it wasn't. If Frank Monohan had become one of the army of souls who simply decided to "drop out," he apparently had done so with only the clothes on his back. He could have lived a sumptuous life for a long time, but he left it all behind.

Strange.

Jelberg went to the stores listed on the American Express, but most of the purchases had been made during the Christmas rush, and the clerks had trouble recalling just who had made these charges. Many were no longer employed there, as they'd been temporary holiday salespeople. For those who did have a vague recollection of the sales, they could remember only that there were "two men."

Next, Standard Oil bills began to trickle in to Monohan's office address. All the receipts showed charges made after December 12. Gas and other items had been purchased in Lynnwood, fifteen miles north of Seattle, and south a thousand miles to Los Angeles, and back again to Sacramento. The license number listed on the slips was not for Monohan's truck but rather for a sedan registered to a California couple, a couple whose home

address was listed in the Seal Beach area —
on Long Beach Harbor.

Jelberg felt he was getting closer. Maybe
his missing man was having a midlife crisis
and had taken off with a younger woman
who had a child. That would account for
the toys someone had bought. Maybe the
woman had signed Frank's name with his
permission.

Jelberg called Sergeant Buzzard of the Seal
Beach Police Department and asked that the
couple be contacted. Buzzard soon reported
back that the man who owned the car in
question — a 1968 Pontiac — was the owner
and manager of a building supply firm in
Seal Beach.

"This guy says he uses only Union Oil
cards to buy gas," Buzzard explained. "But
he has several truck drivers who work for
him and they often have access to his vehicle. When they borrow his car, they put
gas in it."

"You have their names?" Jelberg asked.

"Right. There's four men who live here in
California. There are two headquartered in
Portland, Oregon. That's Al Bryson* and
Don Majors."

Buzzard said he felt the owner of the 1968
Pontiac was telling the truth.

"He seems totally straight and cooperative

with me. I'll see if I can get you rap sheets on the California employees who had access to the Pontiac."

Back in Washington, Detective Jelberg checked for possible criminal records on either Al Bryson or Don Majors. Bryson was clean, but Majors had a current warrant out for him from Grant County, Washington.

The missing persons investigator had pulled the loose end of a string that would keep unraveling. Grant County authorities confirmed that Don Majors also had an outstanding warrant in Wyoming for grand larceny by check. Since Majors often lived in Grant County, the Washington agency was looking for him as an assist to Wyoming. They promised Jelberg they would do a discreet investigation into Majors's background.

In the meantime, Jelberg issued a request to all agencies to search for the still missing canopied pickup belonging to Frank Monohan. No one in Seal Beach had seen it.

The first information on Don Majors came in: Majors had two birthdates of record. Grant County detectives believed that the documents that listed his birthday as September 13, 1922, were probably accurate. "He's very tall — somewhere between six foot three to six foot five," the Grant County investigator said. "And skinny. But his description tends to vary like his birthdays."

"Where's he live?" Jelberg asked.

"Not sure. His ex-wife and twenty-year-old daughter still live in Quincy, Washington, but Majors himself is in and out of town, and usually on the road.

"We're sending you his rap sheet," the Grant County contact said.

How Don Majors might have come to know the missing Frank Monohan was a puzzle to Jelberg. Quincy was thirty-five miles east of Wenatchee. The men lived across the state from each other — separated by a towering mountain range — and Monohan was a respected and wealthy businessman, while Majors's activities seemed to be questionable at the very least.

When Majors's rap sheet arrived, Jelberg was even more surprised. It was thick enough to indicate decades of criminal activity. Majors was presently a fugitive from not only the Wyoming warrant but from a bench warrant in Grant County for not complying with the conditions of his parole release from prison.

"His last known address is in George, Washington," Grant County detectives said in a follow-up phone call. "But the most recent place we have reports about him was in

Portland, Oregon, where he goes under the name of Donald Thompson."

Jelberg studied the mug shot of Donald Majors aka Donald Thompson aka who else? He was thin to the point of gauntness, and high cheekbones and sunken cheeks made his face almost cadaverous. He resembled more than anything an old-time western villain who smoked too much, drank too much rotgut whiskey, and probably had tuberculosis. His eyes were like a fox's, piercing and light-colored. He wore metal-framed glasses and an old-fashioned handlebar mustache.

With twenty-five more pounds on him, he could be handsome. In this mug shot, Don Majors looked as though he had lived his entire life dissolutely.

Bud Jelberg still couldn't figure out the connection between Don Majors/Thompson and Frank Monahan, but they were both missing, and Jelberg asked permission to open the safe in Monohan's office.

In spite of his years of experience in the Seattle Police Department, Jelberg was startled by what he discovered in that safe. As he looked through letters, pictures, and printed material, he found that the highly successful and respected businessman had been leading a double life, a life unknown to his closest friends or his family. Frank Monohan had apparently been deeply involved in "swinging," exchanging sexual intimacies with perfect strangers, the singles and couples who advertised in his collection of erotic publications: *Swingers' Magazine, Sandra's Erotic Journal,* and others of that ilk.

Jelberg sat back on his heels as he thumbed through the safe's contents. He wasn't expecting to find this. He'd thought Monohan might have had tax problems, or been afraid that he'd be caught embezzling, or, most likely, that he had left with a woman much different from his wife.

The magazines and mail in the safe didn't fit with any of that. Would-be sexual contacts had sent their pictures in various stages of undress, including completely naked poses. They were holding whips, handcuffs, black leather masks, and phallic-shaped vibrators, along with all manner of kinky sexual toys. The advertisers' sexual preferences were printed in black and white, although you had to speak another language to understand them. "French, Greek, B. and D. [bondage and discipline.]" The far-out fantasies listed in the magazines required very creative minds to imagine them.

Jelberg lifted out a photo album with dozens of obviously private snapshots that many women had mailed to Frank Monohan.

Some of the women who posed naked for an unknown person's Polaroid camera were beautiful; others would have had trouble being picked up in a dark bar at "last call" by a man who'd had five martinis.

The poses were obscene, and there was no question about the kind of appetites they were trying to whet. There were photographs of men, too: a handsome, powerful-looking man sitting naked on a bar stool in his recreation room, holding a torture device, a cruel smile on his lips. His pretty wife, with a whip in her hands, sat nude beside him.

Don Majors's picture was in the album, too. And as Jelberg studied his photo, he knew he had found the connection to Frank Monohan. Majors was engaged in a perverted sexual act with a female whose face was obscured.

Jelberg would try to identify the other women posing with Majors. Maybe he could build stronger links between the dead man and the missing man.

Frank Monohan had kept not only the correspondence from other swingers but also carbons of his own responses. He had always been an efficient businessman.

Sometime in the past few years, Monohan's life had changed radically: he'd become obsessed with the pursuit of kinky sex. And yet he had apparently managed to carry on his business, too, and to keep his sex-driven world a secret from those who knew him as he once had been. Maybe he'd always been drawn to the forbidden and erotic, and, at forty-eight, had simply decided to leave his marriage and give in to his heretofore hidden impulses.

Jelberg had little doubt now that Frank Monohan was probably dead. He'd been walking on the wild side, a tempting target for people who used the sex trade for profit. But his body had never been found. Legally, it would take seven years for Monohan to be officially declared deceased if his remains were never found or proof of his death wasn't firmly established.

Jelberg believed in his bones that the mysterious Don Majors was involved in whatever had happened to Frank Monohan. But how could he prove it? In those early months of 1975, Monohan's body had not been found. Sometimes, Bud Jelberg doubted his own intuition, and he could almost picture Monohan drinking a piña colada on a balmy beach far away, laughing because he'd pulled of the perfect escape from a boring life in the clammy, rainy atmosphere of the Northwest.

Not likely.

The missing persons detective knew less about Don Majors; he was gone, too.

"Maybe Majors is the dead one," Jelberg commented to Detective Joyce Johnson, who had the desk next to his. "Maybe I've figured it out all wrong."

More credit-card slips came in, and Jelberg added them to Frank Monohan's file. His American Express card had been used at the Holiday Inn in the Duwamish Slough area, just south of the Seattle city limits, on December 13, 1974. Monohan's true signature had been used to sign for a steak dinner for three, and then to pay for two deluxe rooms.

But that was the last time Frank Monohan himself used the card. A day later, a new signature had signed for purchases at a boutique in Southcenter Mall (for black mesh stockings and a black satin waist cincher), at Toys Galore (for electric train equipment and tracks), and for expensive men's clothing at an exclusive men's store. Armed with Majors's mug shot, Jelberg showed his picture and other mug shots to a new group of clerks. This time he hit at least a spoonful of pay dirt. They looked at a "laydown," a collection of photographs including both Monohan and Majors, and they all chose the missing trucker as the man who'd used

Frank Monohan's credit card.

Monohan's truck, an orange 1969 Ford pickup, was located in a towing yard. A man who wanted to buy such a vehicle had spotted it there and called one of Monohan's relatives asking about the price. The truck had been dumped surreptitiously on the huge towing yard lot, and because they took only sporadic inventory, the owners were completely unaware it was there.

Detective Joyce Johnson had the truck impounded and towed to headquarters, where it was processed. Nothing of evidentiary value was found in the truck.

This was the status of the search for Frank Monohan in early June 1975 when Deputy Bill Patterson of Chelan County sent out his request for help in identifying the body found on Blewett Pass.

Bud Jelberg immediately forwarded dental X-rays of the missing Monohan for comparison with those of the corpse. If the body was Monohan's, at least they would solve the first part of the mystery of what had become of him. Jelberg even had a prime suspect — Donald Kennedy Majors — who was still at large.

Moreover, the Seattle detectives already had a handle on the motive for murder. Monohan had been fair game for the swingers he'd been in touch with, and Majors swung with the best of them.

Dr. Bonafaci and Bill Patterson took Monohan's dental chart to Dr. M. L. Westerberg's dental office. Westerberg studied the two charts intently. Finally, he looked up.

"I'm positive it's the same man. There's one chance in a half million that this chart could belong to anyone other than Frank Monohan."

Since the victim's body had been found in Chelan County, Patterson would be the principal investigator in the murder case. He knew who his victim was now, and he knew who the main suspect was, but he still had to find Don Majors. And he had to find some testimony or physical evidence that would bind Majors inextricably to the killing.

Despite Majors's identification as someone who probably used Monohan's credit cards, it wasn't an absolute fact. And that was what Bill Patterson needed to take his case to the Chelan County prosecuting attorney.

That would not be easy.

By the time Bill Patterson finished with Don Majors, he would know more about the wily trucker than Majors's own mother. Some of the people the chief deputy contacted were horrified to find themselves linked to Don Majors. The thought that their hidden sex lives might be revealed left them pale and shaken, and their words tumbled over each other as they hastened to make up excuses. In truth, they were aghast to learn that their "advertisements" in swingers' magazines had now come to the attention of a sheriff's detective. A few admitted knowing Don Majors, while others stoutly insisted the whole thing was a mistake, and they had never willingly participated in such advertisements.

Many were professional people who were "pillars of their communities." One man finally admitted that he'd met Majors through an ad in *The Seekers,* a swingers' magazine. "I met him and his ex-wife in '68," the man recalled. "Majors called me after I answered his ad. I met him at his place in Quincy and he introduced me to a gal. Later on, I worked on the trucks with him."

The embarrassed man said that Majors liked to brag, and claimed to have been a "hit man" in Chicago. "He said he kept a twelve-gauge sawed-off shotgun down his pants leg, but I think he made it all up."

Most people Patterson interviewed still believed that Don Majors was primarily a truck driver. His CB handle was, ironically, "Dudley Do-Right."

"There was one place he always used to show up," the informant said. "Even though I heard he was driving for that outfit in Seal Beach, he never used to miss the fourth Saturday of every month at the Scarlet Circle Dance Club in Portland. That's when the interested swingers get together."

"When was the last time you saw him?" Patterson asked.

"Sometime after the first of the year."

"What was he driving?"

"As I recall, it was a bronze 1966 Chevy Impala with Nebraska plates. I didn't look at the plate numbers."

"Was he alone?"

The informant shook his head. "He had a woman with him — he told me he'd met her sometime in January 1975 in a motel in Nebraska."

Even for a cross-country trucker, Don Majors was peripatetic. He was reported here, there, and everywhere — and always as a faithful fourth-Saturday attendee at the Scarlet Circle Dance Club in Portland, Oregon.

Despite his degenerate appearance and skinny frame, Don Majors seemed to affect women the way catnip did cats. He'd been living with a divorcee, Gerda Goss,* in Quincy, sharing her home with her and her

362

teenage son, Curt,* until sometime in December. Majors also kept up cordial relations with his ex-wife, and had, indeed, used her picture when he advertised in the swingers' magazines (albeit without her knowledge).

He had brought his newest girlfriend, Shireen Gillespie,* to visit his ex-loves in Washington sometime in January, and they had apparently spent their nights in several homes where he'd once been welcomed as a lover.

If any of the former women in his life knew where Majors was, they weren't telling Bill Patterson. Neither his wife nor his former girlfriends professed to know anything about Frank Monohan. They shook their heads and said they had never heard his name. All they knew was that Majors and Shireen had left Quincy in her bronze Impala sometime during the late winter months.

With cooperation from other law enforcement agencies, Patterson arranged for stakeouts to be placed in the locations where Majors was known to visit.

But the Chevy Impala didn't surface.

Patterson tried another tactic. He checked out phone calls that were charged to Monohan's credit card long after he vanished. Many of the people the Chelan County detective called denied that they even knew

Don Majors. And nobody admitted being acquainted with Frank Monohan.

Patterson suspected that he wasn't always hearing the truth, but he understood the swingers' fear of discovery. Finding witnesses was next to impossible.

Patterson began to backtrack on Don Majors's behavior in mid-December 1974. That was shortly after Monohan disappeared. He spoke again with store personnel where Monohan's credit card had been used, and learned that Majors had been accompanied by a younger man.

"I would judge him to be possibly in his thirties," one store owner said. "He didn't say much."

The witness tapped a mug shot photo Patterson held. "This guy — you say his name is Majors — he did all the talking. We thought the young guy might have been his son."

All of the clerks picked Don Majors's picture from a ten-subject laydown as the middle-aged man who had made purchases in their stores.

Don Majors had spent thousands of dollars on December 14 — purchasing everything from sexy underwear to cameras worth three or four hundred dollars. Monohan's American Express card had also been used at a jewelry store in Yakima, Washington, a day or so later. For some reason, Majors was hopping all over the state.

"Maybe he just had the Christmas spirit," Patterson said sardonically. "He seems to have been buying presents for a lot of people."

While he was finding out more about "Dudley Do-Right" Majors, Bill Patterson was also interviewing Frank Monohan's family and friends in depth. They all knew him as a solid businessman, not given to extravagance. When he moved away from his family home, he could well have afforded an expensive apartment. Instead, he had simply put a bed, refrigerator, and a phone into the storeroom off his office. There were no windows there, and it was stuffy and drab.

"Frank always carried his Standard Oil card, the American Express card, and a phone credit card," one close friend said. "He usually carried only seven or eight dollars in cash," another friend added. "But he kept a hundred-dollar bill hidden in his wallet all the time — for emergencies. I don't recall that he ever had to use it."

Monohan's two best friends said they'd had dinner with him at the Duwamish Holiday Inn on December 12 and he had paid for the meal with his American Express card.

"I know he was alive during the day of the thirteenth," one former business associate said, "because I got a question from a ferry company about some work Frank did for them that day."

Frank Monohan's relatives told Patterson that his $300 watch was missing, along with a cowhide attaché case. His wallet — made out of alligator — was gone, too. And his electric shaver.

When Monohan's pickup was recovered, there were only 289.4 miles on the odometer since the last time it had been serviced.

"We know he put about two hundred of those miles on in short trips we were aware of," a young male relative said, "but somebody put ninety miles more on the odometer. That wasn't enough to get up to Blewett Pass and back. So someone must have driven him up to the summit in *their* car."

The letters from potential sexual partners had continued to pour into Monohan's letter drop long after he was dead. They were shocking and disturbing to his family, none of whom had any idea about his involvement with that element of society.

These swingers' letters were turned over to Bill Patterson. Some were from way across America, but several were in the Seattle or Wenatchee area. Detective Jelberg also had a packet of red-hot correspondence sent to Monohan from people he'd already met, and these too were turned over to Patterson.

Was the answer to what had really motivated Frank Monohan's murder buried somewhere in the torrid scrawls on perfume-scented stationery or in the flat-out pornography typed on plain white sheets?

Possibly. There were several letters either to or from Don Majors. Majors mostly wrote about how he was going to set Frank up with his ex-wife. Majors's tactical approach seemed to be a refinement of the old "badger game": he promised much but delivered little. He had kept Frank Monohan dangling, with explicit details of his ex-wife's charms and descriptions of her body. He kept assuring Monohan that their meeting was imminent.

And all the while, the poor woman had had no idea of what her ex-husband was doing.

Patterson felt sure he had found Frank Monohan's killer. All he had to do was find Don Majors.

Word came from a California detective, Wayne Hunter, in Sacramento. A stolen credit card owned by an Elroy Smollett* was being used to buy gas for a car registered to the woman Majors was traveling with — Shireen Gillespie.

The bronze Impala was gone, and they were now driving a maroon 1966 Chevrolet.

"We have copies of gas-charge receipts made from Idaho, south through northern California," Hunter said. "The last address we have for Elroy Smollett was in Sacramento."

"Could you contact him?" Patterson asked. "And ask him what the circumstances were when he lost his gas card?"

Detective Wayne Hunter called back later the same day. "Smollett says he was visiting a man named Ted Aust* in May and that there was a man there named 'Don.' Smollett says he'd left his wallet out in his car while they were doing some remodeling. He didn't notice the card was gone until sometime in June and reported it stolen then."

"Did he describe this 'Don'?" Patterson asked.

"Yeah. The guy is way over six feet tall, skinny, and he has a handlebar mustache. Smollett thinks he's in his late forties or early fifties."

It was Majors. It had to be. Patterson winced as he realized that his quarry now had himself a different car and credit card. At least the investigators looking for him were able to trace him, and Patterson hoped that Don Majors didn't know that.

The hits on Elroy Smollett's gas card came in with steady regularity. Majors was buying gas so often that he seemed to be driving twenty-four hours a day. He was in one town, then another, and soon a thousand miles away.

On June 27, 1975, Majors and his latest woman were still on the run, but Patterson got some startling new information.

The Seattle man claimed to be Don Majors's nephew, and he said he'd had a visit from his Uncle Don on the second of June.

"My uncle said he had a .22 that was misfiring. He brought it in and we looked at it — it was a rifle with a ten-inch silencer. We shot it into a block of wood and it worked all right. He also had a derringer."

The witness said Majors had told him that he'd killed a man, but he hadn't really believed Majors at the time.

"He sometimes tells big stories," the man said.

"Was anyone with him when he dropped by?" Patterson asked.

"Yeah — a woman named Shireen. He said she was his girlfriend. And they had another girl with them, too."

Patterson returned to Quincy, Washington, to interview Don Majors's ex-wife in her home. She denied writing any of the letters to Monohan, or that she'd ever heard of him.

"That's Don's handwriting," she said. "He has a typewriter that he sometimes uses to write this kind of letter, too. Or he'll get his girlfriends to write them. I never wanted anything to do with this smut."

"When did you two divorce?" Bill Patterson asked.

"He left home seven years ago, but he still stops by to visit. He was here on June second with a woman named Shireen. I don't know where he is now. His mother lives in Oregon, and he has a brother in Los Angeles."

She promised to call Patterson if she heard from her ex-husband.

Patterson talked again with Gerda Goss, who also resided in Quincy. She and Don Majors had lived together until late December 1974.

"When was the last time you heard from Don?" Patterson asked.

"He called on the phone and we talked on June second," she said. "He said he was in Idaho — but I thought he was right here in Quincy. He lies so much that you can't believe him. He wanted me to call an attorney in Sacramento about getting one of the Aust brothers out of jail. Aust was supposed to be a Hell's Angel, and I was to tell the lawyer that Don would be down to get him out in a couple of days. I know Ted Aust, too. He used to be Don's cellmate in prison."

The Chelan County chief deputy sensed that Gerda Goss was clearly afraid of Don Majors.

She admitted that that was true. "Don has a key to my house still," she said fearfully.

Patterson handed her his business card, and she promised to call him if she heard from Majors.

The women in Quincy had no reason to worry: Donald Kennedy Majors was far away from them on still another sadistic pursuit. The hits on the Smollett gas credit card were popping up like toadstools as the maroon Chevy headed east. Majors was buying gas, tires, batteries, car parts — anything he could sell. And he was managing to keep one jump ahead of his pursuers.

Majors had another ripe turkey to pluck. He had a voluminous file of letters and notes listing names and phone numbers. He had met them all through ads in swingers' magazines. One man, in Solon Springs, Wisconsin, sounded like a vulnerable target.

Don Majors now had two women with him — Shireen Gillespie, his latest girlfriend, and a pretty young Indian girl he'd picked

371

up in his last swing through Sacramento. Her name was Tana Chippewa.*

Using the women as bait, Majors set out to make money. He would use his most successful MO: entrap the sex-hungry suckers and then rip them off.

Bill Patterson looked at the map on his desk, marking it in red wherever Elroy Smollett's gas card had been used. Majors was heading southeast and then angling off toward the Midwest. From late May through all of June and into July, the stolen credit card had been used in California, Nevada, Arizona, Wyoming, South Dakota, Minnesota, Iowa, Wisconsin, and finally, Illinois. Smollett had been issued a new card, but his first card was kept in force. It was a relatively cheap way to track the man detectives believed to be a killer.

Don Majors and his female traveling companions made a five-day stopover in Solon Springs, Wisconsin. They visited with a well-to-do man who had written an ad looking for some "action."

The man got more action than he bargained for.

While Majors and the two woman enjoyed his hospitality, they never agreed to any sexual activity, finding one excuse after another. Their host became suspicious of his guests, who were eating and drinking him out of house and home, and he confronted them.

That was a mistake. Don Majors forced him into a root cellar beneath his home and bound his wrists and ankles tightly. Then Majors threaded a cord with a lighted lightbulb on one end, trailing it from the root cellar and over the top of the basement door. He left the lightbulb suspended inches above an open container of gasoline. He placed another full container of gas next to the homemade bomb. Majors then nailed plywood over the root-cellar door.

"Now," he'd shouted to the man trapped inside. "If you manage to get free, and try to push this door open, the hot bulb goes into the gas — and that's all she wrote. They won't find you, your house, or most of your block."

With the helpless homeowner tied up, Majors had taken his time clearing the man's home of valuables, including his practically new car.

He'd been right about the gasoline "bomb." Experts said that if the gas and the hot bulb met, the explosion resulting would have leveled the house and the adjoining homes as efficiently as TNT.

However, the man trapped in the root cellar managed to wriggle free of his bonds. He located a saw and tediously cut his way through the ceiling, allowing him to escape without disturbing the booby trap. Local investigators later disengaged the lightbulb very, very carefully.

Then they sent out teletypes asking for information on Don Majors and the two women traveling with him.

At 9:15 in the evening of July 8, 1975, the Sacramento office of the FBI received a phone call from Tana Chippewa's mother.

"My daughter just called me from Illinois," she said nervously. "A man named Don Majors has Tana captive in a motel in Matteson, Illinois. They're in room number eight and he's registered under the name of Wendell Lee. It's the Matteson Motel."

Asked for a few more details, the worried woman repeated what her daughter Tana had told her.

"She said that Majors is planning to kill a man at 9:00 a.m., a man at the motel. All I know about him is that his name is Al and he lives in Crete, Illinois. My daughter says this man she's afraid of — Don Majors — met Al through a swingers' magazine."

The special agent in Sacramento immediately sent a teletype to the FBI office in

Chicago: "The informant says Majors has a .22 derringer and a sawed-off shotgun. Use caution."

Next, Tana Chippewa called the Chicago FBI office and said that she had managed to sneak out of the room where Majors and Shireen Gillespie were asleep and was calling from the motel office. "Please hurry," she begged. "I don't want to help kill a man."

A squad of FBI agents gathered quietly outside the Matteson Motel at 1:30 a.m. Tana Chippewa tiptoed out to meet them, whispering.

"They're asleep," she told the agents. "But Don's got guns in bed with him."

The agents decided not to wait for backup and entered the room through the door that Tana had left unlocked. Majors wakened from a sound sleep to find his bed surrounded by FBI agents aiming guns at him.

When they asked where his weapons were, he gave in and pointed to a spot at the end of the bed where he'd hidden them.

It was a lucky thing that the special agents had been able to sneak up on Don Majors. Had he spotted them, there would almost certainly have been bloodshed. They found a sawed-off .22 rifle loaded, and an operative hand grenade under the covers. The .22 derringer was in Shireen Gillespie's purse.

Shireen was actually Majors's captive, too. She had been more afraid to leave the sadistic con man than Tana Chippewa was. Now, seeing Majors in handcuffs, she gave the FBI agents permission to search the Chevrolet, which was registered in her name. The car was full of more interesting items: a sawed-off bolt-action rifle, the silencer for the rifle, ammunition, rubber gloves, black leather straps used in bondage sex, an empty billfold, blank checks, and stacks of sex magazines, including *The Players, Sandra's Erotic Journal,* and *The Seekers.*

There were thirty-five Polaroid snapshots of potential playmates and/or pigeons. Most of those pictured were nude or seminude. Some were tied up, some wore masks, some were having sex with animals; there were two of a very young girl in her underwear. Young and not-so-young bodies twisted in contortions demonstrating almost every sexual position known to man — or beast — including a few that seemed entirely new, even to the FBI.

Donald Kennedy Majors had an operative seven-point indictment out on him involving weapons violations, and this was on top of the warrants out of Wyoming and Washington. A federal grand jury in Des Moines, Iowa, had issued a bench warrant for Majors on June 25 for violation of the Dyer Act, which involves taking a stolen vehicle across state lines.

His FBI rap sheet went all the way back to 1947, and he'd fallen for almost everything from being AWOL to forgery, unlawful flight, kidnapping, armed robbery, and grand theft. The list was almost an encyclopedia of crime.

Still, although he'd bragged about killing, Don Majors had never been convicted of murder. At least, not yet.

Majors was booked into jail, and FBI agents talked with Tana Chippewa and Shireen Gillespie. Shireen said she'd met Majors sometime in January when he'd checked into the motel in Nebraska where she was the manager. The long, lean "cowboy" from Washington had enjoyed a bonanza with Frank Monohan's credit cards. He turned on the charm for Shireen, a lonely woman who felt trapped and bored in her job in the Midwest motel.

When he checked out of the motel, Majors promised to call and come back. And he did. When he asked her to, Shireen willingly quit her job, and provided her car and her savings for the next meandering trip west to California. If she wondered who the credit cards belonged to that Majors used when her money ran out, or why Don was buying items in one town and selling them in another, she didn't ask questions. Her new lover's sexual charisma had her enthralled.

They'd picked up Tana Chippewa in Sacramento. Tana's "old man" was in jail and she was at loose ends. She'd quickly accepted Majors's invitation to travel with him and Shireen.

But the con games he practiced were much more than Tana had bargained for. The two women were supposed to serve as sexual bait to haul in men whose names Majors had gleaned from the swingers' magazines.

It was a pretty good scam. Victims, fleeced of their valuables, weren't anxious to go to the police. Respected citizens who had kinky sex hangups didn't want them on the public record. Even the man in Wisconsin who had almost been blown to smithereens by the gasoline-lightbulb bomb had refused to file charges.

Majors was full of braggadocio and claimed to be far more accomplished than he really was. One item found on him when he was arrested was a card issued to Frank Monohan showing he had a private pilot's license. Majors had carefully blanked out the "small plane" designation and Monohan's name. He had skillfully changed it to read that he was "Major Donald Kennedy," licensed to fly "multi-engine jets." However, the original printing remained traced in the celluloid envelope the license was carried in.

Tana and Shireen had gone along with Majors's rip-offs of his would-be swinging targets. They had seen his carefully cataloged notebooks, and they weren't in the dark about what his game was. But Tana had balked when it came to killing. That was why she'd slipped out of the motel room in Matteson to call the FBI.

And Majors's promises of a wonderful "vacation" across America had worn thin. They were eating at fast-food joints and sleeping in cheap motels. More than that, Majors constantly told the two women that they were going to have to step up their operation of enticing the secretive weirdos into traps where they could be robbed.

"We were barely making it," Tana Chippewa said. "Even when Don had stolen credit cards from his victims. He wanted money — lots and lots of it — and he didn't much care how he got it. But he just wasn't very good at it."

The case that had begun when Frank Monohan disappeared in mid-December 1974 ended its first chapter in July 1975. Majors was convicted of the charges hanging over him and was safely behind bars; the women were allowed to go free, and they traveled back to Sacramento, where Shireen moved in with Ted Aust, Majors's old prison buddy. Tana decided to wait for her man to get out of jail.

In Chelan County, Bill Patterson still didn't have what he needed to bring charges of murder against Majors in the death of Frank Monohan. Certainly there was no question that the men had known each other, and that Majors had stolen Monohan's credit cards. But that wasn't enough to convince a jury that Majors had killed Monohan. Patterson needed physical evidence or, better yet, an eyewitness. So much time had passed between Monohan's disappearance, the finding of his body, and Majors's arrest in Illinois that finding an eyewitness would be like finding an unbroken egg left on the field after the Rose Bowl.

But Patterson is a most determined man, and his personal conviction was that Donald Kennedy Majors was probably the most dangerous criminal he'd ever come up against. He wasn't about to abandon his investigation.

Majors had bragged to the women and male pals that he'd killed "thirty-three and a half people." Were these only the ravings of an egomaniac, or could his statements be true?

Majors explained the "half" by recalling how he'd shot a man in his Los Angeles apartment with a .22. Majors said he'd gone there to set up one of his "phony orgies." The bullet had allegedly hit the man in the head, but it had only knocked him unconscious.

"I convinced him he'd just had a spell or a fit," Majors laughed to friends. "He left and then he had an accident. The L.A. cops pegged it as a traffic fatality!"

Patterson now had many more names and addresses culled from the notebooks Majors carried in his travels. The stubborn detective was prepared to talk to everyone he could locate in the hope that he could find the missing link he needed. He knew that there had been a "man in his thirties" when Majors went on his buying spree with Frank Monohan's credit cards. Maybe, somewhere in his list of names, he'd find that man. It was even possible that that man had actually witnessed Monohan's murder.

One of the first people Patterson found was the man who counted as the "half" murder. Only he wasn't dead, and he hadn't been killed in a traffic accident. And he didn't live in Los Angeles. He lived in Spokane, Washington, where he held a most respected professional position.

The man, like almost all the other swingers Patterson contacted, didn't want to talk to him. Still, he finally admitted there had been an odd occurrence one evening when Majors came to his apartment. He said he'd bent over to adjust the stereo, and the next thing he knew, he was lying on the floor with a terrible headache and Majors was on top of him, twisting his arm behind his back.

"I had blood on my head, but Don told me I'd had a seizure, hit my head on a sharp corner, and that he was just trying to bring me out of it."

Patterson had little doubt that that man was walking around with a .22 slug in his head. "But he won't have an X-ray," Patterson says. "He doesn't want to know what's causing his headaches; he doesn't want to be involved in any investigation that might blow the cover off his respectability."

As far as the other thirty-three murder victims that Majors claimed, he might well have been telling the truth. More likely, he was starting with the truth and then shading it with his talent for dramatic embellishment.

Bill Patterson was in touch with law of-

382

ficers from New York to Oregon. He found dozens of cases where well-dressed businessmen's bodies were found dumped along side roads, their credit cards missing. Eight of the unsolved cases resembled Donald Majors's MO very closely and were near enough to the itinerary that Patterson charted from the credit-card hits that the Chelan County detective felt Majors could have been involved. Three murders in Tucson, Arizona, seemed to have Majors's stamp on them, and Patterson placed him fifty miles away from the death sites around the same time. There was another in Cicero, Illinois — and more across the country. All were men who had received phone calls, gone out to meet someone, and never returned.

Coincidence? Or validation of Don Majors's boasting that he was a champion killer? The term "serial killer" had not yet been coined in the midseventies, but in the more than three decades since then, several cross-country truck drivers have often proved to kill in a serial manner.

Bill Patterson's main task, however, was to forge the essential link in the Monohan case. Over the next two years, he picked up the burgeoning case file and perused it over and over again to try to find something he might have missed. He talked to hundreds of people, people caught up in Majors's life in both direct and tangential ways. Frank Monohan's murder ate at Bill Patterson, taunting him silently.

In spring 1977, Patterson journeyed to Sacramento to talk again with Ted Aust and Shireen Gillespie. He knew that Majors had stolen a credit card from one of Aust's friends in May 1975 at Aust's home in Sacramento, and he wanted to talk with Shireen again.

Shireen had long since grown disillusioned with the man who'd promised her a new home with all her furniture shipped out from Nebraska. Don Majors had said he would marry her; instead he fleeced her of her life's savings and involved her as a sexual decoy in their headlong flights across the country.

Two years later, she was more than willing to talk in detail about something Majors had once told her. Patterson wondered if it was just another of his fantasies or if it might actually be real?

"Don told me this story," Shireen began. "He told me that he'd driven across a mountain pass with some boy who had his mother's car. He told me about killing some guy and dumping him."

This *was* new information, and Patterson weighed it, hoping that it was Majors's admission to the murder of Frank Monohan.

He was thinking about it as he and Aust tore up the floorboards of a bedroom in Aust's house and crawled down into the space beneath the floor. Majors's former cellmate had suddenly recalled that, when Majors visited him in May of 1975, he'd seen him tear up some papers or credit cards before they'd repaired a sinking floor and boarded it up. That was the day that Elroy Smollett had helped with the remodeling, the day that Smollett's gas credit card vanished.

Patterson remembers that night in Sacramento well: "We were down there with the rats and the black widow spiders, and there was a storm and the lightning and thunder was rattling the house. We didn't find the torn-up credit cards, but I suddenly had a revelation that was stronger than any bolt of lightning outside. Shireen had been telling me about a 'kid with his mother's car.'

"And suddenly I knew who the second man was, the day Majors used Monohan's credit card to go on the buying spree on December 14, 1974. All the time, we thought we were looking for another man — but it wasn't another man. It was a kid, the one kid I'd talked to who'd idolized Majors, the kid who had once thought Majors was a hero.

It had to be Curt Goss! Majors lived with Gerda Goss and Curt — who was sixteen then — right up until the time Monohan disappeared!"

Patterson was on the road and headed back to Quincy, Washington, in no time. Shireen had said a boy was a witness to murder, and the boy had to be Curt Goss.

It was May 4, 1977, when Patterson confronted the now nineteen-year-old Curt Goss. When Patterson asked the youth if he'd gone to Seattle with Don Majors in December of 1974, he answered yes.

"We drove my mother's car, a 1972 Caprice."

Curt said Majors had told him the reason for their trip was to talk to a man in Seattle about the trucking business. Majors had called the man from a pay phone.

"He told me we were going to have dinner with him. And we met him at the Holiday Inn."

"What did he look like?" Patterson asked.

"Middle-aged. He had gray hair, and he was well dressed. He said his name was Frank, and he paid for a big steak dinner for all of us at the Holiday Inn."

"Which Holiday Inn?"

"The one on the Duwamish River. There used to be a drive-in theater across the highway from it."

So far, everything Curt Goss was telling him matched other information they'd had for three years. Patterson began to feel a slight thrill of anticipation. He didn't let Curt see that, though.

The conversation at dinner hadn't been about the trucking business — not at all. It had been about Majors's ex-wife. Majors had described her in glowing terms and convinced Monohan that they should leave that night to drive to Quincy so that the wealthy engineer could meet her. Although they'd already rented two rooms at the practically new motel, charged to Frank Monohan's American Express card, the two men and the sixteen-year-old boy left for Quincy. At least, Curt, who was driving, thought they were going to Quincy.

"The man — Frank — was sitting next to me in front, and Don was in the back. Don told me which turns to make, because I didn't know the roads. I followed his instructions to turn off the freeway into a small town not far from the motel. It was late and it was raining hard. We hadn't reached the Seattle city limits when Don told me to turn into a big place where a lot of trucks were parked and to stop the car. I stopped, and he looked around and told me to drive on.

"We drove all around these little side streets and then he told me to stop again in this place that was mostly vacant lots. That's when he shot Mr. Monohan."

For Patterson, it was almost unbelievable. After years of trying to get Don Majors pinned to the wall, he finally had his eyewitness, someone who had been only inches away from Frank Monohan when he was shot.

"I heard this loud explosion," the teenager continued. "And then Frank just fell over next to me. I almost drove off the road from the shock. I couldn't believe Don had actually killed the man."

Majors had told Curt Goss to keep driving toward Quincy. "He said he would kill me too if I tried to go to the police." Curt believed him; he'd just seen ample proof of what Don Majors was capable of.

They headed up I-90 toward Snoqualmie Pass some fifty miles away. To people in other cars, Frank Monohan appeared only to be asleep, but the terrified teenager could smell the blood that was dripping into puddles on the car floor. He felt as if he was living in a nightmare.

"When we got up to North Bend, Don told me we were going to stop and put Frank in the trunk. We went a little past North Bend and onto the side of the road and parked."

It was pitch dark by then, and fir trees loomed like dark monsters as Curt and Don Majors carried the deadweight of Monohan's body and loaded it into the trunk. The car seat and floor were saturated with blood, but it was dark and Majors figured no one would see it.

"We stopped at a truck stop beyond North Bend for coffee, and Don told me to shape up, that what was done was done."

"So you kept going to Blewett Pass and dumped the body?" Patterson asked.

"No," Curt said. "We turned around and went back to the Holiday Inn south of Seattle. We had those two rooms that Frank paid for, and we were beat. We slept the night there."

"Where was Frank Monohan's body?"

"It was in the trunk."

Curt Goss said they had eaten a leisurely breakfast, and then dumped Monohan's pickup truck in the back corner of a tow yard, where Don Majors didn't think it would be found for a long time.

Patterson was baffled by the thought that Frank Monohan waited in the trunk of Majors's borrowed car.

"So what happened next?" he asked, bending his head over a yellow legal pad, taking notes so Curt couldn't see the expression on his face.

"Then we went Christmas shopping. We went to a clothing store, a shoe store. He got a train set and tracks for his son. He got a camera. We went in a lot of stores."

Around noon, on December 14, they'd headed back home to Quincy. At Blewett Pass, Majors told Curt they were going to dump the body, the body that had lain in the trunk while Majors used the victim's credit card for Christmas shopping.

"I was afraid he was going to kill me, too," Curt said. "So I did everything he told me to. We waited until there were no cars, and Don took Frank's feet and I took his head and we threw him in a snowbank. Then we drove on into Wenatchee and Don made me clean the blood out of the car in the car wash there. Later, when my mom asked why the seat was wet, he told her he spilled a coke on it."

Curt said they'd gone to his mother's home, where they spent the night. He'd been afraid to tell his mother what had happened.

"I didn't tell her about it until six months later, and then we were both too frightened of him to tell anyone else."

"Would you be willing now to testify in a court of law about what you just told me?"

Patterson asked Curt.

"Yes. If it means we could put this nut away."

Frank Monohan had had no warning at all that he was about to die. He'd believed he was on the way to meet a warm and willing woman who was "dying to meet him." He hadn't even been nervous about the side trip they'd made into the little town of Auburn to look at "some trucks."

And he had died without a sound when Don Majors shot him from the backseat of Gerda Goss's car.

Curt said that he, his mother, and Majors had gone to Yakima the next day to do more "Christmas shopping."

"I knew my mother was scared because Don never had any money and now he had all those clothes and cameras, and he was buying more, but she didn't ask him about it."

Even though they hadn't told anyone about what happened, Gerda and Curt Goss had lived a life of quiet dread ever since.

"During the last two and a half years — ever since it happened," Curt Goss told Patterson, "we've had threats from Don Majors on the phone. And strangers have called. My mom and I have feared for our lives. I still do, but I think it's time that I told about this and I think he should be kept in prison."

Curt Goss said that he'd suspected Majors had dark secrets when he was living in their home.

"He changed the lock on the bedroom door and he used it for his 'office.' I could hear him typing in there. He got a lot of letters every time he went to the post office box in George. He told me he was writing a book — but I'd seen some of those magazines with the pictures in them."

"Have you had any contact with him since he went to prison?" Patterson asked.

"Yeah. He wrote me from jail. They were dirty, filthy, obscene letters like the stuff they had in those bondage magazines. I don't know why he wrote to me like that. He just seemed to like to write about it."

"Why didn't you call the police once he was in jail?"

"Because we received a phone call from a man who said he'd been in jail with Don and he said he could arrange a deal to take care of us. We were always frightened. We just burned the letters because they were too filthy to keep."

Oddly, though the case of Frank Monohan's disappearance and murder had been worked principally by Chief Deputy Bill Patterson in Chelan County and Detective

Bud Jelberg in Seattle, this new information showed that Monohan had actually been killed in King County. Patterson forwarded all the information he had to the King County Sheriff's Office, and Detective Mike Gillis took over the case.

Gillis and Detective Sergeant Harlan Bollinger talked to the teenage eyewitness and elicited the same information he'd given to Bill Patterson. He rode with them, pointing out the spot on the outskirts of Auburn where Monohan had been shot, and then leading them along the route to Blewett Pass where the body was dumped.

"Just when did you tell your mother that you'd been with Majors when he shot Frank Monohan?" Gillis asked.

"Not until the first time Detective Patterson came to talk to her. I told her then, and she started to cry. But we were so scared of him, afraid he'd come back and get us."

With the information that Bill Patterson had uncovered on Donald Kennedy Majors and the eyewitness he now had to Frank Monohan's death, King County deputy prosecutor Greg Canova brought charges of first-degree murder against Majors.

In the summer of 1978, Majors was allowed to plead guilty to second-degree murder. When he did so, there were many sighs of relief from nervous swingers all over America who now would not have to testify about their secret sex lives in open court.

Don Majors served two consecutive life sentences, where he no longer had access to a typewriter.

Frank Monohan's fate might serve as a deterrent to those would-be swingers who advertise in a whole new way in this twenty-first century, searching for "love" partners. With the Internet, it's easier to do now, and anyone online has to cope with dozens of unwelcome messages from pornographers and willing sex partners.

A shocking example of the danger of the Internet occurred shortly after I wrote the first draft of this book. A serial-killer suspect, Phillip Markoff, was arrested on charges of murder and robbery after finding his targets on Craigslist. Known as the "Craigslist Killer," Markoff was a promising medical student in New England and engaged to be married. Although the charges against him have yet to go to trial, Markoff appears to have another — secret — life, marked by gambling addiction and crimes of violence against women.

How Don Majors would have loved the Internet with its constant opportunities to find easy victims. If he is still alive, he would be nearly ninety years old now, and probably no longer a threat to anyone.

Don Majors is far past his career as a vicious con artist and killer, but there are others who fill his shoes. Your next e-mail might well be a message from another opportunist not unlike Majors.

Although he never turned down an opportunity for sensual pleasure, Majors's main goal was always to see how much he could milk from the unwary men who answered the phony ads he placed. The number of victims he robbed, beat, or killed probably won't ever be known.

Chief Deputy Bill Patterson did find out that he gained entry into the homes of lawyers, doctors, teachers, and businessmen, all people whose choice of friends — apart from the sexual lure he introduced to them — would never have included Donald Kennedy Majors. But invite him to their homes they did, and he kept their names, their addresses, their pictures, all neatly cataloged against the day he wanted more from them than changing partners.

This is a cautionary tale. Most who read it will have no interest in what Donald Majors was offering in his "sure thing" racket, but the world is full of all manner of con games.

Our trust should be given thoughtfully and only after we have time to evaluate those we meet.

How long Donald Majors would have continued in his wicked ways is an impossible question to answer. But sadistic sociopaths don't change — not as long as they are physically able to carry our their plans. Or until they are locked up. Or they die.

Majors didn't realize he was coming up against the best detectives in Seattle, King County, Chelan County, and the FBI. Nor could he have known that Chelan County's Bill Patterson would never quit until he saw Majors convicted for the cowardly murder he thought he'd gotten away with.

Most sociopaths will only break your heart, steal your money, or take your job. Sadistic sociopaths will kill you without blinking an eye.

■ ■ ■ ■

Run as Fast as You Can

■ ■ ■ ■

Seattle is a paradise for athletes of all kinds — skiers, boaters and sailors, and, of course, joggers. The Emerald City is located in a spot in Washington State where both the Pacific Ocean and the Cascade Mountains are only a little more than an hour away, and King County is rife with parks, trails, and quiet roads where traffic is light and the air is fresh and clean.

And the joggers run — some to rid themselves of pounds accumulated over the years, some to improve their heart and lung capacity, and some for the sheer joy of it. It would seem that there could be no healthier choice for young, middle-aged, and even elderly joggers. Yes, it would seem so, but that wasn't true in the late summer of 1978.

Running the popular trails in Seattle's verdant Seward Park became as dangerous as free-fall skydiving or hang gliding. Someone was watching and waiting in the dense thickets of fir, maple, and madrona trees of the vast park that edges the western shore of Lake Washington, someone consumed with thoughts of violence and killing.

Most people think of Seattle as being cloudy and rainy, but that isn't true in July and August. Temperatures rise into the nineties then, and a hundred-degree day isn't unheard of. Before the heat of these summer days becomes oppressive, many joggers choose to switch their workouts to early morning hours. With so many runners showing up at Seward Park before most people have breakfast, lone female joggers felt perfectly safe. Penny DeLeo, thirty-three, had been part of the "morning crew" — as some runners called themselves — for two months, and she felt no fear at all as she ran along paths that often seemed like tunnels through the trees.

If Penny DeLeo was aware of the murder of a young girl in the park the previous winter, she had forgotten about it. Although the homicide death of seventeen-year-old Joyce Gaunt on February 17 had gone unsolved, it hadn't even been mentioned in the local media for several months.

Everything had been "normal" in the park for so long that the specter of death was the last thing on Penny DeLeo's mind as she scribbled a hurried note to her young son at 7:30 a.m. on Tuesday, August 8.

"I've gone running," she wrote. "Will be back soon. You may watch TV until I get home. Love, Mom."

Then Penny kissed her husband good-bye as he hurried out the front door to catch a bus to work. Shortly after that, she backed her new metallic brown Toyota Celica out of their garage, and drove to Seward Park.

Penny wore a T-shirt, blue and white shorts, and green running shoes — her usual exercise attire. There was nothing unusual about this morning. She expected to be home to fix breakfast for her son within an hour, probably before he even woke up.

But this morning was to be different — earthshakingly different. Nothing in their lives would ever be the same again.

Penny DeLeo didn't return from the park all day. Her son watched television for a while, and then he got dressed and went out to play with his friends. He was curious about where his mother might be, but he was too young to be aware of the dangers of the world.

Shortly before 5:00 p.m., Penny's husband came home from work and found that she was nowhere in their house. He asked his eight-year-old son where his mother was, and was stunned when the boy said he hadn't seen her all day.

Her car was gone, the beds were unmade, and the kitchen counter was a mess of crumbs and peanut-butter smears where the boy had made himself sandwiches.

DeLeo felt the hairs stand up on the back of his neck as a sensation of absolute dread crept over him. Where was Penny? A check with her friends netted no information. No one had heard from her all day. He called Seattle police and reported his wife as a missing person, stressing that Penny had never left home before, and that it was unthinkable that she would leave their son unsupervised all day. Patrolman Dennis Falk drove to the DeLeos' home and talked to her worried husband.

Falk jotted down a description of the Toyota and its license number — IYR-544. He then drove slowly through all the parking areas in Seward Park and found no sign of the vehicle.

Next, he proceeded to parking areas along the beach. The hydroplane races, a big draw for thousands of people who attend Seattle's Seafair, had taken place only a few days before on Lake Washington. Falk checked all the possible places to park from Seward Park to some distance north of the Stan Sayre hydroplane pits.

And he didn't find a metallic brown Celica. He drove the loop road near Lake Washington where Penny DeLeo always ran, and then perused the area around the bathhouse where her husband said she normally stopped for a drink of water after her run.

But Penny DeLeo was gone. It didn't seem possible that someone could disappear from that park, which was alive with people from dawn to long after dusk on such a beautiful summer's day — but, somehow, she had. Her agonized family spent a sleepless night, waiting for a phone call, anything that would let them know she was all right.

The police couldn't take an official missing report until Penny had been gone for at least twenty-four hours. Most adults leave of their own accord, for their own reasons, and come back when they feel like it. But from the beginning Dennis Falk had a "hinky" feeling about Penny — an intuitive cop's slang for something that isn't right, even when they can't say why. And the feeling wouldn't go away.

Shortly before 10:00 the next morning, a bird-watcher tracked an osprey in Seward Park with his binoculars. Edging deeper into the woods, well beyond the trail he'd been on, the man spied what he thought was a pile of clothes. Moving closer, he was stunned to see the almost nude body of a woman lying prone on a carpet of leaves.

Forgetting completely about the habits of water birds, the man ran to a phone. Seattle Police patrol officers, Tact Squad members, and handlers with their K-9 dogs responded within minutes to the "found-body" alert.

The officers confirmed that there was a woman's corpse in the park. They cordoned the area off with yellow crime scene tape while they waited for detectives from the homicide unit to arrive.

And then, incredibly, the activity in the park escalated. A man ran up to them, shouting, "Someone just tried to rape my wife!"

The officers quickly determined that the would-be rape victim was safe at the moment — if hysterical. They obtained a description of the suspect in that attack. Since it had just occurred, they figured he was still in the park.

They wanted to find him as quickly as possible — before he managed to vanish into the crowd that had come to beat the heat of the day.

The descriptions they received from witnesses were quite similar to one another. They were looking for a black male, six feet to six feet two, and slender. According to observers, he'd been wearing a soft white hat, red and white checked pants, and a long-sleeved white shirt. That outfit would certainly make him stand out.

On police orders, Seward Park was immediately sealed off; there was no way for the rape suspect to escape unless he went by water, and that outlet, too, was monitored by boats from the Seattle Police Harbor Patrol Unit. *Air One,* the department's helicopter, was now hovering overhead.

Two of the patrol officers drove the jogging loop road as they searched for the suspect. They soon came across a pretty female jogger accompanied by her large dog. They warned her of the danger and took her safely to the park gates.

"You know," she began, "I did see a man dressed in red and white, with a floppy white hat on —"

"Where was he?"

"Near the bathhouse. He started to go down to the north end of the park as I headed south."

It was a weird situation. The Seattle police might be looking for one man who was responsible for both a murder and an attempted rape. On the other hand, they might be tracking two different men who had erupted into violence during the same twenty-four-hour period. The latter hardly seemed likely.

While the homicide crew headed to Seward Park to start their investigation into what appeared to be a murder, more and more police cars moved in to seal off all exits and to search for the man who had tried to rape the latest victim, who identified herself as Tricia Long.*

Was a killer-rapist stupid enough to return to the park the day after Penny DeLeo vanished, and then assault a second woman? A lot of killers have been known to hang around the rim of a police investigation, reliving the thrill of the murder they've committed. If he wasn't stupid, he was probably obsessed with bloodshed and wanted a front-row seat to watch what came after.

Still shaking, Tricia Long agreed to go to police headquarters to give a statement to detective Merle Carner in the Crimes Against Persons Unit.

Tricia told Carner that she had gone to the park earlier that Wednesday morning with her husband, their baby, and her sister-in-law. The two women planned to jog the loop, as Tricia was training to run in a women's marathon and wanted to scout the course.

"We made one loop together," she said. "and then my sister-in-law got a really bad cramp in her leg and we couldn't massage it away. So I told her I could run alone. My sister-in-law went back to feed the ducks with my husband and our baby."

"What happened next?" Carner asked.

"As I was running, I could see this tall black man up ahead, who was sitting under a tree," Tricia recalled. "When I got within about twenty-five feet of him, he stood up and moved onto the pathway. He didn't look at me — he was facing away from me. He was just standing in the middle of the asphalt path."

"You weren't frightened at that point?"

"No, not really. He didn't seem menacing, but he was acting kind of strange — fidgety — with his hands at his waist. As I passed him, he didn't make any move toward me. I kept right on running. But then, about ten yards farther on, I heard some footsteps running up behind me."

Tricia's words came faster, and Merle Carner noted that her face was washed of color.

"Almost simultaneously," she said, "he grabbed me from behind with his left arm around my shoulder, trying to put his hand over my mouth. He wasn't holding me that tightly, but he said, 'I kill you! I kill you!'"

She said she'd fought the stranger, trying to get free of his grip on her shoulder. She had looked to see if he had a weapon or if he was just threatening her.

"I saw a whitish, plastic handled, short kitchen knife about five inches long — like a steak knife."

"What went through your mind at that point?" Carner asked.

"Naturally, I feared that he was going to rape me. But, when he said, 'I kill you! I kill you,' I believed he would. He was pushing me from behind, trying to get me off the roadway toward the woods. We struggled. I started screaming my husband's name and yelling 'Help!' I was fighting him with my arms and legs as hard as I could.

"It seemed like an eternity, but I think it was only about ten seconds. Then he suddenly let go of me and went running off into the woods."

Tricia Long recalled running faster than she had ever run before, screaming at the top of her lungs, and her husband and sister-in-law heard her and came running. They had tried to call police via a marine radio on one of the boats at the park's dock, but that failed.

It was at that point that the Long family had come across the police officers who were the first responders to the "found-body" report.

Tricia was sure she could identify her assailant if she saw him again.

It was 10:15 a.m. when detectives Ted Fonis and Wayne Dorman checked out the fully equipped crime scene van. The morning was warm and hazy, and the sun was blurred by a smoky overcast caused by forest fires high up in the mountains east of Seattle. Fonis and Dorman were two of the most experienced homicide detectives in their division, having spent many years there honing their craft. They worked together easily, rarely having to speak. They could almost read each other's minds.

After passing through the tight cordon at the entrance to Seward Park, the homicide team was directed to a wooded area close to the bathhouse. It was near the north loop on the lower level of the park, and they were glad to see that it was roped off and closely guarded by several police officers.

The two detectives walked up an inclined path into a thick cluster of trees where the path became a lonely trail. The grass here was matted down, as if a struggle had taken place.

They saw soiled clothing just off the trail: a woman's top, white with blue trim; a pair of running shorts of the same colors; and beige panties.

Her body lay twenty-five feet away. She was nude, save for a white bra, and a pair of green and blue running shoes and socks.

"She can't weigh more than a hundred pounds," Wayne Dorman commented. "She couldn't have put up much of a fight."

The victim lay on her stomach, with her legs spread wide. They couldn't yet see her face but saw that she had chestnut-colored hair, cut short.

"I guess we can say that robbery wasn't a motive," Ted Fonis said. "She's still wearing a couple of thousand dollars' worth of jewelry."

They looked at her left arm where she still wore an expensive wristwatch. She had a gold band ring with a large diamond on the third finger of her left hand. Ironically, the watch was still running and gave the correct time.

"Whoever he was," Dorman said, "he was angry. If it was a 'he.' Either he knew her and wanted to punish her, or he was mad at the world."

They could see that the petite woman had been stabbed again and again, too many times to count — in her back, buttocks, thighs, even her neck. Her right wrist was cut so deeply that the tendons had been severed, possibly a defense wound suffered when she tried to fight back.

Oddly, a pattern was etched in blood on her thighs and back. It looked like the crisscross soles of tennis shoes. The investigators saw that the same pattern appeared in patches of sand close to the body.

"The canine unit just ran by me," a patrolman called to them. "They're tracking someone."

If the dog had picked up on a scent, the killer had probably returned to the scene of his crime, because this woman in front of Fonis and Dorman had been dead for at least twenty-four hours. Rigor mortis was well established, making her joints rigid, and there were other signs that she had lain in the woods overnight.

Looking through recent missing persons' reports brought to the park, the detectives were almost certain they had found Penny DeLeo. The clothes were right, the physical description was right, and she had last been known to be heading for Seward Park.

The King County Medical Examiner, Dr. Donald Reay, responded personally to the scene.

"Doc Reay," as detectives called him, knelt next to the body, examining her back first.

"The bruises near her tailbone and on her

upper right hip occurred before her death," Reay said. "But all these other scrapes on the rest of her back and legs happened after she died. Her killer may have dragged her deeper into the woods so no one could see her."

Penny DeLeo's murderer had shown no respect at all to her body, a significant psychological reaction. And this tended to strengthen the impression that he had been consumed with a terrible rage.

Before they attempted to turn the victim's body over, Reay, Dorman, and Fonis carefully placed bags over her hands, securing them with rubber bands. If she had her killer's skin under her fingernails, or hairs from his head, or anything else that might help to identify him, they didn't want to lose it.

When Penny DeLeo was moved to a supine position, they could see that her white bra was stained crimson over her breasts. And now, more wounds were apparent. In a murderous frenzy, the man who assaulted Penny had stabbed her in her chest, neck, and abdomen. A slender gold chain with a precious stone setting was caught in her hair.

"She's been in the same position since she died," Reay pointed out, tracing the bright purplish-red striations on her chest, stomach, and legs. They had formed when her heart stopped pumping, and blood sank to the lowest portion of her body.

"This lividity pattern is classic for the prone position she was found in," Reay said. "There is no secondary lividity that we'd see if she was moved before the initial pattern was fixed."

Detective Wayne Dorman began to bag the evidence found at the scene: Penny DeLeo's clothing and running shoes, her jewelry, and even some of the matted plants and weeds that were stained with her blood. The detectives also took dozens of photographs of the body and the surrounding area.

Penny DeLeo had been a strong, vigorous young woman in the peak of health, but no woman as small as she was — or even a tall, husky woman — could have withstood what appeared to be a extraordinarily violent attack. A number of the knife wounds had probably penetrated her arteries and vital organs.

From the position of her body, the motive for the young mother's murder appeared to be rape — or attempted rape. Perhaps autopsy findings would tell the investigative crew something more.

Penny DeLeo's car hadn't been found in Seward Park or within miles of it. It was still missing. If car theft was the reason she was attacked, there would have been no need to kill her. It would have been so easy to simply overpower her and take her car keys.

A description of the missing Toyota Celica was broadcast to all patrol units in the city, along with an admonition to avoid touching the vehicle if it was located. "This vehicle may be prime evidence in an open homicide case."

When Doc Reay finished his survey at the murder site, Penny DeLeo's body was removed by the medical examiner's deputies to await a complete postmortem exam.

As detectives Fonis, Dorman, and Moore prepared to clear the scene, they received news that the patrol units had a suspect in custody. "He's on his way into your offices."

A patrol officer searching the southeast portion of the park had seen a flock of crows suddenly take to the air as if they'd been startled. As he watched, he saw a tall figure running toward the water. The officer radioed his position to other police personnel in the park. Tact Squad officers Brian Petrin and Larry Miller were just above the area where the fleeing man had been spotted. They quickly drove their car onto a grassy sweep and spotted the man, who was still running.

But the tall runner had managed to get himself into a dead end when his pursuers drove up to him, blocking him.

He had nowhere left to go when Petrin and Miller leapt from their vehicle with guns drawn.

"Lie on the ground," Petrin ordered him.

The suspect complied and moved his hands to his back so he could be handcuffed. When they searched him, they found no knife — or weapon of any kind.

He wore no hat, so they didn't know if he was the would-be rapist who'd had a floppy white hat, but the rest of his clothing matched the description of the man cops all over Seward Park were looking for: wine, red, and white plaid pants and high-topped tennis shoes. If he'd had a white shirt on earlier, he was bare-chested now. His pants were wet — as if he had been wading in the lake.

Advised of his rights, the suspect said he understood.

Although he was bigger than most grown men, at six feet one and 170 pounds, he told Petrin and Miller that he was only fifteen years old. When they looked at him more closely, they could see that was probably true; he had a youthful cast to his features, and areas on his jaw where whiskers hadn't sprouted yet.

"What's your full name?" Larry Miller asked.

"Lee Wayne Waltham."*

"What were you doing in the park this afternoon?"

"I just came down to swim about twenty minutes ago," he mumbled.

"How'd you get in the park?" Officer Miller asked. "We've had it blocked off for almost three hours."

"A guy I know dropped me off from his boat, and I waded in."

At Seattle police headquarters, detectives Billy Baughman and John Boatman prepared to question the youthful rape suspect. His clothes were taken into evidence, and he was handed coveralls to put on.

Now, three teams of detectives were working on the intricate case — or possibly *two* cases. There was still no way of knowing if the cases were intertwined or mere coincidence. Half of the seventeen men assigned to the homicide unit were deep into one phase or another of the murder or the attempted rape.

Detectives Chuck Schueffele, Merle Carner, and Al Lima were talking with the attempted-rape victim, Ted Fonis and Wayne Dorman were processing evidence from the murder scene, and now John Boatman and Billy Baughman were seeing the prime — and only — suspect for the first time.

Investigators, who had spread out around Seward Park, located a maple tree adjacent to the route Tricia Long had taken. It was an ordinary big-leaf maple and there were scores of them in the park. However, this one had a pile of cigarette butts littering the ground beneath it. Anyone who sat or stood there would have had a perfect view of the jogging path in both directions.

Had the rapist and/or killer waited there? He could have had plenty of time to pick and choose the victims that appealed to him most, and the women were probably unaware of his presence as they came jogging by his look-out spot. The huge tree hid him, and he could also have reassured himself that no one else was nearby to identify him.

Lee Waltham said he lived with his parents a block from the park. Baughman and Boatman spent a great deal of time going over the Miranda rights form with him, and they asked that a detective from the Juvenile division be present during their interview.

The suspect admitted early in the questioning that Waltham wasn't his real name. "My last name is really DuBois,"* he said.

"Why didn't you give the first officers your real name?" John Boatman asked.

Waltham/DuBois shrugged. "I don't know, really. I guess I was scared — Waltham is my real father's name, but sometimes I use my stepfather's name. That's DuBois. And that's the name I use. That's my half brother's name — he's eight."

They let that go; they could check on whether they had his legal name later.

"What did you do this morning?" Boatman asked. "Like when did you get up, where did you go, and so forth?"

"I got up about nine thirty, and walked over to the hydroplane pits. They were still cleaning up from the races 'cause, you know, people leave a lot of trash behind."

DuBois said he'd watched the cleanup crews for a while, and then he'd met a man who'd offered him a ride in his boat.

"Then he took me over by the fish hatchery and let me out in the shallow water," the tall youth said. "I waded in the water, trying to catch some little fish that were there. I kept my shoes on because I was afraid the crawfish would bite me. I was just getting out to take my shoes off when the two policemen

418

arrested me."

"Did you assault a woman earlier this morning?" Baughman asked.

"No, I didn't do it."

"Didn't do what?" Baughman asked immediately.

"Whatever you're asking me about."

"What did you do yesterday?" Boatman asked.

DuBois's answer came quickly, almost as if he'd memorized it. "I got up around six thirty and went to the high school to play basketball. I got home at nine. I met my cousin Reilly Jones,* who's up visiting from L.A., and we went walking over to Boeing Hill. We got home about one thirty. I worked around home, watched TV with my little brother, had dinner, and then did some yard work. When it was dark, I watched the Tuesday night movie and the program after that, and went to bed around eleven."

It was a very precise, complete schedule of the day before, almost too precise.

"Did you kill that girl yesterday?" Boatman cut in, startling DuBois.

"I didn't do that."

DuBois's statements seemed innocent enough, but he'd been wearing pants exactly like the ones Tricia Long had described. There weren't a lot of double-knit slacks in a plaid pattern that featured wine, red, and white. The socks he still wore looked as though they had bloodstains on them. That could be tested in the crime lab. His shoes were Nike tennis shoes with a distinctive ridged pattern. Criminalists would also be able to tell if that pattern matched the marks on Penny DeLeo's back and was etched in the sand near her body.

The investigators pointed out time factors involved in the two crimes and the evidence they had already uncovered.

"There's simply no way that you could have gotten into or out of Seward Park after that woman was attacked by the rapist," Billy Baughman said. "Either our harbor boats or the patrol-car cordon would have stopped you."

The teenage suspect stared at him, shrugged, and made no comment, but little beads of perspiration dotted his forehead.

"Do you want to talk about it now?"

Lee DuBois said nothing.

"The victim from this morning has already identified your pants — she's here in our office, and she says she can identify the man who grabbed her," Lieutenant Bob Holter said quietly. "Did you do it?"

Now, the youth silently nodded his head.

"Did you kill the woman in the park yesterday?"

Again, he nodded his head.

"What did you do with the knife?"

"I dropped it."

DuBois agreed to give Billy Baughman and John Boatman an account of his crimes. Before taking a statement, the detectives tried to contact Lee's family, calling their home every ten minutes for more than an hour.

No one answered.

Although they are always blamed for what their offspring do, no real guidelines exist to predict which parents are going to have problem children. There are so many causes for teenagers going astray, and, sometimes, there is no cause at all. Lee DuBois was a teenager whose actions — whatever they might be — would surely prove agonizing to his parents.

Ironically, Lee's mother was a woman whose many years of education had been spent learning to deal with children's problems. She held a doctorate in educational psychology. Her second husband and Lee's stepfather was a Boeing engineer. The family lived in a very nice house in a wealthy neighborhood only a few blocks from Seward Park.

On the surface, Lee's home appeared to be

stable, happy, and secure.

But that was only on the surface, and like most families, there were secrets no one knew about.

On August 9, 1978, Lee DuBois gave a taped statement to detectives Baughman and Boatman, while Juvenile detective Ron Massie stood by.

"On August eighth," the youth began, "I walked to the tennis courts in Seward Park about six thirty. It was too hot to sleep, and I wanted to find a place to put in my toy hydroplane. I walked halfway around the road that leads around the park. I then sat down in the shade for a while between the road and the beach near the restroom. A Samoan man came up to me. I told him my sinuses were bothering me and he told me he had sinus trouble also, and he gave me a yellow pill."

There were many Samoan families in Seattle, and the University of Washington football squad was blessed with a number of them — who quickly became athletic heroes. Still, DuBois's story had a dreamlike quality to it, and the detectives wondered if it was true.

DuBois said he didn't want to take the pill because it had no "writing" on it to show what it really was. When the "Samoan" told him it was because it was the "improved kind," that reassured him and he'd swallowed the pill.

After the stranger left, DuBois recalled that he saw a girl jogging down the road. "I would say she was about twenty-six, a white girl in shorts which were blue or red. She jogged by me and said, 'He got you, huh?'

"I knew she meant the Samoan as she smiled at him as he went up the trail off the road."

Lee said the woman paused a few moments and then began jogging again. He said he was beginning to feel peculiar from the pill he'd ingested, and he got up and ran after the woman.

"She stopped — as if she had a cramp — and I asked her what she meant by what she'd said, but she didn't tell me. She laughed and started running. I ran after her. I put my left arm around her neck and kept asking her what she'd meant, but she still wouldn't tell me. Then I took my knife out of my pocket and took it out of the case. I pointed the blade at her, saying, 'You'd better tell.' She said, 'Okay, but put the knife away.'"

DuBois had complied, and he described the knife as a "fish" knife, about six inches long, and said it had a wooden case — designed so that it would float.

"I told the woman we were going back to the bathrooms to see if the Samoan dude was still around. The woman was walking ahead of me up a trail.

"She said I'd *ordered* her up the trail, but I denied that. I turned around and headed back down the trail when the knife fell out of my pocket.

"I turned around and saw that she had picked it up. I told her to give it back. She told me to come get it, and began waving it at me. I grabbed one of her wrists and cut myself slightly on two fingers. She fell down during the struggle. She had her back to me as she began to get up. She was about to run away when my mind kept saying, 'Kill her — kill her.' I walked up to her and stabbed her five times in the back. She fell facedown and was trying to get up when I ran away. When I walked out of the trail I saw the Samoan dude and he was shaking his head at me, saying 'Tch . . . tch . . . tch.' I hit him with my fist and then started running. He chased me for a short way and then stopped."

DuBois said he had gone home then.

"What were you wearing at that time?"

"My blue coat and my maroon and beige pants. Prior to running away, I stepped on her neck and her back. I was wearing my

Nike basketball shoes."

The suspect said he had returned to the park the next day to see if he had killed the woman.

"I stayed in the road and looked up, but I didn't go up where she was. I don't know why I killed the girl. Something just kept telling me to do it."

Lee DuBois also admitted to assaulting Tricia Long, but again, he hadn't been in control of his feelings. The voice inside him had told him to "kill . . . kill."

At this point, detectives were finally able to reach the suspect's parents. His mother insisted that all questioning stop, and she said she was going to contact a lawyer. The investigators agreed to her request, and Lee DuBois was taken to the Youth Service Center, where he was placed in the high-security detention section.

Were his violent actions on August 8 and 9 surprising? Not really. When the Seattle investigators checked Juvenile records, they found that Lee had been in trouble before. He'd been a runaway when he was only seven, involved in vandalism when he was ten, and accused of "indecent liberties" when he was just twelve.

He did have a history of sinus problems but had never been known to take drugs of any kind or to drink alcohol. He was active in football, basketball, and track.

It was a dreadful thing to contemplate, but it looked like a boy little more than fifteen years old was behind the ugly murder and attempted rape in Seward Park.

Although DuBois had admitted the murder and the attack to Billy Baughman and John Boatman, he had resolutely denied that there was any sexual motivation in his crimes. He could not — and would not — explain how Penny DeLeo's clothes had come off, and he grew very disturbed when any mention of sex was brought into the interview. Nor would he discuss what had happened to Penny DeLeo's car.

The postmortem examination of Penny De-Leo's body showed that she was five feet, four and a half inches tall, and weighed only ninety-two pounds — no match at all for a youth over six feet tall who outweighed her by almost seventy-five pounds.

Assistant Medical Examiner Dr. John Eisele found thirty-one stab wounds scattered over the hapless woman's body. As Dr. Don Reay and the first detectives on the scene had suspected, many of her knife injuries would have been almost instantly fatal. Her jugular vein had been severed and her heart, lungs, and abdominal organs pierced. Her right wrist had been cut so deeply that the tendons were severed, as well as the ulnar and radial arteries.

If ever there was an example of overkill, this was it. Penny had also been hit hard in the right eye by some kind of blunt object — possibly a fist. The only saving grace for those who loved her was that she had probably not had time to be afraid, and died with the first few knife thrusts. If rape had been attempted, it had not been consummated.

That was very small comfort.

As the news media reports of the murder and attack in Seward Park escalated, homicide detectives received phone calls from several joggers who had seen a man in the park who seemed to be acting peculiarly.

One man said he'd been jogging in the park on August 8 at 7:15 a.m. and he'd observed a tall, slim black male watching two female joggers. The man was obviously trying to keep his face covered. He'd worn a white hat, light jacket, and solid-color pants. Several women had also seen the tall young man wearing the floppy white hat.

At 8:00 p.m. on August 9, the Port of Seattle Police recovered Penny DeLeo's Toyota Celica near the First Avenue South bridge, miles west of Seward Park. The car was taken to the Seattle Police Department's processing room for latent-print examination.

Criminalists found Lee DuBois's fingerprints inside Penny DeLeo's car. They also determined that the ridges on the bottom of the suspect's shoes matched the prints etched in blood on her body.

The net was cinching tighter.

On August 10, detectives interviewed still another young woman who had been attacked in Seward Park — a day before Penny DeLeo's murder. This woman, Janet Carroll,* a nurse employed in a Seattle hospital, told them that she had been jogging in the park on August 7 at 7:00 p.m.

"I was running on the east loop road," she said, "when I saw a tall, dark young man. I jogged by him and then I heard footsteps behind me. He grabbed me and held something sharp against my stomach. Then he threw me over the bank onto the rocks on the lakeshore. I started to crawl back up and saw a male jogger approaching. When I screamed for help, the boy who'd grabbed me ran."

Ms. Carroll said the teenager who'd attacked her wore blue jeans and a light blue top with writing on it.

The MO of the suspect seemed set, although, of course, there was no way of knowing for sure if he had used the same techniques with Penny DeLeo. She could no longer tell police how the man had captured her. From what Lee said of his deadly encounter with her, it sounded very similar to the other victims.

The tall youth's pattern was to stand in the running path, facing away from the joggers, let the women pass him, and then run after them, grabbing them from behind and threatening them with a knife. Now, there was an attack on August 7, a murder on August 8, and a third assault on August 9. There were probably other rape attempts or even completed rapes, but the victims had been too embarrassed to report them.

On August 16, the King County Juvenile Court declined jurisdiction over Lee DuBois; he would be tried as an adult for murder in the first degree and two counts of assault.

Detective Dick Reed joined the probe, and he obtained a search warrant for inspection of the suspect's room. Reed made a list of items that might be in that room, but they could also be somewhere in Seward Park: a long-sleeved sweatshirt believed to have been worn by DuBois during the murder, the car keys to Penny's Toyota, the white-handled fishing knife, a floppy white hat, blue jeans, jean jacket, and a baby blue T-shirt with writing on it.

Lee's room in the handsome residence near the park was furnished impeccably: the floor was carpeted, it had its own private bathroom, TV and stereo, and floor-to-ceiling sliding doors opening onto a lushly landscaped yard. Lee could clearly come and go through the sliders without his parents knowing.

The room was very neat, and Lee DuBois's clothes hung on hangers in the closet — all pointing the same way. He had a wardrobe any teenager would envy.

Accompanied by the suspect's mother and his lawyer, Dick Reed and Ted Fonis searched for the missing clothes. They found several pairs of blue jeans, jean jackets, and a light blue shirt with "Adidas" printed on it. All the clothing had been washed, and at this point it would be hard to isolate blood spots if they had been there. Still, some of the jeans bore dark stains, worth analyzing to check for any vestige of blood.

Dick Reed checked off just a few items listed in the search warrant, but there weren't many left. Next, they did a grid search of Seward Park, beginning at the spot where Penny DeLeo's body was found. They failed to turn up any of the items sought. The knife, car keys, and floppy hat were gone, perhaps hidden in the waters of Lake Washington or somewhere in the thick vegetation.

Reed received a call from still another female jogger who had seen a tall black male in the park early on the morning of August 8 — just about the time Penny DeLeo would have been jogging.

"He was sitting under a big maple tree," she said, "and watching joggers on the trail. I was alone, but there were several people running near me. I guess I was lucky."

"Yes, you probably were," Reed said, wondering if she really could fathom just how lucky she was.

Clearly, Penny DeLeo had been chosen for attack, possibly because she had the misfortune to be jogging alone and rounded the trail loop at a time when no one else was around.

And possibly for her shiny new car.

Lee DuBois's only alibi for where he was at the time was Reilly Jones, his cousin from Los Angeles. Jones had already returned to L.A., but the Seattle homicide detectives asked that a Los Angeles Police Department detective interview him.

Reilly Jones's statement to the California detective filled in many of the blank spots during the three-day period when DuBois allegedly brought down a reign of terror on females in the park.

Reilly said he'd been in Seattle since the middle of July, and had spent a lot of time with his cousin Lee. They'd gone to Seward Park on the afternoon of August 7.

"Lee told me that he would have a car the next day from one of 'his girls,'" Reilly recalled. "I wasn't sure what he meant by that, but he took off about seven p.m. and headed toward the jogging trail. I didn't feel like going with him, so I went home. He came home at eight and told me again he was going to have a car tomorrow."

(Janet Carroll, the nurse, was seized on the jogging trail at 7:00 p.m. on August 7, and got away from her attacker.)

Jones said that he had seen his cousin tuck a short-bladed fishing knife in the elastic anklet band of his right sock on either August 6 or 7. "He told me he carried it for protection."

Reilly Jones said he thought Lee was just blowing smoke about getting a car — he wasn't even old enough to have a driver's license. But on August 8, Jones said that Lee wakened him by tapping on his window at 11:00 a.m.

"He was tapping with car keys. There was only one key on the ring."

DuBois had bragged, "I told you I was going to get a car!"

Lee changed his clothes, and Reilly saw him throw a pair of green corduroy pants into the closet. Then Lee insisted on taking Reilly for a ride in the new shiny-brown Toyota Celica.

"It was hidden down the street so Lee's mom — 'Dr. Sue' — wouldn't know about it," Reilly said. "And he told his little brother who's eight to keep quiet about it."

Reilly had his doubts about where the car had come from. As far as he knew, Lee didn't have any girlfriends, much less one who would let him drive her brand-new car. But he went along. They drove to a drugstore to buy candy, and then cruised aimlessly around the southwest section of Seattle for about an hour.

"We were headed back toward Lee's house when the car ran out of gas. He told me we were going to have to walk home. I saw him throw the car key into some brush. When I asked him why and told him 'That dude's gonna get you for throwing his key away,' he wasn't worried at all.

"He just said, 'No. Sh— *he* won't.' "

They were miles from Lee's house, and it took them several hours to walk home. They spent the rest of the day watching TV, and

Lee DuBois never mentioned just how he'd gotten the car.

"What was his mood?" the LAPD detective asked. "Did he act different than he usually does?"

"Naw. He was just his usual self."

"Did he have any scratches on him?"

"I didn't see any."

The next day — August 9 — Reilly Jones hadn't seen his cousin at all.

"He was gone at eleven that morning when I woke up. I haven't seen Lee since we went to bed on the eighth. We were tired from walking miles after the car ran out of gas."

Was it possible that DuBois had seen Penny DeLeo in the park before, knew she ran every morning before 8:00, and had coveted her new car? Even if that was the only motive, it didn't explain why he had attacked women the day before and the day after her murder.

Although the category wasn't yet known in 1978, in retrospect it's clear that Lee DuBois had all the traits of a "spree killer." "Serial killers" weren't categorized at the time, either. Until the early eighties, every killer with multiple victims was considered a "mass murderer."

Spree killers erupt suddenly, striking day after day after day — until they are caught.

Often they take suicidal chances. Lee DuBois was captured three days after he began raping and killing, and it was extremely fortunate that he was. He might have run up a toll even more devastating than he already had.

Lee DuBois went to trial twice. His first trial, in February 1979, answered some of the questions about why and how a fifteen-year-old boy could have grown up to be a spree killer.

As his jury listened, transfixed by the perversity and cruelty of Lee's crimes, the testimony detailed his horrendous early years. He hadn't had the safe and secure childhood that most people assumed he had. His mother's first marriage — to his natural father — had been marred and then destroyed by the "outrageous outbursts" of Lee's father.

The crux of DuBois's defense plan was that he was mentally ill and unable to differentiate between right and wrong at the time of his crimes. Under Washington State law, this means "unable to perceive the nature and quality of the act."

The prosecution did not deny that the defendant was *clinically* mentally ill, but the State contended that he was *legally* aware of what he was doing as he stabbed Penny

DeLeo thirty-one times and assaulted the other two joggers.

Now, his mother dabbed at tears as she painfully recalled her first marriage. She testified that her former husband's outbursts usually began as he sat in silence at the foot of his bed. Predictably he would get up and begin to beat his head against the wall.

When this happened, Lee, who was only a toddler, screamed in terror. At one point, when he was eighteen months old, his father had pulled a gun on his mother.

"I grabbed the barrel of the gun and was shot through the hand," she recalled. "Then I shot my husband. I don't remember how many times."

Their one-and-a-half-year-old child was showered with his parents' blood, still warm as it saturated his clothing. Although his mother had carried him from the bedroom, he continued to scream so frantically that she could not calm him down. It was a major emotional trauma for the child.

The couple had been treated in the trauma unit of Harborview Medical Center, and they both survived. No charges were brought, but their union was shaky from then on. They eventually divorced after a five-year marriage.

"When my husband got that way," Dr. Sue

DuBois testified, "I'd reach for a pitcher of ice water I kept in the refrigerator. Throwing it on him was the only way to get him to come to his senses."

She made no attempt to diagnose what was wrong with him, but it's likely that he was bipolar, with a tendency to be depressed more of the time than ebullient. His violent rages could not be controlled without his getting a face full of water and ice cubes.

It is quite possible that Lee had some genetic input from his father's mental health issues, but it was difficult to say whether nature or nurture had turned him into what he had become.

Dr. DuBois told the court that she herself usually jogged in Seward Park each morning.

"What do you think would have happened if you had gone to Seward Park the morning of the eighth of August?" defense attorney Aaron asked.

"It's very scary to me," Lee's mother replied. "Based on his unusual behavior — he stares at me blankly and sits on his bed the way his father did sometimes — and because I'm a jogger, it could mean, I guess, it could have been me."

For the lay members of the jury, the possible psychological aberrations were getting very heavy indeed. An Oedipal attachment, perhaps? A teenager who felt both dependent on and resentful of his mother?

The psychiatrists called to testify all had opinions about what was wrong with Lee DuBois. Those testifying for the Defense said that he was a paranoid schizophrenic who heard voices and believed himself to be possessed by evil spirits. Those speaking for the prosecution deemed him sane under the M'Naughton Rule and fully responsible for the consequences of his actions.

After twelve hours of deliberation, the jury signaled that they were hopelessly deadlocked on the question of legal sanity as it might apply to the defendant. A mistrial was declared. Ten jurors had voted for conviction, with two holding out for acquittal by reason of insanity.

They were dismissed, and plans for a new trial began.

In late April 1979 DuBois went on trial again for the same charges. The second trial, like the first, was lengthy and involved. It lasted for two and a half weeks. But the outcome was different this time. On the third of May, the jury deliberated only five hours before returning a guilty verdict.

Lee Wayne DuBois faced a life sentence.

■ ■ ■ ■

Justice for Penny DeLeo, Tricia Long, and Janet Carroll was dealt with under our criminal justice system. But never for Joyce Gaunt.

Joyce Francine Gaunt never had much of a chance in life. She was mentally challenged from birth owing to fetal alcohol syndrome. Her mother had ingested far too much alcohol during her pregnancy, damaging Joyce before she was born.

Joyce's murder has never had closure. Detectives worked hard on her homicide, but there were still a number of questions that demanded answers — especially in light of the August crimes in Seward Park. And, indeed, of other homicides that came years later.

Joyce spent her short life being shuttled from one foster home to another. Her last was in a group home on Capitol Hill in Seattle's central district. She attended Pacific School, an institution for special needs children. It was hoped that she might one day be able to live on her own, and even hold a job. She was able to take buses by herself, to perform simple chores, but her lack of reasoning power hindered her. She was often stubborn, confused, and unhappy over her mental limitations. On occasion, she ran away from the group home, resentful of the discipline and restrictions there.

On February 16, 1978, she was seen waiting for her regular bus at 4:30 p.m. as dusk settled over Seattle. She should have been home by five or a little after. Her houseparents became anxious as the hours passed and she didn't arrive at the group home. A few minutes past midnight, their phone trilled and they leapt to answer it. It was Joyce, and she talked to the housefather. She would not say where she was, but she didn't sound as if she were in trouble. If she was in danger, she didn't realize it.

Her houseparents urged her to come home, and she quickly hung up. Or perhaps someone with her hung up the phone.

Nine hours later, Joyce Gaunt's pathetic body was discovered in Seward Park — close to the bathhouse and only a short distance from where Penny DeLeo would be found six months later.

Joyce, too, was nude, and lying on her face. Someone had crushed her skull with a heavy object, and she had been strangled.

From that day to this, no one knows where Joyce Gaunt spent the night of February 16 or how she reached Seward Park, many miles south of the group home where she lived.

She would have been as trusting and naive as a child of eight or ten, yet she looked like a fully developed woman.

Seattle detectives have wondered if there is any connection between the death of Joyce Gaunt and Lee DuBois's spate of violence six months later. The crime scene is the same, the MO is very similar, but DuBois declined to discuss this earlier killing. And so the case of Joyce Gaunt remains open. It's even possible that she was an early victim of the Green River Killer — Gary Ridgway — who also left victims in Seward Park as he prowled King County in the eighties, leaving at least fifty young women dead.

Each of these teenagers — Lee and Joyce — met a tragic end. DuBois, whose background was full of promise, who came from brilliant parents, and who lived in an apparently happy home where finances were never a problem, served years in prison.

Joyce Gaunt, whose life was blighted even before birth, had no life ahead of her at all. Perhaps each of them was so scarred by early influences that there could be no other fate for them than what they drew.

Penny DeLeo's fate is harder to contemplate. The little boy she left a note for is close to forty now. Nothing can ever make up for the loss of his mother during his formative years.

Several of the detectives who worked on DuBois's case(s) have passed away, and all the rest have retired.

Dr. Susan DuBois remained married to Lee's stepfather until the elder DuBois passed away in 2007.

As far as I can determine, Lee DuBois has been out of prison for years. He is listed in local phonebooks. There is no public record of his re-offending.

■ ■ ■ ■

THE DEADLY VOYEUR

■ ■ ■ ■

Except for the fact that it is often torn by violent winds and thunderstorms, Enumclaw, Washington, has always been considered one of the safest towns in the state. Set in the far southeast reaches of King County, it's a small town in the very nicest, homiest sense. It snows more there, and summer gardens freeze over sooner there than in the rest of the county, because its elevation is higher. Only 6,000 people lived in Enumclaw in the midseventies; some commuted thirty-five miles to Seattle or to Tacoma. More were farmers or worked in the businesses that serviced the town itself. Enumclaw wasn't known for anything but the county fair and a bakery with the best homemade bread in the state.

In short, it has always been the kind of town where a city dweller will go for a Sunday drive and inevitably begin to think about selling his split-level house in Seattle's spreading megalopolis, to opt instead for the quieter life of Enumclaw.

Only a generation or two ago, it was the sort of town where you could send your kids down the road to the store and never have to worry about it.

That was back in the day.

But then in the eighties and nineties, the elusive Green River serial killer left the bodies of some of his hapless teenage victims near Enumclaw. It was a tempting place to hide his forbidden carnage because the town sits surrounded by designated wilderness areas, dams, and rivers, all in the massive shadow of Mount Rainier.

But long before Gary Leon Ridgway began killing his estimated four to five dozen victims, there was another killer who tracked the innocent near Enumclaw. He was so angry and frustrated that he didn't care who he attacked, who died, or who would live with jagged scars on their memories forever.

The Enumclaw killer woke about 9:30 on the morning of Friday, March 22, 1974. He'd decided that he wasn't going to work that day at the lumber mill. His wife and their two little girls were already up and eating breakfast in the kitchen, but he didn't feel like talking to them. His plans were none of his wife's business.

He took a bath and then dressed in a print shirt and a pair of jeans.

He felt edgy, so he gulped down three tranquilizers and waved his wife away when she asked him how many eggs he wanted. Gradually, he felt the pills begin to do their magic, although they didn't work as well as they once had.

Less than half an hour after he'd awakened, he was headed away from his wife and babies in his 1974 Pinto station wagon. Maybe he knew what he was looking for all along. Maybe he didn't consciously think about it. He hated the Pinto already. He'd been proud of having a new car, but then he'd read that Ford Pintos were flawed and sometimes broke into towering flames if they were even so much as tapped from behind. He felt like he'd been taken, and now he was saddled with three years of payments for a piece of junk.

He drove the new station wagon carelessly down State Road 169 to the neighboring small town of Black Diamond. He was looking for a tavern, but it was early, too early for most of them to be open. Finally, around eleven, he found a beer joint open for business in Black Diamond.

He drank a lot of beer. Later he'd say "a dozen — maybe a half dozen." He played a couple of games of pool. He left at half-past noon or shortly after and went looking for more beer. He found a supermarket and bought three twelve-ounce bottles, figuring he was saving money rather than buying it at the tavern.

It wasn't working anyway.

Neither the beer nor the pills made him feel any better. As he drove, he began to think about all the things that were wrong in his life. Nobody ever cut him a break. He had bills — lots of bills — and that bugged him.

He regretted now that he'd yanked his two tiny daughters' arms. And he'd spanked them too hard. In spite of that, they still loved him and were happy to see him come home. That ate at his conscience.

He sipped the beers and drove and thought about all the bad things he'd done; he counted all the people who'd been on his back — at least it seemed like somebody was always riding him for something.

The green Pinto prowled the streets of Enumclaw as the afternoon passed. He wasn't going anywhere. He could have taken any road out of town and it wouldn't have mattered. His black thoughts kept him from seeing and appreciating the signs of spring in yards and green stretches along the highway: daffodils, bright orange-red quince sprouting on stalks that had seemed dead a few weeks earlier, pussy willows. Even the skunk cabbage that bloomed velvety yellow in the bogs beside the road were pretty from a distance. Up close its cloying smell was overpowering, and anyone who picked it found that out in a hurry.

For this man, even spring was a miserable season. He might have decided to go home, but he kept driving. Without willing it, he wound up on the Enumclaw-Buckley highway. State Road 410 would eventually take him to Crystal Mountain, where there was a popular ski area, and mounds of snow still covered the ground.

The teenage girl and the boy walking along Highway 410 in Enumclaw were enjoying the first faint aura of spring in the air. And that's about all it was, too. It was still cold, freezing at night. Although the day before had officially brought the season into being, the trees in the wilderness woods were as leafless and dry as they'd been in November. But it wasn't raining, and it wasn't freezing in the daytime.

And it was Friday afternoon, the best time

449

in the week for high school students. The store they were headed for was a half mile or so down the road, and they neither wanted nor sought a ride.

Camilla Hutcheson* was sixteen, auburn-haired and pretty. Keith Person was only fifteen, but he was already five feet, ten inches tall, while carrying 140 pounds on his lanky frame. He was still as slim as an arrow, but there was promise there of the man to come.

The high school sophomores enjoyed each other's company, although they weren't a particularly romantic duo. They'd known each other since grade school, and they still liked each other. Sometimes, one or the other of them would entertain thoughts of moving their relationship ahead, but they each figured if that was meant to happen, it would — all in good time.

Keith was born in Seattle, but he'd lived his whole life in Enumclaw. He was popular with his fellow students and president of the school's ski club. His dad ran a local real estate firm. Camilla's father worked as an aircraft mechanic for the Boeing Company. They were typical Enumclaw teenagers, they'd gone to school there since they were kindergartners and attended church there, and their idea of high excitement was at-

tending a pep rally before a football or basketball game, or going to the county fair in
Enumclaw, or the Western Washington Fair
in Puyallup.

Instead, these two attractive teens were
about to walk, all unawares, straight into
hell. There was no one around to warn
them, and they weren't prepared to defend
themselves.

The man in the green Pinto cruised along
410, spotted them, and executed a U-turn in
the middle of the road so he could head back
toward them.

He had been driving without purpose, but
now he had a plan.

It was 2:14 on that Friday afternoon when
the communications center of the King
County Sheriff's Office received a report
from Harry A. De Lashmutt, a forest ranger
assigned to the Mount Rainier National Park
Service. The initial report mentioned only
that there had been a shooting, something
not at all uncommon in the wooded foothills. It could have been a poacher, someone
target shooting who'd missed, or even the
result of a fight.

The location given was noted as being
three-fourths of a mile east of the Mud
Mountain Dam Road on Highway 410.

Homicide and robbery detective Sergeant Len Randall was notified by radio, and he directed detectives Ted Forrester and Bruce Morrison to proceed to the scene. Detective Rolf Grunden headed for the hospital in Enumclaw to interview a victim who was reportedly under treatment there. After he'd alerted Special Operations that the team from the sheriff's office would probably need auxiliary lighting at the scene — whatever it turned out to be — Randall himself drove to Enumclaw.

Homicide, detectives live their working lives on the edge of a powder keg. Days, even weeks, may go by when nothing happens, and there are also times when murders are almost predictable.

No murder can be called routine — but a drunken husband shooting a drunken wife, or vice versa, is what might be considered a predictable killing. A mentally ill person with paranoid delusions, untreated, often becomes a predictable killer. Holiday gatherings, old resentments, and too much liquor usually collaborate to keep detectives away from their own family celebrations.

Although those who care about both the killers and the potential victims have worried about what might happen and even asked police to step in, the truth is that law enforcement's hands are tied. Police cannot arrest someone for something they *might* do without invading the rights of a suspect-to-be; they can only pick up the pieces after it's too late.

Yet there are occasionally crimes so atypical, so senseless, and so heartbreaking, that even the most outwardly tough detective has trouble controlling his emotions. Perhaps that's why a homicide unit is any police department's "Ulcerville."

There would be witnesses waiting at the hospital to talk to Randall and Grunden, witnesses who, for once, had not been afraid to become involved.

One was the Reverend Thomas J. Tweedie of Gig Harbor's United Presbyterian Church. He and a friend, Robert McCleod, had been driving along Scatter Creek Road toward the Crystal Mountain ski area at about 1:30 on March 22. As they headed up toward the mountains, the air grew chill.

Suddenly, as if she were indeed an apparition, the two men were startled to see a young girl run out onto the road from some bushes to their left. She was completely naked, and a thick scarlet rivulet of blood ran down one of her legs.

The girl was crying hysterically and waving her arms.

As they drew beside her, Reverend Tweedie and Bob McCleod stopped their car. The terrified girl immediately leapt into the backseat.

Fighting to be understood through her shuddering sobs, she tried to explain what had happened.

"A crazy man was chasing me, and he has a gun. He made me take all my clothes off," she blurted, keeping her head below their car's windows. "He's still around here. We have to be careful!"

"Don't worry about that," Reverend Tweedie said, while he handed the girl his jacket to cover herself.

"No, no," she said urgently. "You don't understand. We have to get help for my friend. Please!"

Even in her deep shock and terror, it was not her own safety the auburn-haired girl was thinking of. They wondered if there was another girl back in the deep woods.

She was impatient with them, but they put that down to whatever emotional trauma she had suffered.

"It's not a girlfriend," she cried. "It's my boyfriend, Keith — he's still in there. He's still in the woods with a madman. He's beating Keith with a shovel!"

As Reverend Tweedie pulled across the

bridge, prepared to try to rescue the girl's boyfriend, he heard the cracking sound of a pistol shot.

Then there was only silence.

The sobbing girl was covered with a shirt and jacket now, but she trembled violently. Her benefactors didn't know what to do. Should they go into the dark copse of trees to save the boy? Or was it too late? They didn't know how badly the girl was injured. She obviously needed to get to a hospital at once, yet there still might be a chance to save her friend, as she kept begging them to do.

But they weren't armed — ministers seldom are — and they knew the maniac in the woods ahead was. It would be foolhardy to walk into a hail of gunfire; they were all likely to be killed.

They decided to flag down the first car that came by. Fortunately, it was Ranger De Lashmutt driving the next vehicle. He stopped as he saw the two men in a red Volkswagen frantically signaling him.

"We're not sure what happened," Reverend Tweedie said. "We came across an injured girl — she's in our car over there. She says her boyfriend is out there in the woods, and that a 'madman' is beating him. I guess he held both of them at gunpoint. Then we heard a shot —"

"Has the girl been shot?" De Lashmutt asked.

"I'm not sure. She's bleeding from a wound on her leg. She surely needs an ambulance."

The ranger had a shortwave radio in his car, but the area was so isolated and blocked by mountains that he could not get a message out to ask for deputies and an ambulance. The signal was swallowed up repeatedly by the mammoth rock walls and cliffs.

While the ranger was trying different bands on his radio's reception, they heard one more shot from the woods. And then there was a terrible silence broken only by the girl's soft crying as she sank deeper into clinical shock. De Lashmutt grabbed his first aid kit and tried to stem the flow of blood from the wound in her thigh.

They knew they could drive the wounded girl out, but that would leave the boy at the mercy of the stranger in the woods. They breathed a sigh of relief when the next rig to approach the chaotic scene was driven by a husky truck driver.

"I've got a citizens' band radio setup in my truck," he said after they'd explained what was going on. "Let me give it a try."

But he couldn't raise anyone, either.

Tweedie and De Lashmutt sent the truck

driver out to Highway 410, where he was more likely to make radio contact with sheriff's deputies.

As the churchmen and the ranger waited, a lime green station wagon pulled out of the woods. The driver was headed straight for them, and they could see he was a heavy-set white male who appeared to be in his mid-twenties.

He drove toward them, gaining speed.

"That's him!" the girl shouted. "That's him!"

Thinking quickly, and with considerable courage, Reverend Tweedie pulled his car across the road, almost completely blocking it. The trucker followed his lead and pulled his rig next to Tweedie's, closing the rest of the gap.

There was no way the Pinto station wagon was going to exit Scatter Creek Road — short of plowing into the VW Beetle and the truck. It skidded to a stop.

Tweedie and De Lashmutt grabbed the man. For some reason, his clothing was soaking wet — both his blue jeans and a brightly patterned shirt. The helpful trucker saw the pistol protruding from the man's right rear pocket. He grabbed it and placed it on the roof of the ranger's car. Next, he checked the rest of the stranger's pockets, but he didn't find any more weapons.

With his arms pinioned by a minister and a forest ranger, the man who'd driven the Pinto was swearing violently. They smelled alcohol on his breath; it was almost oozing out of his pores. He was behaving weirdly, and he seemed to be out of touch with reality. But his manner was not the main concern of the group in the woods. It was the boy they cared about.

Was he alive or dead?

Bob McCleod and the trucker grabbed the first aid kit and headed into the desolate area as far as they could in the truck driver's rig. They had to park and set out on foot when they came to a turnaround on the forest road. First they went down the Scatter Creek bypass road.

They found nothing, and they heard nothing but poplar leaves quivering in a faint wind and the cry of birds.

Next, they headed in a northward path from the turnaround area. When they got to Scatter Creek itself, they saw the teenager. He lay facedown just above the creek itself. And he too was nude. He was bleeding from several areas on his body, and most of his skin was either scratched or bruised.

The two men climbed over to him, praying that somehow he would not be dead at all but only unconscious.

It was a forlorn hope. They touched his carotid artery under his ear, his wrists, and even his feet for a reassuring pulse.

But there was none. Keith Person was dead.

Gulping down the impulse to cry, they looked around the creek-side area. They spotted two piles of clothing — one obviously belonging to a teenage girl, and the other to the dead boy, who had probably given his life to save hers.

None of it made any sense to these laymen, nor would it compute for the sheriff's detective either. The captured man, who smelled like a brewery and struggled with the men holding him, swearing obscenely, had to be at least a decade older than the victims. A love triangle didn't seem likely.

They would have to wait until the injured teenager felt well enough to talk about what had happened next to Scatter Creek. She was the only living witness.

While the burly suspect was being held for the arrival of the King County deputies, Reverend Tweedie and his friend Bob McCleod headed into Enumclaw with the injured girl. Enumclaw Sergeant L. E. Robinson met them and led them to the hospital.

Camilla Hutcheson had suffered extensive scratches all over her body as she made her desperate bid for freedom in the woods. At the hospital's ER, physicians verified that she was suffering from severe shock.

"She's been shot, too," the doctor on duty said.

"She was?" Tweedie asked anxiously. "We didn't know."

"She has a wound in her left thigh that was caused by a small-caliber bullet," the attending doctor said to the minister and the deputies. "It's a through-and-through wound. She was extremely lucky. If the bullet had hit a bone instead of flesh, she might have been crippled and unable to escape. I believe this will prove to be a .22- or .25-caliber bullet. They tend to tumble over and over — bounce around inside — if they strike a bone, and they can destroy vital organs. It's much better for the patient to have a small bullet pass through only soft tissue."

Camilla would be held overnight in the hospital. But there was nothing that could be done to help fifteen-year-old Keith Person, who lay in the woods. The EMTs hadn't yet arrived with an ambulance; in fact, they had been told to turn back until they got further word. Although Keith was thought to be dead, his age and his reputation around town made every man connected to the case surreptitiously check for himself. The quick pressure of warm fingertips against cold flesh. The impossible hope.

There had to be a heartbeat. Good kids like this shouldn't die.

In a town the size of Enumclaw, news spreads like a lava flow. Already, the news (albeit a bit garbled) of what had happened at Scatter Creek was circulating in town.

"We have to get to the boy's parents," Enumclaw police sergeant Robinson said quietly. "They must not find out on the street."

Fortunately, they located Keith's parents rapidly, and they listened with horror and disbelief as police told them that he was dead.

Death notification, especially of the young who have perished as the result of criminal violence, is the hardest assignment any detective or police officer ever has.

But someone had to tell Keith's parents that their fine, healthy, popular son had been killed with two gunshots.

"But why?" his father asked. "Why?"

No one really knew why yet. None of it made sense. But the teenager was gone forever, and there was no way to bring him back. While his parents grieved, the search for answers had already begun.

Back at the crime scene, King County deputies Mark Fern and Herb Duncan had reached the scene in the woods near Scatter Creek, followed shortly by patrol sergeant Harlan Bollinger. They saw the red-eyed, disheveled-looking man who was still held tight in the grip of a forest ranger and a citizen who looked as though he should have been in church. Ironically, he should have, but Reverend Tweedie was determined that the stranger must not escape. Fern and Duncan handcuffed the suspect and placed him in the backseat of their patrol car.

The deputies then attempted to further secure the area where Keith Person's body lay facedown. It had to be held sacrosanct until homicide detectives could begin their inch-by-inch crime-scene analysis.

However, an odd individual refused to move on, and kept creeping closer to where Keith's corpse lay. He was about to cause them a good deal of trouble.

The man explained that it was he who had calmed the suspect by putting him into "an hypnotic trance." Fern and Sergeant Bollinger exchanged glances; the prisoner hadn't seemed at all "calm" to them.

Now, the self-styled psychic insisted on

remaining at the spot next to Scatter Creek. Finally, with the aid of state trooper Earl Gasaway, the weird man was secured in the trooper's vehicle until he could give a statement.

As the investigators had suspected, the man's meandering explanations proved that he had nothing whatsoever to do with the case; he had merely been passing by and wanted to become involved in "the excitement."

Deputy Fern, too, had checked Keith Person's vital signs, hoping as they all had that he might still be alive. Fern then took possession of the gun retrieved from the man in the green Pinto. It was a Colt .25-caliber semi-automatic. The deputy marked his initials on the butt of the gun with a green felt pen and later turned it over to detective Rolf Grunden to be placed into evidence. Fern also found a .25-caliber bullet in the suspect's pants pocket.

With instructions from Sergeant Len Randall, Fern transported the suspect to the Enumclaw Police Department headquarters, where he was advised of his rights under the Miranda Rule. He agreed to take a Breathalyzer test to determine the percentage of alcohol in his system. The results showed a concentration of only .02, nowhere near the legal level of intoxication.

The suspect, whose wide, bland face and rosy cheeks made him look like anyone but a murderer, said his name was Jerry Lee Ross, and that he was twenty-six. He was currently working as a ripsaw operator at Harris Pine Mills, a local firm. He was five feet, eight inches tall, and weighed a hefty 180 pounds.

Ross told detectives that he lived with his wife and two toddler daughters on Pioneer Street in Enumclaw.

He seemed proud of his service as a U.S. Marine and said he'd received an honorable discharge. After that, he'd attended Green River Community College in Auburn, in the hope of finding another career; lumber mill jobs were fine for young men, but he had seen the hard physical work wear down men who'd stayed too long at the mill.

Why had Jerry Ross shot two high school kids? That was the question in everyone's mind. Detective Rolf Grunden checked to see what might be on Ross's rap sheet — if, indeed, he had one. Jerry Ross did, but it was for penny ante stuff and showed only numerous traffic arrests, including a few DWIs. Nothing that could be considered a violent crime.

There was not the slightest explanation for

the horror that had erupted in the woods.

Jerry Ross was asked to remove his clothing while he stood on a clean white sheet. Often minuscule pieces of evidence can be found as they drop to a sheet. There were a few evergreen needles, some dirt, but those would only tend to validate Scatter Creek as the site of the murder — and the investigators were already pretty sure of that.

Ross then dressed in clean coveralls and awaited transportation to the King County Jail.

It seemed that this one day was at least a week long. It was getting dark, but that was natural in March. Back near Scatter Creek, detectives Ted Forrester and Bruce Morrison surveyed the crime scene. The dead youth still lay facedown, his slight frame stretched along the ground. Someone — maybe a deputy — had thrown a blue shirt across the youngster's back as if to protect him from the cold he no longer felt.

The two piles of clothing told the graphic story that inanimate objects often do: a green plaid jacket, a pair of boy's shoes with socks tucked inside, a pair of jeans with a watch in the back pocket, a pair of boy's jockey shorts; the girl's brown leather jacket, her blue jeans with bloodstains on the thigh, a blue sweater, a white bra, a pair of blue and white panties, a pair of small blue tennis shoes, a red cloth purse. And a copy of *The Story Bible.*

"Someone forced those kids to undress — and you can see they took as long as they could, delaying what was coming," Ted Forrester said. "See how carefully everything is folded?"

Forrester took pictures of the evidence and the surrounding scene. There were tire tracks — distinctive impressions left by relatively narrow new tires. After Forrester finished, Morrison made plaster moulages that showed the treads, tire size, and even small marks that indicated where rocks or stones had marked the tires. In many ways, tires are like teeth when used as identifying factors. Wear and tear, scars, distance measurements, placement of teeth and treads.

Morrison and Forrester found bullet casings, too, from a small-caliber weapon. Ballistics experts would be able to tell them exactly *which* weapon, more precisely.

As Keith Person's body was removed to be transported to the King County Medical Examiner's Office in Seattle, an angry crowd gathered outside Enumclaw Police Department headquarters. Jerry Ross sat inside the police headquarters in a tightly secured room. He had requested to talk with a minister, and investigators had arranged for one to visit him.

Still, the situation had all the elements of an ugly confrontation, one not dissimilar from old-time lynchings. The crowd outside was growing bigger every minute, and they wanted to get their hands on Jerry Ross. To forestall a possible rush on the building by citizens caught up in the mob mentality, Lieutenant Richard Kraske and Sergeant Len Randall decided that the suspect must be removed at once through a rear entrance.

They managed to distract the furious throng out in front of the police station, while they rushed a disguised Jerry Ross out to Rolf Grunden's car. Grunden drove out of town on back streets, with a deputy following close behind in another vehicle.

The Seattle jail was high atop a building, and much more secure. During the ride into Seattle, Ross spoke about his life as a marine.

"I was a rifleman in Vietnam," he said, almost wistfully. He spoke of his years in the Marine Corps, the camaraderie, and somehow managed to make even war sound like a good place to make friends.

After fifteen minutes, Ross's voice trailed off.

"I think I would like to think a little

bit," he said.

"Go head," Grunden said. "You probably do have some thinking to do."

There was, of course, one person other than the suspect who knew exactly what had happened in those bleak woods that edged up to Scatter Creek. And that was sixteen-year-old Camilla Hutcheson. Somehow, she gained the strength to give a statement to detective Jerry Harris. The investigators hated to ask her to remember the horror she'd been through, but they also knew that her memory might well become flawed as time passed. Jerry Ross was a dangerous man, and they wanted to be sure he wasn't out on the street within a matter of months.

They felt he would soon be stalking other vulnerable victims.

"Start by telling me about your afternoon," Harris said. "Just tell me what you remember?"

"It was about one p.m.," Camilla began. "I was walking down the highway with Keith Person. And I saw a guy drive by once in a green Pinto and then he drove by again. [When we were] near the Safeway he stopped and rolled down his window, and asked if we wanted a ride. Keith looked at me and I said 'No.' I asked Keith if he knew the guy. He said he thought he did."

She closed her eyes as she recalled what had been a deadly decision for them. She and Keith had walked over to the car smiling, but as they drew closer, Keith touched her arm — firmly enough to let her know he wanted her to stop.

"I don't know him at all," he whispered out of the side of his mouth. "Let's take off."

Camilla said they'd half turned away from the green Pinto, ready to run toward the shopping section.

"It was too late," she said faintly. "When we looked back to see if the man was driving away, we saw that he was still there, and he had a little gun in his hand. He was aiming it right at us."

"You're going for a ride with me," the stranger ordered in a menacing but authoritative voice.

"We felt as if we didn't have a choice," Camilla recalled. "We thought he was going to shoot us."

They got into the front seat of the Pinto, and the man started driving toward Crystal Mountain. He turned off the main road near the Mud Mountain Dam, but there was another car on the road ahead. Their captor had muttered that it was "too light out," and he turned around.

Camilla hadn't known what he had in mind, but she knew it wasn't anything good and she begged him to let them go. If he would just let them out on the highway, they'd find their way back to Enumclaw.

"Just let us go," she said. "I promise we won't tell anyone!" she had pleaded.

"It's too late" was their captor's cryptic response.

While Camilla tried to reason with the man, Keith was trying to get the door open and jump out, pulling Camilla with him. He signaled his intention with his eyes, and she understood — and was ready to jump with him.

"But Keith couldn't get the door open without the man knowing," she said. "He had these seat belts, and they buzzed really loud if they got unhooked. The guy would have been alerted right away if we tried to jump out."

Their kidnapper kept driving along narrower and narrower roads. It was daylight, but the trees surrounding them hid the sky and made it feel like dusk. Maybe it was, she'd thought. Maybe they'd been driving for hours; in her terror, she had lost track of time.

Camilla continued to plead for their release, but she got on the stranger's nerves.

Suddenly, she heard the gun fire and felt a stinging pain in her thigh.

"I was facing Keith when he shot me. I felt it and I could see the blood and I screamed. The man said if I didn't shut up, he would do it again."

When they were an estimated two or three miles past the Mud Mountain Dam, the driver turned the car down a gravel road. Evidently, he had found it dark enough and secluded enough to serve his purposes.

"He made us get out of the car, and then he reached into the backseat and came out carrying this collapsible shovel. That was scary, because we wondered why he needed a shovel?"

Camilla drew a deep breath and tried to keep her voice from trembling. Their abductor's next request had first struck them as so ridiculous and humiliating that they didn't believe him at first.

"He ordered us to take off our clothes. He was holding the gun in his right hand. And it was a very small gun. He'd already shot me with it, and I was still standing up.

"Keith and I looked at each other and laughed."

But they'd soon learned it wasn't a joke. "He said we'd better do as we were told."

And so they removed their clothing, taking as much time as possible, taking off their jewelry, watches, tucking socks inside shoes, folding garments very slowly and carefully. They were both terribly embarrassed, and hoped the man with the gun would tell them to stop before they were totally naked.

But he said nothing, watching them with glittering eyes until they were both completely nude.

"Now you've got to make love to her!" the man barked at Keith Person.

"We just stood there and looked at each other," Camilla recalled from her hospital bed. "We just couldn't do that. Neither of us ever had. It was crazy."

When the stranger realized that the teenagers were adamant in refusing to have sexual intercourse despite the gun he held on them, he ordered Camilla to perform an act with a beer bottle. She had never heard of such a thing in her life. She was shocked and incredulous.

Again, Camilla courageously refused, staring defiantly at the madman in front of her.

Their captor was angry, but Keith was angry, too. He moved in front of Camilla to protect her. The man he faced not only had a loaded gun but outweighed Keith by about forty pounds. He'd been trained as a fighting marine, and Keith was only a sophomore in high school.

Camilla told Detective Jerry Harris that the "crazy man" picked up his shovel then.

"He started to hit Keith on the head with it," she said, tears running down her face. "I knew I had to get help. I didn't see Keith fall, but I knew that both Keith and I together wouldn't be a match for the 'madman,' and his gun and his shovel."

While their kidnapper was distracted by beating Keith, Camilla ran for the bushes and then leaped and rolled down the twenty-five-foot cliff into Scatter Creek. She remembering blacking out when she hit the water. She felt as if she were drunk, or dizzy, or in a nightmare where nothing made sense.

Half walking and half floating in the icy water, she worked her way toward the bridge ahead. Several times, the dark waves of oblivion rolled over her and she sank beneath the water, but the frigid water helped to snap her back to consciousness.

"And then I looked up and I saw the man with the gun above me. He'd been following me along the bank."

Somewhere she'd heard the term "like shooting fish in a barrel." She felt like the fish, trapped without any protection at all.

"He told me to get out of the creek and come back up the bank," Camilla said. "And

473

I did what he said, but I didn't stop when I crawled up. I figured that somehow I'd survived the first bullet, and maybe the next one wouldn't kill me either. I knew he was going to shoot me."

As Camilla reached solid ground, she said she'd begun to run, ignoring the shouts of the man behind her. She heard him fire the gun again, and waited for the sting in her back, but this time the bullet didn't hit her.

And then, mercifully, she broke out through the brush and ran to the safety of the minister's car.

"I knew he would have killed me if he caught me . . ."

Camilla said she had never seen the man before but knew she would recognize him again. Despite his bizarre demands that she and Keith perform sexually for him, he had not touched her himself.

Why on earth had the suspect taken the helpless teenagers for that forced ride?

Detective Grunden tried to sort out some of the answers as he took a statement from Jerry Lee Ross. Again, Ross had been fully advised of his rights and, after talking to his pastor, he said that he wanted to tell the truth about what had happened.

He recalled that he'd seen the two young

people walking toward Enumclaw. He wasn't sure of the time, but he decided he'd ask them if they wanted a lift. He denied he had forced them into the car.

"As we were driving the girl asked me where we were going. About that time I pulled out a gun alongside the driver's seat. I had put the gun next to the seat before I left home in the morning. The gun is a .25-caliber automatic, a Colt. I'd loaded it with seven shots.

"I told them to keep their mouths shut — that we were just going for a ride."

But, as he continued his statement, Ross admitted that he was thinking about the girl as they drove. At first, he'd considered "laying her" himself.

"Then I thought about watching them do it," he said. "I also thought I could tie the boy up and 'play' with the girl. I already had a leather shoestring in my car that I planned to use.

"As we were driving, the girl asked for a cigarette. The gun went off accidentally when I reached for one."

Jerry Ross's version of the attack grew more tangled as he spoke, the wheels spinning in his mind almost visible to Grunden as he wrote down the words.

"I think the bullet hit the horn because

it was honking. The bullet struck the girl's left leg. I unscrewed the horn and stopped it from honking. The girl was screaming. I said something like shut up or I would do it again — or something like that."

Ross recalled how he turned off onto a dirt road and drove to the end. He described getting the shovel from the back of his car because he planned to knock the boy out so that he could molest the girl.

"We walked to an old bridge site. We walked about a hundred feet. I told them to take off their clothes. They were reluctant at first. The girl asked me to let them go — I told them no."

Ross told how he watched while the teenagers shed their clothing.

"I ordered them to have sex with each other," he continued, "but they wouldn't do it. When they refused, I offered the beer bottle to the girl."

Ross's statement of the attack was so depraved that it was difficult for even veteran detectives to listen to it.

When Keith's back was turned, Ross said he'd hit him twice on the back of the head with the shovel. "He kind of dodged the blows, but I knocked him to the ground. Then he got up, sort of ran or turned around.

"The girl started running down the hill. I shot at the boy."

Ross said he had chased the girl until he couldn't see where she was. Then he said he had disarmed his gun. He'd returned to the scene and found Keith Person lying face-down. "I didn't see any blood. He wasn't moving."

No, Keith Person wasn't moving. Even had he lived, he would not have moved again. He'd been shot — not once, but three times, with one of the slugs lodging in his spinal column.

That may very well have been the first shot that hit the brave teenager, and it would have paralyzed him from the vertebrae it hit, taking away any feeling below that level. A .25-caliber slug is not all that large, but it would have severed forever the vital nerve pathways needed to walk, run, ski. A second shot had perforated his right pelvis and small bowel. The third shot entered Keith Person's head near the midline in the back. It was a near-contact wound, characteristically star-shaped, marked with smudging and searing of the tissues.

It now looked very much as though someone had deliberately placed the gun close to the boy's head and fired while he lay helpless from the spinal wound. This was probably the shot, coming from deep in the woods, that Reverend Tweedie, Bob McCleod, and Camilla had heard.

And the investigators understood now why Jerry Ross's clothing was soaking wet when he came barreling out in his car; he'd gone into Scatter Creek to try to grab Camilla, but her youthful agility had given her the strength to get away and dash up the bank.

Processing of Jerry Lee Ross's car substantiated statements taken from Camilla and from Ross himself. Among the items found were: an expended shell casing (from the shot that penetrated Camilla's leg); a brown holster next to the driver's seat; the horn's rim that had been struck when the bullet was fired at Camilla; the green collapsible shovel; the leather thong that Ross had planned to use to tie up Keith while he molested Camilla. The tire measurements matched the photos and moulages made at the scene.

Jerry Lee Ross had had the .25-caliber automatic since March 8, 1974 — only two weeks before. At the time he obtained a permit to carry it, he had listed "self-protection and sports" as his reason for wanting a gun.

There wasn't much doubt that he had premeditated a sexual attack on someone. He just hadn't known who at the time he bought the gun. Filled with rage, Ross had been a prowling, stalking, killing machine.

Charged with first-degree murder and first-degree assault, Ross was denied bail by Justice Court Judge Evans Manolides.

On April 26, 1974, Jerry Lee Ross pleaded guilty to both counts. Later, he received a long prison sentence — but not a life sentence. When he was released, he spent the last of his free years living about fifteen miles from Enumclaw.

What insidious tracery of cruelty moving through Ross's brain caused the death of a young man of great potential and the emotional scars on a heretofore trusting young girl is something that a psychiatrist might be able to explain. He wasn't intoxicated when he shot Camilla and Keith. He might have suffered from post-traumatic stress disorder after serving in Vietnam, but that diagnosis was seldom accepted in courtrooms in 1974. He might have been a run-of-the-mill sociopath, capable of neither empathy nor guilt.

For the parents and siblings of the two kidnapped youngsters, it really doesn't matter anymore. Their losses are irreplaceable. And, for the community of Enumclaw, there is a diminishment, too: gone forever are innocence and trust and the feeling that violence happens only in the big cities.

If there was any good to come out of the tragedy of March 22, 1974, it is the knowledge that passersby did help, and that they cared enough to stop and risk their own lives in an effort to save Camilla Hutcheson. Without them, she might very well be dead, too.

Today Keith Person would have been fifty years old. He never got to graduate from high school, go to college, marry, become a father, or have a career he enjoyed.

Camilla Hutcheson is fifty-one, but she has disappeared from the public eye, cherishing her privacy. Certainly, she has carried the weight of a tragic and ultimately frightening memory over the thirty-five years that have passed since Keith died. To maintain her privacy, I have changed her name.

All the detectives who worked to unravel this unbelievable case have long since retired, and a few are deceased.

Jerry Lee Ross died on January 14, 2006, at the age of fifty-nine. The one thing in his life he was proud of was his service as a corporal in the Marine Corps. He lies buried among other soldiers, sailors, and marines in Tahoma National Cemetery in

Kent, Washington.

The reason why he shot at two helpless kids died with him. And maybe even he didn't know why.

DARK FOREST: DEEP DANGER

The state of Oregon voices a philosophy about tourists — only half in jest: "Visit us but don't move here." Native Oregonians and "near-natives" cling to the fond hope that they can keep Oregon's natural glories free of the megalopolis congestion that chokes other parts of America, and keep the air as crystalline and pure as it was in pioneer days, when weary travelers first glimpsed what was indeed a promised land. Oregon may very well be the ideal spot in America to raise a young family, and the Medford-Jacksonville area in the southwestern part of the state is one of its choicest regions.

Those Harry and David fruit baskets sent for Christmas and other celebrations — every juicy piece wrapped in tissue paper — come from the orchards growing around Medford.

In Jackson County, the thick stands of towering fir alternate on the horizon with dry chaparral, and gold and green rolling hills give way to emerald-shaded mountains that rise higher and higher and then disappear into clouds or, perhaps, infinity. Until the recent recession, jobs were almost always plentiful for an able-bodied man willing to work in the orchards, the woods, computer companies, and the many industries necessary to maintain the comfortable standard of living local residents enjoy. In the last thirty years or so, myriad businesses have expanded to cater to the burgeoning tourist trade. Fishermen, hunters, campers, and those who seek to recapture a sense of how it was more than a century ago, vacation in Jackson County.

The Rogue River and the Applegate River wind their way through the county, although today a section of the Applegate has long been dammed up to become Applegate Lake, flooding small hamlets such as Copper, which no longer exists above water. Sturgis Fork and Carberry Creek also flourish near Jacksonville.

None of the main characters in this very sad true story were tourists, however; most were native born, descended from Oregon families who have been around for generations.

Some had chosen Oregon to be their home state.

In the case — or rather, cases — below, we

will follow three families. One was to be admired and emulated, at least until they met up with pure evil in a deceptively peaceful setting. The next was downright odd — and violent. The third family was small, only a mother-to-be and the infant she carried in her womb. There was a common denominator among them, of course.

Their lives became inexorably linked, their fates entwined, all their names noted in media reports and newspaper articles. The five victims might have avoided their fates if the dates or times they met with a stalker were changed just a little. If they had shopped for groceries a half hour earlier, if it had rained, if a car hadn't broken down . . . so many minute aspects of anyone's day can change fate.

Or, possibly, they are fate?

The first victims had no reason to be afraid. They were virtually home when they met unimaginable cruelty and danger. They trusted the land, the woods, their neighbors, and even strangers.

Their stalker wasn't afraid, either. Nonetheless, he trusted no one and had no sense of guilt or conscience in the dark places behind his charismatic smile.

The last victim should have died, and would have died — had she not been incredibly brave. She clung to her life and her baby's life, as she realized to her horror that she was the only one who could save them.

In the summer of 1974, twenty-eight-year-old Richard Cowden and his family lived in White City, Oregon, a town with about 6,500 residents. Like his brothers, he was a handsome man. Cowden was a logging truck driver, handling those behemoths of the blacktop with their loads of felled timber giants as easily as another man might pilot a Volkswagen Bug. It was hard work, but the pay was excellent and he enjoyed the woods, with the pungent smell of evergreens mixed with sawdust and the sound of keening chain saws.

Cowden had a family to support and protect, and he cherished them. There was his wife — Belinda June, twenty-two, a pretty, dark-haired woman; five-year-old David James; and the new arrival, five-month-old Melissa Dawn. They lived in a three-bedroom, two-bathroom home, complete with mortgage, of course, but they were chipping away at that. They had two cars, one a 1956 Ford pickup that they used for camping, they were making payments on the 1970 sedan, a vacuum cleaner, and some new household furnishings. They still managed to maintain two savings accounts.

Richard and Belinda were close to their extended families. This solidarity helped them all get through a spate of serious family illness. Three sons had been born to the elder Cowdens; the oldest brother died of cancer when he was only twenty-five. Richard was born next, followed thirteen months later by his brother Wes. They had a sister named Susan. Because he'd started school at four, Richard was held back a year, so he and Wes ended up in the same grade, and they went through school together, further cementing the already close bond between them.

Richard Cowden was content and at ease in his world, but in late summer 1974 he faced someone unlike anyone else he had ever known.

By Labor Day weekend that year, the Cowdens' freezer was filled for winter, and Belinda's vegetable garden still thrived. They had just finished redecorating young David's bedroom, and he was looking forward to starting kindergarten. Their first Christmas with baby Melissa lay ahead. It seemed as if they had the perfect life.

The Cowdens loved to camp out, but they hadn't planned to go camping on the Labor Day holiday. Richard had arranged to borrow his boss's truck to haul a load of gravel for his driveway, and he expected to spend the weekend spreading the gravel.

The irony of fate, bad luck, or chance, or whatever we choose to call it, intervened. The truck broke down, and no amount of tinkering with it got it going. Secretly, Richard wasn't really disappointed, because it meant they could take a few days for fun instead of spending them shoveling gravel.

Belinda fixed a picnic, and they packed up kids, their dog, Droopy, supplies, fishing poles, and disposable diapers for Melissa, and they all headed for Carberry Creek, twenty-five miles southwest of Medford.

The camping area in the mountains is isolated. The town of Copper had yet to be flooded, and it was close by. But "town" meant a crossroads, a country store, and a few houses. A scattering of farms popped up downstream from the campsite the Cowdens picked on Carberry Creek, but upstream the land became deep woods.

The drive to reach Carberry Creek was part of the fun of the outing. The Cowdens' old pickup passed through Jacksonville, once a booming gold-rush town. Many of the fine old homes built in the last century still stand in Jacksonville, with turrets, gables, and intricate fretwork all advertising that they once belonged to men who had struck it rich. The old county courthouse is there, too, now a museum, filled with the rusting tools of the men who sought gold in the streams and earth of Jackson County. The Cowdens were aware that even in the 1970s, the challenge of a fortune still waiting in the ground drew miners, but they were only looking for a quiet spot to fish and picnic.

Richard turned in to their favorite site along Carberry Creek Road, and he parked the pickup on the road above their campsite. There was a picnic table close to the creek, trees for shade. The creek itself was less than a foot deep this late in the summer, and as clear as glass.

They planned to camp until Sunday and then stop at Belinda's mother's house in Copper for dinner on Sunday, September 1, before returning home. The weather was so perfect and the scenery so beautifully peaceful that they were glad the gravel truck had broken down.

Melissa played happily on a blanket while young David and the basset hound, Droopy, scampered around. Then Richard and David fished while Belinda prepared lunch on the camp stove.

Even though the Cowdens knew the area well and had been to Carberry Creek many times, there was always something new to discover. Belinda and Richard kept a close eye on David; there were still mine shafts around from the old days, as well as wild animals and deceptively deep spots in the tranquil creek.

Belinda's mother lived just under a mile from where they camped; her home was one of the few in Copper. If it grew cold or rainy during the night, or if one of the youngsters became ill, they could always pack up and be under a sheltering roof in no time.

The thought of danger was probably one of the farthest things from the Cowdens' minds as they enjoyed the lazy Labor Day camping trip. Beyond the normal caution that any young family takes while camping outdoors, they had nothing to fear — or believed they didn't.

On Sunday morning, September 1, David and his father hiked the mile into Copper and visited the general store. They bought a carton of milk and walked off toward their camp. They appeared perfectly normal — happy, certainly not under any pressure, nor anxious about Belinda and Melissa, whom they had left alone back at camp.

Later in the day, in Copper, Belinda's mother prepared a big family dinner and waited for her daughter's family to arrive. The hot dishes grew cold and the cold ones warm as time passed. Too much time. It just wasn't like Belinda to be late for a dinner; she knew how much trouble it was for the cook when guests were late, and she was a considerate young woman. At length, the older woman took off her apron and drove to the campsite. She had no trouble finding it. The Cowdens' pickup truck was parked up on Carberry Creek Road, headed down toward the general store. Richard had been doing that lately, in case the battery failed.

She walked down to the creek, fully expecting to see the family.

They weren't there, and she felt the first niggling pricks of panic. All their lives were so predictable, and they kept in touch as often as they could. There were, of course, no cell phones in 1974, and she had no way to call her daughter and son-in-law. She was positive that they wouldn't simply have forgotten about having dinner at her house and driven on home.

Belinda wouldn't do that. Besides, it was obvious that they hadn't packed up their campsite. And their truck was still up on the road.

A plastic dishpan full of now-cold water sat near the picnic table. And on the table itself was a carton half-full of milk, dishes and silverware stacked neatly. (The milk would turn out to be the same milk that Richard and David had purchased Sunday morning, and it would help to establish a time line.) The keys to the pickup were on the table. Belinda's purse was in plain sight. Fishing poles leaned against a nearby tree. Even little Melissa's diaper bag was there, and the camp stove was nearby, still assembled.

It looked as if the family had taken a walk into the woods, expecting to come back momentarily. Belinda's mother called their names, and her own voice hung in the air, startling and eerie in the silence that followed. No one answered. Even the birds stopped chirping.

When does one begin to be really afraid?

She walked closer to Carberry Creek itself. She was somewhat reassured to see how low it was, barely wading depth. They couldn't all have drowned, although she knew Richard and Belinda would have jumped into deep water to save their children. They would do anything to save their children.

And then her eye caught sight of something else. Richard Cowden's wallet lay on the ground. His mother-in-law picked it up and saw that there was twenty-three dollars inside. Close by, she found his expensive wristwatch, and an opened package of cigarettes, her daughter's brand.

Even if the family had decided to go into the forest to explore or to pick berries, she doubted that they would have left such valuable items as a purse, wallet, watch, and truck keys behind.

Belinda's mom moved back to the truck. All the clothing they had brought with them was there — with the exception of their bathing suits. And bathing suits and blackberry thorns don't mix. If they'd meant to go hiking, they would certainly have changed into more appropriate clothing.

Puzzled and more than a little frightened now, she sat down at the picnic table to wait. She tried to tell herself that they'd all be trooping into camp in a minute and she wouldn't have to admit how worried she'd been. She tried to be angry because her supper was ruined, but her gnawing fear overcame the anger.

What could have happened? Was there a deep hole beneath the calm surface of the creek — or maybe even a whirlpool? Could David have fallen in and Richard and Belinda gone to his aid? Could they all have drowned? But what about Melissa? Left alone on the creek's edge, she would be helpless; she couldn't yet crawl, could barely turn over. And she was always kept in her plastic infant seat. Where was that?

Her grandmother's mind raced, picking up and then churning all kinds of thoughts about tragedy and disaster. All right. Face it. If they all drowned, where was Droopy? A dog could survive where a human couldn't.

And Droopy was gone, too.

She strained her ears for the familiar hoarse whooping sound of the basset hound's bark — but all she heard was the gentle sighing of the fir trees and the lapping water in the creek.

Although summer days are long in Oregon, Belinda's mother could see the sun sinking in the west, and she knew she had to get help before it was fully dark. With one last look around the deserted campsite, one last hard listen to the woods that might hold a terrible secret, she ran to her car. Ten minutes later she called Jackson County Sheriff Duane Franklin's office.

The dispatcher listened to her story, tried to comfort her, but thought privately that the report didn't sound good. Sheriff's men and troopers from the District 3 office of the Oregon State Police arrived at the Carberry Creek scene. It was just as Belinda's mother had described it. Certainly the young family had been there — and recently — but they were not there now. The men's voices echoed in the wind as they called out the

Cowdens' names, and their shouts drew no more response than had hers.

An accident could have happened, of course — but to an entire family? They doubted the creek was either deep or swift or wide enough to cause them all to drown. At any rate they agreed that the dog would have survived, but he was gone.

There were animals in the deep woods — brown bears, coyotes, cougars, some poisonous snakes.

There might have been human "animals," too. Prowling, stalking voyeurs more dangerous than bears and cougars. Still, the lawmen, too, figured there had to be a reasonable explanation. Maybe one of the Cowdens had been injured in an accident or a fall, and other campers had taken them all to a hospital.

When it became too dark to effect a thorough search, the investigators departed for the night, with officers left behind to guard the spot. A full-scale search would begin in the morning.

One member of the Cowden family did show up the next morning, but he couldn't talk. Early Monday morning, September 2, Droopy, the basset hound, scratched at the door of the general store in Copper. Perhaps the only living witness to the fate of the Cowden family, Droopy had no way of telling the officers what he had seen. The dog was hungry and tired but did not appear to have been injured in any way. Where had Droopy been all night?

The Cowdens, however, did not show up. There has probably never been a more massive search effort in the state of Oregon than the search for the Cowden family. Oregon State Police, Jackson County sheriff's officers, the Oregon National Guard, Explorer Scouts, the U.S. Forest Service, and scores of volunteers were sure — at least in the beginning — that they could find them.

Lieutenant Mark Kezar, assistant commander of the Oregon State Police's District 3 division, took on the overall coordination of the search and the subsequent investigation. A year later, he remarked wryly, "I felt like that campground was my second home."

In retrospect, Kezar regretted that the investigation didn't start at top speed immediately and was delayed "for maybe a day" because there was no sign of violence at the Cowdens' campsite. No blood, nothing broken. Nothing stolen. He agonized for months over that delay.

Scores of police personnel and reserves searched the Carberry Creek campsite for a few weeks, and almost a dozen detectives worked the case as a task force for five months.

The U.S. Forest Service rangers checked every road and trail within a twenty-five-mile radius of the campground. Planes and helicopters flew as low as they dared, taking infrared photographs. If the Cowdens had been killed and buried, the freshly turned dirt and dying vegetation would appear bright red on the film, although it might well be invisible to the naked eye.

Investigators at the campground looked in vain for footprints, tire tracks, or for a pattern of scuff marks in the dirt that might indicate a struggle had taken place. But there was nothing at all.

Oregon, the pioneer state, has long been known for a very modern skill. The state has outstanding forensic science labs, and their crime scene investigators are well trained. But they have to have something to work with. There *were* no footprints, no tire tracks with which to form moulages. On their hands and knees, CSIs sifted the dirt at the Cowdens' camp, looking for metal fragments (from slugs and/or bullet casings), cloth, buttons, ID, and any other infinitesimal clue that might still be there.

They found nothing that would help solve

the disappearances. Someone — or some "thing" — had entered the Cowdens' camp and taken the family away, literally without a trace.

It was almost as if some craft from outer space had hovered, landed, and carried off a typical American family to examine in some far-off planet. But would they ever bring them back?

Law enforcement investigators think in far more pragmatic ways and tend not to believe in such things as psychics, crystal balls, and alien abductions. They continued to search for the Cowden family.

More and more, it looked as if someone had kidnapped the Cowdens. But why? Robbery obviously hadn't been the motivation. Richard's wallet, his watch, his truck — complete with keys — were there. A sexual attack was quite possible. Belinda Cowden was a lovely young woman; left alone at the campsite, clad in a bathing suit with only a friendly basset hound for protection, she could have inspired lust in the mind of someone hiking in the area.

But wouldn't that mean that only Belinda and Melissa should be missing? And, if Richard Cowden and David had walked back to find intruders in the campsite and a fight had ensued, wouldn't there be evidence of a struggle? Why would the entire family be missing now?

Lieutenant Kezar and his fellow Oregon State Police officers — Lieutenant George Winterfeld, Sergeant Ernie Walden, and troopers Lee Erickson and Darin Parker — set up task force headquarters at the camp. They called for aid from state police technical experts in Salem, the state capital.

Sheriff Franklin cut down on some patrols and shifts so that he could make every man possible available for the search that was becoming more baffling by the day.

They searched the abandoned mine shafts, as well as both sides of every creek, river, and gully for miles. If, however improbably, the Cowdens had drowned, their bodies would have surfaced and been caught in the rocks and debris downstream in Carberry Creek.

But none of them did — nor was even a shred of cloth from a bathing suit found.

They brought in bloodhounds and necrosearch dogs — the canines trained to pick up scents of either living creatures or dead bodies. They were given the scents of the Cowden family from clothing left behind at the campsite. The dogs started out enthusiastically, but they soon ran in circles, then stopped and looked at their trainers as if to say, "What is it you want us to find?"

State police detectives talked cautiously to the press, who soon sensed a story of highly unusual circumstances. Erickson commented, "That camp was spooky; even the milk was still on the table."

Sergeant Walden agreed. "It's getting to look really strange. It's not logical that a couple like that would take off with two young kids and leave all their belongings."

As the weeklong intensive search continued, there wasn't a person in the whole Northwest who could read or watch TV who hadn't heard about the missing family.

The closest thing to a clue was a report that hikers had seen a dog, a basset hound, on September 1 some four to six miles upstream from the campsite. But they hadn't seen anyone with him.

The Carberry Creek area is only a short distance from the California border, and it is literally crisscrossed with logging roads, honeycombed with abandoned gold mine shafts — some of them sunk as long as a hundred years ago. Lieutenant Kezar and his men realized that the Cowdens might never be found if they had been killed and hidden in some mine whose existence had been known only to old-timers — now long dead — with the mine's entrance grown over with underbrush.

Kezar did not believe that an entire family could have stumbled and fallen into such a mine.

A few other possibilities, more shocking — if that was possible — had to be considered. Could the Cowdens have chosen to vanish voluntarily? Or had either Belinda or Richard murdered their own family and disappeared? It has happened in other cases. People do run away for private reasons: to avoid financial responsibility or some personal situation. They crack under pressure, shocking everyone who knows them.

The investigators scrutinized the Cowdens' past thoroughly. They had no more debts than any couple in their twenties, and they weren't behind on any payments. Moreover, Richard Cowden's paycheck was more than adequate to meet their monthly bills. Belinda was a good manager — as evidenced by the full freezer and the garden she kept up. Cowden was considered a valuable employee on the job, and he hadn't had any beefs with other drivers or loggers.

As far as the marriage went, it was described as very happy by friends and relatives. The handsome couple were devoted to each other, probably even more so since the birth of Melissa five months before. If there had been any breath of scandal about their marriage, it would have been well known in a town as small as White City — but there was none.

No, there was no reason in the world for the Cowdens to choose to disappear. Lieutenant Kezar was convinced that wherever they were, they had been taken against their will.

The searchers abandoned the organized efforts near the campsite in the Siskiyous a week or so after Labor Day. They had not found one scrap of physical evidence that might help find the Cowdens, much less the family themselves. They realized that the couple and their two children could be thousands of miles away by this time . . . if they had left of their own accord.

But no one who knew them believed that theory. Neither Richard nor Belinda would put their families through such pain — especially since Richard's parents had already lost one son, and they were waiting to hear if another son had cancer. Richard's brother Wes had started out Labor Day weekend with a reason to celebrate. He had just been released from the hospital after exploratory surgery on a tumor that his doctors feared was malignant. With the memory of his oldest brother's death from cancer at the age of twenty-five, Wes had been prepared for a similar diagnosis.

But his lump was found to be benign, and he was tremendously grateful. Within a day, he learned that his beloved brother Richard and Richard's family had disappeared.

The Oregon State Police and the Jackson County Sheriff's Office were flooded now with clues, suggestions, theories. Some were too ridiculous to consider, but others were checked out thoroughly. In the months to come, Kezar and his men would interview 150 people, compile a file on the Cowdens' disappearance case, and come to know the family as well as if they'd known them personally for fifty years.

As soon as Wes Cowden recuperated enough from surgery, he and his father, who had once been a trapper and knew the mountains, ravines, trails, and campsites of the upper Applegate Valley by heart, began their weeks-long search for Richard, Belinda, David, and Melissa. They were both eager to find some answers, and afraid of what those might be.

It was probably the worst heartbreak any family could go through: not knowing. None of the Cowdens' relatives slept well, and their minds kept returning to terrible imaginings about what could have happened to them. They tried to protect each other, and many suppressed their own feelings so that they wouldn't hurt each other more.

A $2,000 reward for information was set up. Just before hunting season began, another plea for funds went out. The grieving friends and relatives of the missing family felt that deer hunters might be in a position to unravel the puzzle, which grew more inexplicable with each passing day.

On October 3, Richard Cowden's sister wrote a letter to the editor of the *Medford Mail Tribune,* appealing to hunters to be on the alert for "anything that could be connected to a man, a woman, a five-year-old child, or a five-month-old baby. Even though we try not to let our hopes dwindle that they will be found alive, we ask that you will even check freshly turned piles of earth. We will truly appreciate any clue or help that some hunter may find."

It was a tragic request, proving once again that there is nothing worse than not knowing. At the time, eight young women were missing in the Northwest; all of them had vanished completely in Washington and Oregon, but the concept that a whole family could disappear was incomprehensible. (The missing women were later determined to be victims of serial killer Ted Bundy.)

Two hundred concerned citizens wrote to

Oregon Senator Mark Hatfield, asking him to have the FBI actively enter the probe. But there was no evidence that the Cowdens had been kidnapped or taken across state lines. Senator Hatfield and Lieutenant Kezar stressed that every law enforcement agency asked to assist in the case so far had responded with full strength — but there was so little for any of them to go on.

The hunting season came and went, with no trace of the Cowdens. Christmas arrived, but no one in their family felt like celebrating. Richard and Belinda's house sat dark and empty. Snow covered the hills where they had picnicked, and then the rolling slopes brightened with lupines, wild mustard, and wild iris, and a torrent of spring rains washed the snow and topsoil away.

On Saturday, April 12, 1975, two men from Forest Grove, Oregon, were taking advantage of the spring weather as they made a trip to the Carberry Creek area to do some prospecting for gold. They looked for the precious ore in the upper Applegate region, six and a half miles upstream from the campsite where the Cowdens had disappeared seven and a half months earlier.

Forest Grove is a long way north of Medford, and the men were not nearly as aware of the disappearance of the Cowdens as were local residents. Their thoughts were only of finding gold as they approached a steep, timbered, rocky hillside about three hundred feet above the old Sturgis Fork campground. But they soon forgot all about striking gold.

They found first one bone, and then another, and were horrified when they saw what appeared to be the skeleton of a human being. It was tied to a tree. Animals had scattered some of the smaller bones over a hundred feet in every direction.

The modern-day prospectors had no idea how long the remains had been there, but they noted bits of clothing, faded by weather, in the area, too, and were pretty sure they weren't looking at the skeleton of a long-dead miner. They ran back to their vehicle and called the Jackson County Sheriff's Office.

It was 3:30 p.m. — and over seven months since the Cowden family had vanished.

Sheriff Franklin dispatched deputies and notified Lieutenant Kezar and the Oregon State Police team. The officers were fairly certain that they knew what they had — at least one member of the Cowden family. From the length of the femur bones and the configuration of the pelvis, the body would appear to be that of Richard Cowden.

Kezar knew that it would take extremely careful criminal investigation to preserve what evidence was left after almost eight months. He requested assistance at once from technical experts in Salem and from Dr. William Brady, the Oregon State medical examiner.

The troopers and deputies searched the hillside for the rest of the afternoon but had to quit as shadows began to fall. They had waited out the winter and the spring; they didn't want to risk losing some vital clue because of darkness.

At dawn the next morning, they were back. At 9:30, they came upon a cave, a cave whose entrance was nearly obscured by an outcropping of rock above it. It had obviously been almost totally sealed up with rocks and dirt, either by nature or a human being. But the fierce Oregon winter rains had pelted the barricade, and a small rock-slide had resulted, letting slices of light into the cave itself.

The officers looked into the opening, trying to focus as their eyes adjusted to the dark. There were bones inside, obliquely reflecting the filtered light of the forest. Carefully, sifting the debris as they worked, they unearthed a body inside. It, too, was the skeleton of an adult, this skeleton smaller, though, than the one tied to a nearby tree, and most likely a female with short, dark brown hair.

They lifted the decomposed form out and shone their flashlights into the dim interior of the cave. There were other bones. Small bones that would prove to be those of a small child, and the tender bones of an infant.

At last, they were looking at what they were sure was the Cowden family, buried away from all the searchers until Mother Nature herself revealed at least part of the answer to a terrible secret. The lost family had undoubtedly been here, seven miles from their campsite, since the previous fall.

Kezar, Franklin, and their men fanned out over the hillside. They went over every inch of ground, finding more clothing and a plastic baby carrier, its gay pastel coloring grimly incongruous to its grisly surroundings.

Everything found — no matter how small — was bagged and labeled; the Oregon State Police forensics laboratory would analyze all of it. Metal detectors were brought in, and the entire area was scanned in an attempt to find the murder gun and or bullet casings — with no success. For days Kezar and his men literally sifted the earth of the cave and hillside, but the killer had been meticulous in leaving no sign of himself behind.

The investigators sought a gun — because the bodies of the woman and little boy in the cave appeared to have been shot. If, for whatever unfathomable reason, Richard Cowden had killed his wife and children, and then killed himself, the weapon would be there.

There was no death weapon in the area. If it was there, anywhere within the radius that a dying man could throw it, Kezar's men would have found it.

No, someone had taken the family far, far upstream from their camp, probably at gunpoint and, once there, killed them. The woman and children were stuffed into the cave then, and sealed up like characters in an Edgar Allan Poe horror tale. Cowden's body would have been too large to fit into the cave, and the killer or killers had left him where he was tied, helpless to protect his family.

Positive identification of the remains was made by comparison of their teeth with dental records. Dr. Brady performed the postmortem exams in an attempt to determine the specific cause of death. He confirmed that Belinda and David had succumbed to .22-caliber bullet wounds — Brady found spent slugs in their bodies — and tiny Melissa had perished from severe head wounds. But it was impossible to determine cause of death for Richard Cowden. He could have been shot, too, with a bullet piercing soft tissue that had disintegrated with the passage of time, but Dr. Brady could not be sure.

Without body tissue, lethal methods like strangulation and stabbing are often impossible to establish so long after death. Sometimes, .22-caliber bullets do little damage — unless they hit bones, which change their path within the body. Then, they can injure vital organs fatally.

They knew the weapon was a .22 — rifle or handgun — but they weren't able to do ballistics comparisons because they didn't have the murder gun.

Lieutenant Kezar made a somewhat cryptic statement to the press, saying he believed the killer probably was a person who either lived in the area or had once lived in the area, because the bodies had been stashed in such a hidden, murky cave, a cave only a local person would be likely to know about.

The $2,000 reward for information leading to the finding of the Cowden family was paid to the two gold prospectors who had found Richard Cowden's remains. Another reward, totaling $1,697, remained for information leading to the arrest and conviction of the killer.

It seemed that Droopy, the family pet,

might be the only living creature — beyond the killer himself — who knew what had happened. Campers had seen the basset four to six miles upstream on the creek, very close to where the bodies were eventually discovered. Questioned again, they shook their heads helplessly. That's all they had seen — a dog.

Droopy had probably made his way back to the town of Copper, looking for his family.

One Copper resident recalled that he had talked to a young family on September 1. He looked at the Cowden family's photo and shook his head. It wasn't the missing family he'd seen; they were tourists who said they were from the Los Angeles area.

"I remember they said, 'We're camping right across from you,' which would have meant the old campgrounds."

The witness said that the couple were in their late twenties or early thirties, and very friendly. The man had said he was in the computer field — possibly as a programmer in Los Angeles. He'd had a beard.

The California couple were traveling with children. "They had three children," the other camper said. "They all had biblical names. I can't tell you just what they were, but they were old-fashioned, from the Bible — maybe Joshua or Jason, Sarah. I can't recall. One of the kids was just a baby in one of those backpack things."

The investigative team wanted mightily to talk to that family. It was possible that they had seen someone in the area on the fatal September 1, but the team's requests for contact, published in Southern California papers, drew no response at first. The campers weren't suspects, but they might have seen someone who was.

Eventually, the investigators did locate the California tourists. Yes, they had arrived at the campgrounds about five o'clock on the night of September 1. The Cowdens were believed to have been abducted about midmorning that day, so the Californians wouldn't have seen them.

"Two men and a woman pulled up in a pickup truck, though," the father of three recalled. "They acted like they were waiting for us to leave, and, frankly, they made us nervous — so we moved on."

A man from Grants Pass contacted the state police after he heard that the Cowdens' bodies had been found. He was puzzled.

"I was helping in the search last September," he said, "and I searched that cave. There were no bodies in it."

Kezar figured they were probably talking about two different caves. "I asked him to take us to the cave he meant, to make sure we were talking about the same thing — and he did."

And it *was* the cave that had become a crypt. Was it possible the killer had begun to worry that someone would find the bodies, and he returned to where he'd originally left them, and moved them into the cave?

It wasn't impossible. Murderers had moved bodies before for that reason.

For every answer, it seemed, there were more questions.

In the meantime, Lieutenant Kezar and Lieutenant Winterfeld, Sergeant Wilden, and trooper Erickson continued to wade through mountains of tips, clues, and speculations.

They checked out known sex offenders and psychiatric patients recently released from the Oregon State Hospital in Salem, and followed up on both known and anonymous informants' messages. It seemed as if every small town in southern Oregon had a few "grotesques," as novelist Sherwood Anderson described residents of villages who didn't fit in. Most weren't dangerous; they just marched to different drums.

One of the routine reports from the Oregon State Board of Parole turned out to be anything but routine. They notified the state police team that they might have a possible suspect for them, one who certainly seemed capable of such a brutal crime.

Dwain Lee Little, twenty-five, had been paroled from the Oregon State Penitentiary on May 24, 1974, less than four months before the Cowdens vanished. Little was somewhat of a felon celebrity as, at sixteen, he had been the youngest prisoner ever received into the prison system.

Yellowed newspaper photos published in the midsixties showed Dwain Lee as he looked at the time. He had a sweet baby face then, and a sweeping pompadour with one unruly cowlick that brushed the middle of his forehead. He was five feet, eight inches and weighed only 150 pounds. Those who kept up with crime had found it was almost impossible to picture Dwain Lee carrying out the act for which he was convicted: first-degree-murder.

The Little family was living in Lane County, Oregon, in November of 1964, on rural property. Orla Fay Phipps was sixteen, a pretty neighbor girl who lived on nearby acreage. Dwain Lee might have had a crush on her, but thus far he hadn't indicated it to his family or mentioned it to any of his friends. He was also said to have had a thirteen-year-old girlfriend.

Dwain was a poor student who had a serious reading problem, failing grades, and an IQ between 89 and 94. He was not developmentally disabled, but he was at the lower end of normal. Even so, he was captain of the eighth-grade football team and president of his class.

He could be charming and polite. He said "sir" and "ma'am." He was a pretty good-looking kid who was popular with the girls at the Springfield Junior Academy near Eugene. He made a positive first impression, and teachers tried to help him. As far as anyone knew, he didn't know Orla Fay Phipps very well at all.

Dwain Lee spent a lot of time in an orchard near his home. He was a loner who usually went there with his dog. He called this orchard his "second home," and he explored animal trails, hunted, and watched birds. He did hang out in the orchard sometimes with an older cousin whom he idolized, and the two of them had a trap line together.

"Dwain Lee would rather have had a quick-draw pistol," his cousin said, "than anything in the world."

The teenager had a few male friendships, but he terminated those he did have abruptly. He and Orla Fay's brother were close for a while, but Dwain walked away from that relationship.

Orla Fay Phipps was a well-developed and very pretty blonde. She often wore shorts — which Dwain's sister, Vivian,* thought were too provocative — when she rode past the Littles' property.

"Dwain always went to his room when she showed up," his sister said.

On November 2, 1964, Orla Fay left to ride her horse, and her family became concerned when she didn't return home, although her horse did.

Orla Fay couldn't come home. She had been brutally murdered, although it was clear she had put up a tremendous fight to live. She had been struck on the head with a blunt object, sustaining skull fractures, and then her throat had been slashed and stabbed several times with a very sharp knife.

Autopsy results proved that Orla Fay had been raped after death.

At the time she died, Dwain Lee was only fifteen, but both physical and circumstantial evidence indicated that it was he who killed Orla Fay.

The legal question after his arrest for first-degree murder was whether he should be tried as an adult or as a juvenile? After his arrest, he was placed first at the Skipworth

Home — a juvenile detention facility — as psychiatrists and psychologists prepared to evaluate his mental status and look at his background.

The elder Littles distrusted mental health professionals, feeling that they had been betrayed by them in the past, and Dwain shared their apprehension. His attorney and Juvenile caseworkers asked Dwain to get to know the doctors scheduled to evaluate him before he made his judgments.

The doctors looked first at the Little family's background and interpersonal dynamics.

And it proved to be a checkered background for a boy of fifteen. His entire life had been one trauma after another. The Little family was far from ordinary.

When Dwain was seven, he was accidentally struck in the head with a baseball bat, and it left a depression in his skull that remained visible. He was hospitalized for a few days and had to wear a protective helmet for five months. For several years after that, he was forbidden to participate in contact sports. He also had headaches, and there was some question that his injury had caused his extreme difficulty in spelling and writing.

In an effort to help him learn, his parents had placed him in a Seventh Day Adventist school. Sometime later, his mother and sister were baptized into that religion. Dwain, however, often gave the impression that he was the most religious member of his family, attending church services and reading his Bible.

The elder Littles — Stone* and Pearl* — were a curious pair. From the time Dwain was born in 1948, their lives were marked by paranoia, going way over the edge of people who "saw a glass half empty."

Dwain's father alleged that he had been threatened by a man named Si Hopkins,* and Hopkins intended to kill his whole family. Stone's brother, Jackson,* had told him that Pearl was cheating on him with Hopkins, and that Hopkins would happily kill him if he could have Pearl.

Despite frail health, Pearl was a good-looking woman and so was her daughter, Vivian. While Si Hopkins had lusted after Pearl, Stone's brother, Jackson, was besotted with Vivian — his stepniece. The objects of their lust had found both of them "coarse, vulgar, and repulsive" and had never wanted anything to do with them.

Afraid of both Si Hopkins and Jackson, the Littles had lived in virtual hiding. The children were taught to shoot a gun by the time they were five or six. A loaded gun was kept in the house at all times, they hauled water in because they were afraid their water supply might be poisoned, the children were never allowed very far from the house unaccompanied, and they occasionally lived for as much as a year under assumed names.

Shortly after Dwain was born, Pearl Lee Little was charged with arson, accused of burning down a friend's house. She was jailed temporarily, but the charges were later dropped. Two years later, the Littles' own house burned down and they lost everything. Apparently, there were no arson investigators who correlated this to the earlier fire.

In 1956, old records indicate, Stone Little was shot by a foster child, and he lost one testicle, part of his penis, and partial use of his right leg. Between that time and 1961, the Littles reported that nine of their cows were poisoned, other cows were shot, and two of their dogs were poisoned. Someone — apparently the mysterious Si Hopkins — had deliberately felled a tree on Dwain's father, crippling him for life, and that was followed by yet another mysterious fire that destroyed $32,000 worth of their logging equipment.

Stone Little cried as he described his misfortunes to a Lane County social worker, and explained why it was no wonder that his family had lived in fear for years.

Stone was committed to Eastern State Hospital in Washington State in 1961 after he shot his brother, Jackson, fatally. He was diagnosed as criminally insane with "paranoid reaction, paranoid state."

Some versions of the Little family history say that it was Jackson who shot Stone in his genitals, and not a "foster child" at all.

Whether all of this bizarre series of events actually occurred, state workers didn't know. They wrote, "Regardless of the source, it has been experienced by all of this family as real."

Jackson Little *was* shot to death, and Stone *had* been committed, and for a spate of time there was relative peace in the family. But two years later, Stone Little escaped from Eastern State Hospital, gathered his family together, and fled to Tennessee. He was arrested and jailed there, awaiting extradition to Washington State, but nothing came of that and he was freed!

Dwain Lee was glad; he hated the time he spent in Medical Lake, Washington. Being the son of a patient of the mental hospital brought a stigma with it, and he was taunted by schoolmates. He didn't like Tennessee much, either. But most of all, he said he had missed his father.

The Little family had moved to Oregon to start over in 1964.

Somewhat ironically, a social worker assessing the family that November wrote with vast understatement: "The family reports that the past year in Oregon has been the most secure, happiest year of their lives. Since being shot and having a tree fall on him, Mr. Little has been handicapped with a lame leg and has experienced considerable recurrent pain but rarely complains and has managed to hold a steady job."

Dwain Lee's mother, Pearl, had her health problems, too. She told a court worker that, before she married Stone in 1946, she had suffered from childhood arthritis which developed into Legg-Calvé-Perthes syndrome in her hip. She was hospitalized when she was ten and was placed in a body cast and traction for nine months. When she was released, she had to wear a brace from her armpits to one foot, to keep her affected leg stiff. This went on for several years.

When Pearl became pregnant with her daughter, Vivian, she had to wear a brace again, and recalled that she was paralyzed for some time after Vivian's birth. When she was expecting Dwain, she had had a kidney infection. Throughout her life, she'd undergone several surgeries for "female problems" and "tumors" and was on crutches when Dwain Lee was arrested.

According to her family, Pearl Little never complained either.

Pearl grew up on a farm in Arkansas and had only a third-grade education, although she could read quite well. She was self-educated and "small, friendly, outgoing," according to her interviewer.

Pearl told social workers that her family "is my whole life. All the threats and tragedies we've suffered have just brought us closer together than families usually are."

Vivian was not Stone's child, but he had accepted her, and they didn't tell her about her real parentage until she was sixteen.

Pearl admitted that she had always felt closer to Dwain than to "Vivi," probably because her daughter was rebellious. According to Vivian, Dwain always did what their parents said.

Pearl outright spoiled and babied Dwain, and people said he was tied to her by her apron strings. She gave him a baby bottle until he was four years old. He recalled carrying it in his hip pocket until he got disgusted with it and threw it away. Pearl never allowed Dwain to be away from her for any length of time, and had an anxiety attack when they were once separated for a whole week. The Littles never left their children with babysitters.

Dwain, "the good child," obviously hadn't done well with all the "smother love" and the constant threat that some sort of disaster might be just around the corner. Whatever feelings of resentment and inappropriate thoughts he might have held were hidden deep within him until that day in November when he found himself alone with Orla Fay.

With Dwain under arrest for first-degree murder and locked away in detention, his mother was beside herself with worry. She visited him whenever she was allowed to, and correction workers noted that not only did he kiss her hello and good-bye, they exchanged kisses frequently all during their visits.

Their physical connection didn't seem normal; Pearl asked her son, who was now sixteen, to sit on her lap, and she held his hand, ruffled his hair, and even caressed his leg. Observers saw that this was sexually arousing for him, which embarrassed him — especially when the other boys in the unit teased him about it.

(This inappropriate behavior between mother and son was also noted in psychiatric studies of Gary Ridgway, the Green River serial killer, who confessed to more than four dozen murders of young women.)

Dwain Lee seemed to see himself as an extension of his parents; he told them everything he thought and felt, even to the point that he shared sexual jokes with his mother.

But he told psychologists that he was closer to his father than his mother. While his affect was almost always flat and without empathy for other people's feelings, he cried when his father had to leave Lane County to find work.

His reactions to other situations were strange. When he had entered detention, having been charged with murder a few hours earlier, he was smiling and friendly, seemingly oblivious to what would have shocked most teenagers. A few days later, a detective came to the detention facility to interrogate Dwain about Orla Fay's murder. He showed Dwain a color photo of the nude dead girl, marred by blood and terrible wounds, and said, "You did that! Look what you did!"

The detective was shouting and could be heard at the far end of the corridor. He next showed Dwain a knife that was identical to one the teenager owned, but Dwain calmly denied any connection to the homicide.

When the investigator left the interview room, Dwain shook hands with him and thanked him. He was completely unruffled and said the detective was only doing his job.

And when he was told that his parents and grandparents were selling almost everything they owned to pay for his defense, he appeared to have no emotional response. He simply changed the subject and didn't seem to understand that this was a crisis for his closest family members.

He seemed more an automaton or a robot than a human being — unfailingly polite and saying whatever he thought would please people, but without any feeling at all.

He told his parents the kinds of things that most teenage boys would share with each other — but he had no male friends. There was one thing, however, that Dwain Lee Little didn't tell either parent. He would not confess to killing Orla Fay Phipps.

Stone Little told Dwain that if he was guilty of killing Orla Fay, he should reveal it to him, and Stone would see that he got away and would never be found.

Pearl Little announced that although she might have some questions about Dwain Lee's innocence in the murder of Orla Fay Phipps, she wouldn't believe any evidence against him as long as he said he wasn't guilty. She believed in her "perfect boy."

Pearl wore blinders a lot, and she clearly did not like conflict of any kind, wanting only to please and win the approval of others.

"When Stone and I argue, we always try to make up before bed," she said. "Stone, he kind of withdraws into himself when there's a problem and cuts himself off from people. I just feel hurt real easy and I want to make up quick."

While he was in detention, Dwain worked hard to impress the adults in charge. Like his mother, he seemed to thrive on approval and shrink from criticism. He would take on jobs that other inmates wouldn't do, and he was a tattletale, reporting any misbehavior among the other boys. Some supervisors found him "almost self-righteous" at times, but most adults who met him viewed Dwain as an "innocent child" caught up in something he didn't understand. This was especially true of women, who tended to dote on the handsome teenager.

Dwain had his supporters who vowed he was innocent — that he couldn't do such a thing as had happened to Orla Fay. His girlfriend, now fourteen, wrote to him regularly and tried to get authorities to let her visit him. Her mother liked Dwain, too, and their family had put up $1,500 to help pay for his attorney.

As part of his pretrial evaluation, Dwain was interviewed after being injected with sodium pentothal (truth serum). His attorney agreed to that if no one was present with Dwain except the psychiatrist and one other physician. Results would be given to both the district attorney and the Defense, and to the judge.

Dr. George Saslow of the University of Oregon Medical School was given a list of questions on December 28, 1964, to try to find answers.

Who was Dwain Lee Little?
1. A description of Dwain Lee's personality.
2. Is the nature of his personality such that it would permit the commission of this kind of crime?
3. Would a person with his kind of personality be more likely to commit this kind of crime than a person with a different mind or personality?
4. How disturbed is Dwain at this time?
5. Are treatment facilities available in Oregon today [1964] adequate for the restoration to community life within five years of persons found to have

committed a crime such as charged in this case?

6. How long would a course of treatment in an institution usually require most people such as this to [be safe to release into] the community?
7. Would people who have committed crimes such as this usually require lifetime supervision?
8. How likely is a person to commit such a crime again if he does not receive treatment?

In retrospect, it was an impossible task. Who could possibly know what Dwain Lee Little might be capable of, or, indeed, if he was truly insane under the M'Naughton Rule?

In the end, a grand jury handed down an indictment charging Dwain as an adult. The jury at his trial handed down a verdict of guilty of first-degree murder, and he was sentenced to life in prison.

On February 11, 1966, Dwain Lee Little became the youngest prisoner ever to enter the Oregon State Penitentiary in Salem.

He made headlines for a while, and then most of the Oregon public forgot about him, reassured by the "life" sentence.

Dwain was first assigned to the prison's

garment factory, where he was under very close supervision by the staff and was also watched over by older inmates. Apparently, there were enough men who were truly concerned about the safety of a young and handsome inmate that he was not sexually exploited by predatory convicts. He attended group-therapy sessions and appeared to be benefiting from them.

After his first year in prison, advisers in the prison convinced him to go to school. He continued attending classes in the Upward Bound program until 1968.

"The reports of his activities and his attempts to help himself were excellent," one unit manager wrote.

In 1972, he worked as a clerk in the Group Living captain's office, and joined the "Lifers' Club." He was more sure of himself and relaxed, and corrections officers felt "his self-image was improving greatly."

Now he was permitted to go on "outside trips" with the Lifers' Club. "I have gone on trips with him," a prison staff member noted, "specifically to observe his relationship with women. He treated all persons with respect and understanding.

"Little has learned to live with his remembrance of the antisocial behavior of his parents, of the rejection by his peers and others in the areas where he resided. I've watched him change from a somewhat cocky and bewildered young man into still a young man — but one who has a high level of social awareness and of his responsibility toward maintaining his place in society. I am certain of his remorse for the offense that he committed and the girl he killed. I would welcome him as a next-door neighbor."

Many people who had met Dwain Lee in the eight years he spent in prison felt he was a prime example of a young man who would never return to captivity; instead, they expected him to become a good citizen. He had been on scores of supervised trips outside the walls and never caused any trouble.

They recommended him for work release. He was transferred to the Portland Men's Center on February 6, 1974, and began work at a concrete products plant, where he made $2.50 an hour and received glowing evaluations.

He was allowed four passes to Portland homes, all of them sponsored by his mother and his sister. And on May 24, 1974, Dwain was released on parole. He was, of course, forbidden to carry any deadly weapon, and would not be allowed to enter Lane County — where he had killed Orla Fay Phipps — or adjoining Benton County.

By the fall of 1974, Stone and Pearl had moved to Jackson County, and Dwain was living in Jacksonville. He was doing well as a warehouseman for a steel company in Medford, earning $4.75 an hour and reporting regularly to his parole officer. He spent a lot of his free time on the Applegate River, swimming and visiting friends. Although his parole officer wasn't happy about some of those friends and counseled him continually about the trouble they might bring him, Dwain didn't seem to listen.

"Little's only apparent problem at this time," the PO wrote on September 3, 1974, "appears to be that he is not very discerning of people around him and is too anxious to accommodate others' needs and wants above his own."

As he wrote that, it was Tuesday, the day after Labor Day, and the Cowden family had been missing approximately forty-eight hours.

And Dwain's parents lived in the area where they'd disappeared.

When the Oregon State Police investigators and the Jackson County sheriff's detectives learned that Dwain Little had been in the Copper area at approximately the same time the Cowdens had vanished, they located him at his parents' home and questioned him. He denied any knowledge of the Cowden family, said he didn't know them, had never seen them, and had no idea what might have happened to them.

Dwain Little was only one of scores of people they talked to. His prison and work release record were spotless, and they could find nothing substantive that might link him to the crimes.

Dwain Lee and his girlfriend, Roxanne Feeney,* were living with his parents during the summer of 1974. Roxanne had a secret that she chose not to tell anyone. She had seen Dwain with a .22-caliber gun and knew he wasn't supposed to have access to firearms. However, after Christmas, she discovered that Dwain was cheating on her with another woman, and she told police that she had personally observed him with the .22 pistol and seen him load it, and that they had used it for target shooting together.

Dwain's parole was suspended on January 12, 1975, and revoked completely in May. He had been out of prison for one year — less one day — when he went back into the Oregon State Pen on May 23, 1975.

Once more, he set about convincing the authorities that he had changed. And that was one of his talents — the "lacquer coating" that one psychiatrist had described, smooth and impenetrable. He got his old job as a clerk back, and, again, he was a model prisoner.

Dwain Lee was married now, and he had a wife, Linda,* waiting for him on the outside. He first tried to get paroled to California, but that state refused responsibility for him, and he also considered Idaho — but he finally submitted a request to be paroled to his wife's parents' home near Hillsboro, Oregon. He had a job waiting for him with a potato-chip company; he never had trouble finding work.

It was surprising how many corrections officers backed Dwain's parole. He had made a positive impression on them, and they failed to see who was behind the mask he presented to the world. He'd always been clever at hiding his emotions, and after more than a decade in prison, he had become extremely con-wise.

Oregon State Prison Warden Hoyt Cupp was not among those who believed that Dwain Little was no longer a danger to the community, nor were many of the psychiatrists who had examined him over the years. However, they had not considered him psychotic — except perhaps when circumstances made him explode.

"A person who is so unknown to himself

emotionally," Dr. Saslow wrote, "generally gives others no signals that he is about to lose emotional control, and he may lose it quickly."

One psychiatrist thought that the only chance of healing whatever was wrong with Dwain Little would be for a mental health therapist to spend "quantities of undemanding love for the long time that it would take to convince him that it was not a trap . . . Without therapy, the outlook is dark."

Most of the others feared there was no treatment that would work — inside prison walls or out. He seemingly had no conscience or empathy, and was far more likely to kill again than were most prisoners who had gone to jail for murder.

He was paroled for the second time on April 26, 1977. He now had more "special conditions" attached to his parole. He had to become involved in a mental health treatment program (at the discretion of his parole officer), he could not associate with known felons, he could not enter Lane or Jackson counties without his PO's permission, and he would maintain an independent living situation.

He had had the same parole officer for years, and the man never lost faith in him. Although Dwain would be living and working hundreds of miles north of Jackson County, his parole officer would remain in charge of his case.

For over three years, Dwain Little evaded the eye of the law.

In the Tigard–Beaverton–Lake Oswego area south of Portland, on the morning of Monday, June 2, 1980, Margie Hunter,* twenty-three, got up early to look for a job. She had been employed at a company named Metalcraft but was temporarily laid off. She also needed to pick up a check for two weeks' pay at Metalcraft's employment division.

Because the dark clouds overhead looked more like March than June, Margie drove her twelve-year-old white Karmann Ghia, even though she'd been having some trouble with it. Her life was in a state of flux; she needed to find a smaller apartment, and she suspected that she might be pregnant. If she was, she felt she couldn't be more than a month along. She was happy about the pregnancy, although surprised.

After she finished her errands, Margie visited a girlfriend, leaving at about three p.m. She passed through Tigard and had made it onto Old Highway 99 when her car broke down. The gas pedal had broken off. Discouraged, she pulled over to the side of the road, turned on her flashing lights because it was almost as dark as dusk with the threatening storm, and got out to walk to a phone booth.

She was having a really bad day, and then the sky opened up and hail bounced on the road and on her. A hitchhiker ran up behind her and offered her a jacket he had in his orange backpack. She accepted it thankfully. He was a little taller than she was, and he looked like a lot of hitchhikers: brown curly hair, mustache, beard, and glasses.

She wasn't afraid of him.

The pair bent their heads and started trotting toward shelter as the hail continued to pelt them.

At that point, another Good Samaritan came along. The driver of a blue Honda Civic stopped and waved at them to get in. They didn't hesitate, and still Margie felt safe, more so when she settled in the backseat and realized she recognized the driver. She didn't actually know him or even his name, but he had worked at Metalcraft, too, on the day shift as she did. That had been during the fall months of 1979. He was a "grinder."

She asked him to drop her off at the next phone booth they came to, and he nodded. She noticed that his car was only a year or so old, but it was dirty and filled with trash: fast-food containers, old newspapers, cigarette butts.

They soon came to a phone booth by a Catholic school, and Margie got out. The driver said he would take the hitchhiker on the few miles to King City, his destination.

Margie called her mother, who wasn't home, and a male friend who didn't answer, either. She was out of change, so she walked a little farther to a gas station, got change, and tried calling her mom and more friends. Nobody was home. She gave up, crossed the highway, and started walking back toward her car. Even if it wouldn't start, she wasn't that far from her apartment.

The hail had stopped, but it was raining hard when she saw the blue Honda approaching from the south. The hitchhiker was no longer in the car, and the driver pulled over in front of her and offered her a ride again.

She'd seen him at Metalcraft, and he'd let her out readily at the phone booth twenty minutes earlier. He seemed safe. She got in, telling him she hadn't been able to reach anyone to pick her up.

He didn't talk much, but he told her he'd give her a ride home.

"He asked me where I lived," Margie recalled. "And I told him. I told him where to turn into my driveway, but he went right past it. As soon as he went past it, he said, 'Oh — well, I'll turn around and come back.' But he never did, and I kept telling him to turn off on streets, so he could go back, but I thought he was just going around the whole street to take me back. And he never said any words after that."

Margie realized that she didn't know him at all. He was a stranger, and he had no intention of taking her home.

"Then he asked me if I was smart," Margie continued. "And I said I tried to be. Then he pulled out this switchblade, and he said, 'Then you'll do what I want you to do.'"

She thought the knife was a switchblade; it was black and shiny and about eight inches long. It had been right there underneath his seat.

Margie told him she was pregnant, and begged him not to hurt her.

"Well, then you think about your baby," he sneered, "and you'll do as I tell you to."

They were heading away from her apartment now — toward Tigard and Tualatin, and onto an overpass over the I-5 freeway toward Lake Oswego, and then back again onto the freeway. The driver demanded that Margie fellate him, and she complied. She wanted to live, and she would do what she had to do.

He asked if she could "stomach it" if he ejaculated into her mouth, and she said no, and he said she didn't have to.

That was odd, because he had been so mean before.

Now she felt the car turn again, and she saw that they were about to head northeast on Highway 205 toward Oregon City. She asked him where they were going, and he told her he was looking for a place where he could take her off the side of the road where no one could see them. He gave her strict instructions: she was to get out of the car on the driver's side and hold his hand as if they were a couple.

They had barely left the off-ramp on a winding road with sharp turns when he pulled over. She followed his instructions, noting that he had hidden the long knife under his sweater. He pulled her up the hill into a grove of trees.

She was trying to remember everything about him so she could tell the police later. He was medium height, chubby, clean-shaven, and wore blue jeans, the gray pull-over sweater, and black work boots.

Her memory was as clear as ice. She thought of everything she could, to get through the sexual attack that began too far above the freeway for anyone in the cars below to see. He made her take off her brown turtleneck T-shirt, her orange sweater, blue jeans, and blue high-heeled sandals, and then her bra and panties. She wished devoutly that she had worn her Nikes — she would be able to run so much better if she got the chance.

Her captor wanted romance, and he insisted she French-kiss him and respond to him. But she was terrified and filled with revulsion, and she couldn't respond. He was unable to enter her because her vagina was absolutely dry. He asked her to perform oral sodomy on him again, and she obeyed.

When nothing worked, he masturbated to ejaculation.

Margie felt a glimmer of hope when he told her to get dressed. He was going to let her go!

She bent over to put her shoes on, and he held out his hand to help her up. She grasped it, and suddenly he was behind her, holding her throat in an arm lock. Then his hands were grasping both sides of her neck, and she saw black clouds descending on her.

Margie passed out. She didn't remember anything until she came to, feeling as if she were suffocating in the dark. She first thought she was dreaming. But, finally, she realized that her sweater was wrapped around her head. She tried to pull it off with her right hand, but she couldn't feel her right hand at all. She used her left hand, although it felt terribly weak.

"It took five minutes for me to get my sweater down from over my head," Margie said. "And then I tried sitting up, but I was too weak."

At that point, she saw her right hand and realized it was slashed, her wrist cut almost halfway through.

The man who had hurt her was gone, but he had pulled her into a blackberry thicket, virtually hiding her.

Margie knew she had to get help before she bled to death. She tried to move her legs and discovered she could not feel her left leg. She took off her shoes. "I knew I had to walk out of there, and I tried to stand, but I couldn't," she said.

She couldn't use her right hand, and she couldn't feel her left leg — but she began to crawl out of the trees and brambles that hid her. Because of her injured right hand, she scuttled on her shoulder on that side in a crablike movement. She made it to the top of the grassy bank, and when she couldn't crawl anymore, she rolled.

"I kept that up until I could get where the

grass was cut down and people could see me. And I kept waving to them, and about fifteen or twenty cars went by before someone finally stopped," Margie said. "By then I couldn't wave anymore; I was just laying [*sic*] on the ground. I couldn't move anymore."

The Tualatin Valley Fire Department responded to the 911 call, and EMTs found Margie barely conscious and bleeding profusely. She was rushed to Meridian Park Hospital in Tualatin, where she was admitted in critical condition. Oregon State Trooper Les Frank went directly to the hospital. Dr. Michael McCleskey told him that the victim had bruises and swelling in her neck, a stab wound at the base of her skull on the rear right side, deep lacerations — including tendons and nerves — in her right wrist, and deep cuts to the nerves and tendons of her left ankle.

When she arrived, she had virtually no blood-pressure readings and had lost one-third to one-half of the blood in her body. She would need surgery to get blood to her right hand and her left leg, and there would be nerve damage to repair later. For the moment, they had to stabilize her condition before they could operate.

Amazingly, she was now conscious and

quite lucid, and Trooper Frank could interview her. A Clackamas County deputy — Robert W. Smith — happened to pass by where she had waited for an ambulance, and had spoken briefly to her. Margie wanted to be sure that the police knew who had raped, stabbed, and strangled her. She had gasped out details to Smith, too.

She told Frank that her attacker was a short, heavy white male with close-cut dark brown hair. He was in his thirties and driving a new-model two-door blue Honda Civic.

The best news of all for the Oregon State investigator was Margie Hunter's absolute belief that her rapist had worked at Metalcraft, where she worked. She was positive.

Dwain Lee Little had made a huge mistake when he chose Margie Hunter as a victim. She said they had even talked about working there. He could have simply taken her home, but he must have planned to kill her all along, knowing that she could identify him.

One thing Margie commented on was that her captor seemed to have "no feelings at all." He didn't care about her baby, her life, about anything but what he wanted. Trying to get through to him was like pleading with a robot.

Dr. McCleskey categorized Margie's wounds as "devastating." They had to get blood to her wrist and her ankle. Along with Drs. Tongue and Barnhouse, the surgeons isolated the severed tendons of both extremities, along with the damaged nerves. Her injuries were full of dirt and grass, and these were all painstakingly irrigated until they were clean; antibiotics were given to prevent infection if possible.

After resection of all the tendons of her wrist, and their grateful discovery that her radial artery was intact, the doctors felt the repair was "most satisfactory," and they wrapped her wrist in a short arm cast.

Next, they turned to Margie's ankle. There they found only two severed tendons, including the Achilles tendon — which was probably what had prevented her from standing or walking when she came back to consciousness in the bushes.

The surgeons put a cast on Margie's leg and moved on to the two-inch-deep neck wound. Fortunately, it wasn't as dangerous as the deeper slashes in her arm and leg. It was closed with sutures.

It took eight hours of surgery to perform the first procedures on Margie Hunter's knife wounds. She came through the operations well, and was upgraded from "critical" to "serious" condition.

Margie's pregnancy was intact; indeed, when she was well enough to have a pelvic exam, she learned that she was really twelve weeks pregnant — almost three months. Whether she would be able to maintain her pregnancy was still iffy. She had been choked, beaten, and cut to the bone, and had lost so much blood. And there was the shock factor to be considered, too.

Only time would tell.

While Margie Hunter was in surgery, law enforcement officers in the Tigard-Tualatin area looked for a new blue Honda, and detectives planned to contact Metalcraft in the morning to see if they could find the names of former employees who had worked as grinders, and matched the description Margie had given. Workers' parole status might or might not be known to the company.

It turned out that that wouldn't be necessary. An Oregon state trooper had pulled over a blue Honda recently on a routine traffic violation. When he heard the bulletin broadcast to all police agencies, he realized the description matched the car and the driver he had stopped earlier. He'd recognized the driver instantly: Dwain Lee Little, who had become infamous and familiar in the minds of many Oregon officers. After his last parole, he had moved to the Tigard area.

Dwain had had the same parole officer for years, a man who had started out with great hopes for him. The PO confirmed that Dwain had worked for Metalcraft during the fall and winter of 1979. He promised to obtain a mug shot of Little to include in a photo laydown when — and if — Margie Hunter was well enough to look at it.

At 8:00 p.m. an Oregon state trooper spotted the blue Honda, and Dwain Little was arrested on a charge of attempted homicide.

A search warrant for his home was executed, and investigators seized six knives, several items of men's clothing, and a handwritten log of his activities. A subsequent search produced ten thousand rounds of .22 ammunition.

His parole officer said Dwain Little had been on his latest parole for three years and one month without any serious problems. He had seemed to be an average citizen and was consistently employed at the Sweetheart Corporation until July of 1979, when he quit his job there because he couldn't get along with a new supervisor. Next, he moved to Idaho to work in a steel factory with his brother-in-law, but that relationship deteriorated after two months, and he came back to Oregon — and Metalcraft. Little was laid off because he sustained a hand injury that required surgery. He had been unemployed for five months.

His wife, Linda, had given birth to their first child — a son — only five weeks before his vicious attack on Margie Hunter.

"Most facets of their everyday life," Dwain's parole officer said, "were being met in an appropriate manner."

Or seemed to be.

Dwain Lee Little hadn't spent much of his adult life outside prison walls, and his joblessness and having a baby to care for might have caused him to disintegrate into violence once again, although that explanation was certainly no excuse for what he had done to Margie Hunter.

Dwain was thirty-one now, and he still didn't know who he was; he knew only what he wanted, and, as always, he had seized it. He was a mad dog behind a smiling face, a walking, breathing time bomb. Even though he had gone back to prison before for having a deadly weapon in his possession, he had apparently been unable to give up guns and knives. What on earth was he intending to do with ten thousand bullets?

It made the investigators shudder to

think of it.

Even his heretofore trusting parole officer recommended that his parole should be revoked at once.

Dwain Little was held in the Washington County Jail for only a week; in the interests of public safety, he was set to be transported to the Oregon State Penitentiary in Salem on June 9. Corrections officer Clarence Hedrick and Virginia Wolff of the Washington County warrants division accompanied one female and two male prisoners — including Little — in a van headed south on the I-5 freeway. Dwain Little and the other male prisoner were chained together with leg irons, and they each wore handcuffs attached to a belly chain.

They hadn't gotten more than twenty miles on their forty-five-mile trip when Dwain said the jail nurse had given him a diuretic pill that caused water to build up in his system.

"I have to go every few minutes," he said, as he begged Hedrick to pull into the next rest stop.

Hedrick refused. At that point, Dwain became hysterical and threatened to urinate in his clothes and all over the van.

Hedrick wasn't happy, but he stopped at

the rest stop just south of the Tualatin River. He explained the radio system to Ms. Wolff, and told her to call for help if anything untoward should happen, gave her their exact location, and then locked the van doors so no one could get in or out while he was in the restroom with the two male prisoners.

When they were inside the restroom, Dwain Little said he was getting sick and his bowels were loose. He wanted the chain around his waist removed. Using the extra set of handcuffs from his own belt, Hedrick handcuffed Dwain's left hand to the bar in the handicapped stall, and then removed Little's right hand from his belly chain, allowing him to defecate. When he was finished, Hedrick put the right cuff back on Little's belly chain.

Hedrick moved to unhook his left handcuff, but suddenly Dwain Little wrenched free of it and kicked Hedrick in the groin, and a struggle ensued. If both inmates had turned on the corrections officer, he might well have been a dead man — but the other prisoner chose to help Hedrick instead of Little.

Hedrick had Dwain around the neck and then in a hair-hold against the wall, and the helpful prisoner removed Hedrick's extra handcuffs and snapped them around both

Little's wrists.

Dwain Little looked at the other prisoner and hissed, "You're dead . . ." They didn't doubt he meant the threat, and the convict who had saved Hedrick's life was soon housed in protective custody.

Little's futile escape attempt may have been his last hurrah. He was now charged with attempted murder, first-degree rape, first-degree sodomy, and first-degree kidnapping. He initially pleaded not guilty to all the charges. Under a plea agreement, the sodomy charge was dropped.

On November 11, 1980, he was sentenced to twenty years for attempted murder, twenty years for rape, twenty years for kidnapping; each had a ten-year mandatory minimum. His terms would be served consecutively. The earliest he could be released would be in thirty years, when he would be over sixty years old.

As he pronounced sentence, Judge Ashmanskas said, "I find the case here are crimes involving great violence, bodily harm, extreme cruelty, or callousness. I do believe Mr. Little is dangerous, by whatever criteria, whatever formulas they may invoke; I find that he is an unusual risk to the safety of the public — based upon his psychiatric evaluations . . . I also find this to be supported by the nature of these particular offenses as well as his prior criminal history. Two victims are enough, Mr. Little, and I am not going to chance a third victim."

But were there only two victims? Orla Fay, yes. Margie Hunter, yes. But deputies and troopers looked closely now at the still unsolved Cowden case.

Dwain Lee Little had long been the prime suspect in the deaths of Richard, Belinda, David, and Melissa Cowden on Labor Day weekend, six years earlier. He was out on parole at that time and living with his parents in Ruch, Oregon — eighteen miles downstream on the Applegate River. He was found carrying a .22-caliber pistol a few months later and returned to prison. The California tourists had seen two men and a woman who resembled the Littles in the Cowdens' campsite area after their family disappeared. Even their description of the strange trio's pickup truck matched the one Stone and Pearl owned. An old miner who lived in a cabin farther up Sturgis Fork Creek said that the Little family had stopped at his place on Monday morning, the day after the Cowdens disappeared. The Littles had even signed a guestbook the miner kept to remind him of his visitors.

When questioned, the Little family members all denied any knowledge of the Cowdens' disappearance. Dwain Lee said he had been away on "business" that weekend on the southern Oregon coast, and had returned to meet up with his parents for a trip "into the mountains" on Sunday morning.

Dwain Little had refused to take a lie-detector test. If he had, and if he passed it, the charges against him for "felon in possession of a firearm" would have been dropped. But he had chosen to go back to prison rather than submit to a lie-detector test.

Why was he so afraid of the polygraph test? Maybe he had something more to hide, something that was far worse than the gun charges. . . .

The tiny town of Ruch, where the Little family lived in the fall of 1974, was the closest town to Copper. And yet when asked what route he'd taken from the Pacific coast to Ruch, Dwain repeatedly said he took the road that did not go through Copper, even though that would have been the shortest way.

Investigators had seized the Littles' truck and processed it for any possible evidence linking it to the Cowdens. They found it was as clean as if it had just rolled off the production line in Detroit. They had never seen a truck so meticulously cared for.

Dwain Little had been back in the Oregon State Pen for almost a year when there seemed to be a break in the Cowden case. A convict who had shared a cell with Little sent a message through the corrections staff that he needed to talk to detectives.

Rusty Kelly* had a story to tell. He swore that Dwain Little had admitted to him that he was the one who killed the Cowdens. He had given him details. Moreover, Little was spearheading an escape plan that involved sixteen prisoners. Kelly said he was one of those, but he'd never really intended to follow through. He offered to show officials a cache of weapons that were being saved to use in the mass escape.

Jailhouse informants aren't the best source of information, and they can be reduced to mincemeat by defense attorneys, but the detectives gave Kelly a polygraph test regarding the escape details — and he passed easily. They deliberately didn't ask him any questions on the Cowdens' massacre during the lie-detector test.

He led them to the hidden arms.

The media announced that the grand jury in Jackson County would consider this new information, and a "true bill" indicting Dwain Lee Little in the four murders would be handed down any day.

But it never came.

Lawmen in Jackson County still had no physical evidence that would absolutely link Little to the murders of a family who met a monster as they camped out. He was already in prison for what would probably be the rest of his life. Unless he escaped, he wasn't a danger to anyone — except, perhaps, to Rusty Kelly, who had snitched on him.

Today, the handsome, slender youth of 1964 is an old man, barely recognizable. He is overweight, with skin the greenish gray of prison pallor, and thinning hair; the lines on his face have solidified into a sullen stare. The charm he evinced in his youth no longer works. While laymen in Oregon may not remember him, there are few police officers — working and retired — who don't recall him instantly. Their first comment is always: "Yeah, I remember him. He's the one who killed the Cowden family."

But that has never been proved. The circumstantial evidence against him is voluminous; the hard evidence is still missing. No one had heard of DNA matching back in 1974. Today, there is nothing left to use for comparison.

Little continues to file requests and legal papers as he still hopes to be released. His thirty-year minimum sentence is up in 2010, but there is no guarantee that he will be paroled. He could be locked up until 2040, when he will be over ninety years old.

It would be a great kindness to the Cowdens' extended family if Dwain Lee Little would confess to their murders and ask forgiveness.

It might shorten his sentence somewhat, but it's not like him to confess. He never really has. Within his family Dwain Lee could do no wrong, and, as Pearl Little said once, "As long as he tells me he's innocent, I will believe him."

Margie Hunter impressed her doctors with her sheer grit and determination. She faced many operations, and even after they were accomplished, she was left with a number of permanent handicaps. Her left foot and lower leg had lost most of their sensation, and there was some atrophy that might get worse. Margie's right hand and wrist had been slashed to the bone, and with all the tendons severed, she had a profound lack of feeling there — a far more difficult situation in a hand than a foot. Her thumb was trapped in her palm because the muscles at its base were cut. She could tell the difference between hot and cold, sharp and dull, but her finer dexterity and motor skills would be compromised.

"I anticipate," one of her surgeons wrote, "in the future, she will become left-handed and use her right hand only as a 'helping hand.'"

Margie also had some scars that were not crippling but were cosmetically damaging.

She worked hard at physical therapy to make her hand and leg as strong as they could be. She would need them more, soon. Her baby was still alive and well inside her. She gave birth just before Christmas 1980.

She would never forget Dwain Lee Little or his cruelty, but she was ready to move ahead with her life. One thing that Margie didn't know was that Dwain might have been stalking her. A Christmas card that Metalcraft sent out in 1979 featured a group of employees. Detectives saw that Dwain Little was standing right beside Margie Hunter in the photo on the card. She may not have noticed him — but it was quite possible that he had noticed her, learned where she lived, and made a practice of driving the roadways near her apartment. On June 2, 1980, he had no business at all there as he drove up and down the Old Highway 99. No business, perhaps, but watching Margie.

Wes Cowden, Richard's brother, has gone

over endless possibilities of what might have happened to Richard, Belinda, David, and Melissa, or why anyone would target them. It was possible someone had been watching Belinda while Richard and David were at the country store — and Richard walked in on an attack on his wife. More likely, he had looked first at the killer carrying a .22 rifle as just another camper. Wes described Richard as "trusting" and thought he'd probably struck up a conversation with a stranger.

"You don't want to get in my brother's situation," Wes said. "Because I'm sure things were out of control before he even knew there was a problem.

"My brother was different than me," he continued. "On an outing like that, he wouldn't have been carrying a weapon. And I wouldn't think about being up there without one."

Wes Cowden's children and other members of their extended family still live with the threat that someone might have a grudge against them. Someone who walks free. Wes Cowden isn't convinced that Dwain Lee Little killed Richard and his family. "I'd still like to know for sure who did it, and that if Little did do it, he'll never be freed from prison."

It is a terrible legacy for Wes and his sister,

Susan, to live with. And it's a chilling fear in the small communities and homes near Carberry and Sturgis creeks and the Applegate Valley area, especially when the Spanish moss droops from the trees, ground fog covers the forest floor in autumn, and old memories come back.

Some old-timers there say the campground is haunted.

There is still the chance that some infinitesimal evidence or a rusted .22-caliber gun is up there, and that elk hunters, loggers, or campers who have never heard of the Cowden family will find it.

If they do come across something that seems useless to them, but which might be purer gold than any amateur miner could find there, they should contact the Oregon State Police.

ABOUT THE AUTHOR

Ann Rule has written thirty books, with thirty-five million sold, and all titles still in print. A certified instructor for law enforcement and prosecutorial training, she has twice testified before U.S. Senate subcommittees on victims' rights, women who kill, and serial murder. She lives near Seattle, Washington, on the shores of Puget Sound. Visit her website at AnnRules.com.

1/10